THE ROAD TO GEZI

Resistance and Counter-Publics in 21st Century Turkey

edited by Gamze Yücesan-Özdemir

© Red Quill Books Ltd. 2016
Ottawa

www.redquillbooks.com

ISBN 978-1-926958-32-3 (paperback)

Library and Archives Canada Cataloguing in Publication

The road to Gezi : resistance and counter-publics in 21st century
Turkey / edited by Gamze Yücesan-Özdemir.

Includes bibliographical references.

1. Demonstrations—Turkey—Istanbul—Taksim Maydan».
2. Demonstrations—Turkey—Istanbul—Gezi Park».
3. Demonstrations—Turkey—History—21st century.
4. Protest movements—Turkey—History—21st century.
5. Social movements—Turkey—History—21st century.
6. Taksim Meydan» (Istanbul, Turkey).
7. Turkey—Politics and government—21st century. I. Yücesan-Özdemir, Gamze, editor

DR738.5.T64R62 2016   363.32'30949618   C2016-900143-1

RQB is a radical publishing house.
Part of the proceeds from the sale of this book will support student scholarships.

TABLE OF CONTENTS

PART I: RESISTING NEOLIBERAL PUBLICS IN 21st CENTURY TURKEY

PART II: STRUGGLING FOR COUNTER-PUBLICS
IN 21st CENTURY TURKEY

LIST
OF TABLES

1.
THE ROAD TO THE GEZI UPRISING

Resistance, Struggle, and Counter-Publics in Turkey

Gamze Yücesan-Özdemir

We have entered the new century with worldwide resistance and uprisings. What we once called 'the neoliberal onslaught' has become old-fashioned in left/socialist analyses. Indeed, it is now neoliberalism itself—so long at the center of social, economic and political life—that is now under critical onslaught. At the same time, the practical and political experiences of working classes in many countries cannot be expressed through the narrow horizons of the bourgeois public sphere. The need for overcoming this entrenched sphere and finding new forms of publicity for working class interests has become clear. Urban streets that were so long the site of consumption or mere routes for getting from one place to another have begun to host the voices and protests of those who want to reclaim their lives from the neoliberal order.

The Gezi Uprising in Turkey (also known as the 'June Uprising') was the catalyst of this resistance. In June 2013, the most massive and glorious civil uprising in Turkey's history took place, sparked by the authorities' attempt to transform a small park into an industrial complex. Young environmental activists took the initiative in the park's Taksim Square, standing up against the demolition of the park. From this small and modest park, at the center of Turkey's biggest city, Istanbul, a massive civil insurrection was born. Hundreds of thousands of people came together on the night of May 31, 2013, to protest the brutal police attacks against people sleeping in their tents. Millions of people from all around Turkey took to the streets simultaneously. The protest sparked that night continued throughout the month of June. With tents pitched all around, Gezi Park became the symbolic lifeworld of the resistance. Quite remarkably, every section of the social opposition lived and existed side-by-side in the park for days, resisting state violence. This was no less than a short-lived communal utopia.

The Gezi Uprising has since been the subject of many academic analyses, which have focused on the historical and spatial conjuncture of the movement and its class characteristics (Tuğal, 2013). Although these analyses are certainly valuable, the challenge remains to think through 'the road' to the Gezi Uprising; that is, to consider the processes by which it was made possible. Without this approach, we could become trapped in a perspective of the Gezi Uprising that tends to set it apart from the historical and social totality by confining it to a sole moment and place. Consequently, questions pertaining to the uprising become narrowly posed as, 'Was it a middle-class uprising?' or 'How many people were there in the streets?' If we ask instead, 'What paved the way to the Gezi Uprising,' this allows us a broader perspective with relevance for many different counter-publics. By posing this question in terms of process, we begin to see significant points of connection between movements that have thus far been separated analytically and politically, such as the student movements, anti-Hydroelectric Power Plants (HES) resistances, movements against urban renewal, doctors who object to the Full Day Law,[1] teachers who are not appointed, the white collar workers who came together in the 'Plaza Action Activists Platform,'[2] and the blue collar workers who resisted the TEKEL (Turkey's former alcohol and tobacco monopoly). The argument of this book is that resistance practices of fractions or strata of the working class in all fields of social life created the Gezi Uprising. This is to reclaim Marx's (1852) well-known mole metaphor: While describing a revolutionary moment, Marx addresses the mole that digs silently underground without ever popping out, '*Well dug, old mole!*' We want to show how the digging of different segments of the working class and the tunnels they opened up played a significant role in paving the way to the Gezi Uprising.

---

1   The Full Day Law went into effect in October 2011 and stipulates that doctors employed at university hospitals must work a full day in their state positions and cannot work in private practice at the same time.

2   IBM Turkey employees have created the 'Plaza Activists Platform' with other employees working with large and prestigious companies in big plazas with high salaries but bad working conditions.

To shed light on the actually existing resistance and the construction of counter-publics in 21st century Turkey, we take three specific positions: First, there is a need to counter the darkness and pessimism, as well as the theoretical abstraction ingrained in the mainstream reading of politics in Turkey. The latter is limited by a preoccupation with the neoliberal onslaught on the public, which eventually results in a negative and narrow emphasis on the collapse of the public sphere and public politics. Yet, it is crucial to see the signs of hope—resistance and the making of counter-publics—in this rather dark picture.

Second, a social totality-based approach to public politics is crucial. The mainstream reading is characterized by an attempt to understand the neoliberal profile of the public in a patchwork style. In other words, the analyses offered from within the mainstream literature are conditioned by the neoliberal 'bits and pieces' approach, which relegates each and every public issue—social rights, gender rights and civil rights—to seemingly distinct spheres. This book, on the other hand, by offering a social totality-based approach, sheds light on the possibilities for the combined effect of resistances in the publics.

Third, an analysis of resistance and counter-publics needs to offer creative and useful ways of materializing the theoretical discourse on the public and political-public activism. Understanding resistance and counter-publics has often focused on *praxis*, preferring the greenness of political-public activism over the grayness of theory.

Facing and Standing against the *Silent Violence* of the AKP

The Justice and Development Party (AKP) has certainly deployed violence during its past 12-year rule. There are, of course, various forms of violence: Violence deployed by repressive state apparatuses; violence committed by men against women; violence deployed by imperialist powers against underdeveloped societies; and violence generated by religious and ethnic tensions. Nevertheless, the most destructive and harshest one among them is silent violence (Coşar & Yücesan-Özdemir, 2012). Neoliberalism and Islam are intertwined and deeply embedded in the silent violence that the AKP deploys. Neoliberalism resorts to right-wing ideologies all over the world, the specific formations of which—nationalism, conservatism, Islamism, Christianity—serve to make the violence of neoliberalism more tolerable. Joining hands under AKP rule, neoliberal violence is made livable through references to Sunni-Muslim life worlds and beliefs. More-over, Islamism is becoming neoliberal to survive and reach greater segments of the society.

There are identifiable economic, political, and ideological bases of the silent violence of the AKP. One of the main economic bases is marketization and commodification. All fields of life in Turkey are adapted into market relations. The AKP has introduced constitutional, institutional, and legal changes promoting commodification and marketization (Coşar & Yeğenoğlu, 2009; Yeldan, 2006). Three trends are notable: state withdrawal from welfare provision, employers' increased flexibility over labor, and the marketization of social security (Arın, 2002). The separation of economic decision making from politics helps governments to empower markets against society. Further, legal reforms in Turkey are made to conform to the neoliberal economic rationality, which is fixed to the goal of capital accumulation without regard to those suffering from economical, ideological, and political facets of social inequality and insecurity (Özdemir, 2012). Turning education, healthcare and social security into sellable entities through money is a major systemic violence against the people (İnal & Gürkaynak, 2012).

Another economic base of the silent violence of the AKP is precarization. An increasing segment of Turkish society is caught in the trap of precarity and faces an indefinite future in the labor market. The working class experiences precarity in many fields: Work precarity, precarious employment forms, social precarity, income precarity, and union precarity. We can describe work precarity as situations in which it is unclear whether one will have the same job tomorrow. A growing number of employees in Turkey are experiencing precarity that is not in line with international standards. For example, the Labor Law of Turkey does not provide any protective measures against dismissals (Özdemir & Yücesan-Özdemir, 2006). Moreover, precarity of employment is also on the rise in the form of subcontracted work, home-based work, on-call work, temporary contract work, and part-time work. In fact, it has become the most common employment form (Bölükbaşı & Ertugal, 2013; Süral, 2005).

Social precarity is also on the rise. Turkey is experiencing quite unstable growth and poor investment prospects in the new century: Worsening distribution of income and social equality, a paralyzed financial system, and an informal labor market expand day by day (Yeldan, 2006). A significant part of the population is making a living from informal activities in the cities. According to the data of the Social Security Institution, 38 percent of employment in the whole economy was informal in 2013.[3]

Income precarity refers to having no income after being fired and/or having no income after the completion of working life due to the absence of social security. Income insufficiency is also a factor of this form of precarity. Within

---

3   'Monthly basic indicators December 2013', http://www.sgk.gov.tr/wps/wcm/connect/ce5dc5c5-ba77-468d-8074-cab48d024bcc/2013_12_Temel_Gostergeler.pdf?MOD=AJPERES (10.03.2014).

the post-1980 era, suppressing wages became the main course of conduct. Within an economic vision based on the ideas that production would depend on foreign markets, a domestic consumption market would not be needed. Low and lower costs would enable competitiveness in international trade, and wages would be suppressed to increase competitive power (Bahçe et al., 2011; Yeldan, 2006). Union precarity is also an important factor of precarity patterns. Both unionization rates and the share of employees who have the right to collective bargaining have been dramatically decreasing in recent years in Turkey.[4]

An important political base of the silent violence of the AKP is its governance of poverty. In Turkey, policies for addressing poverty since 1980 in some ways parallel the transformation in the economic program and the accumulation regime. In this respect, the paradigm that offered grounds for the strategies of reducing poverty was initiated by the January 24, 1980, decisions.[5] Furthermore, the establishment of the Fund for Promoting Social Aid and Solidarity (SYDTF) in 1986, and the initiation of the Green Card service in 1992, can be considered within this framework,[6] and certainly as a product of the *populist concerns* for addressing liberal policies. In December 2004, the SYDTF was transformed into the *Sosyal Yardımlaşma ve Dayanışma Genel Müdürlüğü* (Social Assistance and Solidarity General Directorate, SYDGM). The social assistance activities are now run through a total of 973 *Sosyal Yardımlaşma ve Dayanışma Vakıfları* (Social Assistance and Solidarity Foundations or SYDV) under the authority of governors in 81 provinces and administrators in 892 districts (Yazıcı, 2009).

One of the ideological bases of the silent violence of the AKP is the 'individual.' The AKP aims to abolish all collective structures, framing these as an instrument of oppression that emphasizes uniformity over diversity, suppresses

---

4   Statistics about unionization rates in Turkey and union membership are multipartite and contradictory. According to the data of the Ministry of Labor and Social Security, from July 2008, 3,179,510 workers (except public sector labor unions) are members of labor unions and the unionization rate is 55.7 percent. This rate is very close to the average of OECD countries. On the other hand, when statistics released by the Social Security Institution in July 2008 are examined, only 6 percent of workers in the private sector are members of labor unions. It should be highlighted at this point that paid and salaried workers shown in the statistics of both institutions are registered to social security institutions. Therefore, when the snowballing informal sector is taken into account, the reality that unionization rate is below 6 percent becomes evident.

5   The process has evolved through 'the liberalization of domestic financial markets, commodity market, foreign trade regime and exchange rate regime' (Ansal et al., 2000, p.5) and through the policies directed toward the privatization and reduction of labor costs.

6   The SYDTF is an institution that should assist citizens in absolute poverty and other persons that have been admitted to Turkey. One of the major projects introduced by the SYDTF is the Green Card program. The objective of the Green Card program, enacted in 1992 following a protocol between the SYDTF and the Ministry of Health, was to provide health services to poor people that were ineligible for social security and that had a monthly income of less than one-third of the minimum wage. In 2006, approximately ten million people were entitled to green cards (WTO, 2006).

the individual, and subordinates the minority to a tactless mass (Yalman, 2012). 'Individual responsibility' is privileged and the statement that 'there is no right extrinsic to responsibility' is emphasized (Yücesan-Özdemir, 2012, p. 130). In other words, a balance of individual responsibilities and rights is promoted. This amounts to replacing the 'rights' that are acquired through collective struggle as members of the working class with a 'right' that can be obtained individually (Özuğurlu, 2011). In other words, by narrowly focusing on individual initiative, the class nature of society is denied—along with the constructive and creative role of labor (Castel, 2003). As the neoliberal construction is socially accepted, the 'individual' will consider itself an entity that exists independently of the relations of production. The individual will not act as a part of the working class collectivities, and therefore it will contribute to the production of the current boundaries.

This constrained emphasis on the individual undermines all of the advancements and advantages of the republic, including citizenship, collective rights and solidarity. The advancements and advantages of the republic, such as the socialization of healthcare services, secular education, industrialization and development plans, 'social state' and employment policies were bringing people together on common grounds and integrating them (Boratav, 2014).

Another ideological base of the silent violence of the AKP was the direct attack on the connection of place and identity through the creation of forms life that enable human and planetary flourishing in unison (Özuğurlu, 2011; Savran, 2010a). Laborers lost their belief in the value of acting together and having their own say. Taking the right to speak away from citizens is an act of silent violence that, in turn, imposes silence.

Those in power—along with their supporters—are not strangers to the concept of 'democratization'; in fact, they use it in their own discourse. It is probably the case that the more it is mentioned by those in power, the greater the indication of democracy's absence. 'Democratization' was released into circulation from two main points, both of which were in line with seeding neoliberalism in Turkish soil. The first was the attempt of the Islamic-oriented capital fractions to create an urban counter-self (Tuğal, 2009). The second one was the 'democratization' discourse that was generated by left-liberalism. It should be highlighted at this point that liberalism has never been a strong political ideology in Turkey. For this reason, it made efforts to survive by cooperating with conservatism and/or nationalism according to the conjuncture. In the past 10 years, liberalism has struggled to survive by cooperating with the left. Therefore, the infamous marriage of 'our people who are enamored with democracy on the periphery and the bureaucratic, Kemalist elites in the center' (Çarkoğlu, 2007) is nothing but a liberal narrative that totally ignores capitalist relations of production, class relations, and capitalist accumulation of capital. The aggressive rhetoric of political power against every kind of opposition and the Prime Minister's authoritarian and totalitarian approach clearly exposes an absence of real 'democratization' in Turkey.

The greatest destruction that the silent violence caused for the working class is the loss of willpower. Laborers who dread tomorrow, who are not confident with the future of themselves and their families, and who cannot interfere in this process are at risk of losing their self-respect. In mainstream labor studies, concepts such as honor, self-respect, and self-esteem are very popular. These concepts contain methodological individualism and give meaning to laborers through moral and sentimental associations. They also strengthen the tendency to become dull to analyzing laborers as members of a class. In this context, I prefer the concept of 'willpower' over these other concepts. Ambiguity of the future is the common ground of the seven fields of precarity that I discussed above. Willpower precarity is part of this precarity pattern. Institutionalizing precarious work led to a loss of willpower among workers in Turkey. Changing jobs often—a widespread phenomenon—leads to a perception of 'being a loser' (Özuğurlu, 2010). Özuğurlu (2010) writes that, 'I'd like to stress that the explanatory *code* of the behavior of the working class in Turkey is 'fear.' Laborers use this multi-layered code. The fear felt in the first layer is to lose their job and not find another. A little bit deeper, there is the fear of failing to fulfill the requirements of the basic role s/he undertake (dutiful child, precious spouse, responsible parents, etc.). Putting this into the terms of psychology, a major fear of *'loss of self-respect'* is the point in question' (p. 52). Loss of willpower creates bending the knee and obedience.

'The darkest day does not go dark' says Orhan Kemal (2007) in one of his novels. While we are talking about 'silent violence,' we are making 'dark' analyses indeed. The AKP government cannot reproduce the social integrity in the society. The ground upon which the AKP is based has been significantly disturbed. On the other hand, life is being built within opposition and resistance. Resistance movements in Turkey can be read as efforts of the working class to regain their creativity and confidence toward defending their lives. We should deem it a challenge to the impression that there is no alternative. People of the working class have started to mobilize power over their lives and destinies. In short, collective self-confidence of the working class is being repaired. In our dark analyses, we should recall the words of Lenin: 'History has a much more broader imagination than you attribute to it.'

I want to point out two tendencies within the context of resistances and struggles that I have mentioned above. First is that which says 'no.' The Gezi uprising, TEKEL resistance, anti-HES struggles, student dissent, the resistance of the urban poor against urban regeneration projects, and the struggles of unappointed teachers all reveal the strong collective tendency towards refusals and objections. The second tendency is that which says 'no' to existing structures and then endeavors to create alternatives. This is a tendency in search of alternatives, which is demonstrated in various attempts at unionization, local government, organizing via social media, and new journalism practices.

Resistance and Struggle: Voices of 'No' from the Street

It is clear that the diggings of different segments of the working class and tunnels they opened played a significant role in paving the way to the Gezi Uprising: Student movements, anti-HES resistances, movements against urban regeneration, doctors who object the Full Day Law, teachers who are not appointed, white collars who came together in the plaza action platform, blue collars who resisted in TEKEL resistance. Thus, resistance practices of fractions and strata of the working class in all fields of social life offered significant contributions to the Gezi uprising.

Thinking about collective resistance certainly means thinking about class struggle and class-consciousness. It is not incorrect to say that few Marxists have gone beyond theoretical analysis to studying the class-consciousness of real workers[7] in particular in recent years (Ollman, 1993). This is due to the belief, among Marxists, that such consciousness is a necessary by-product of capitalist economic crisis or the belief that class-consciousness can only be observed in political actions (Ollman, 1993). However, it should be emphasized that class struggle and class consciousness are constantly produced within irreconcilable conflicts of capitalist social formation and within all moments and fields of life. Class struggle is the life itself.[8]

7　Non-Marxist social science has made class-consciousness one of its main topics of study (Ollman, 1993). Ollman (1993) mentions four approaches that investigate class-consciousness within non-Marxists social science. The first one is the attitude surveys that are directed to measuring how workers feel and think. The second is the public choice literature examining the practical reasoning that leads individuals to make decisions on whether to participate in class actions or not. The third is the fact of increasing fragmentation of the work force that follows from changes in the structure of the job market. The fourth is the approach that looks for an answer to the question 'Why is there no socialism in the U.S.?'

8　While I was discussing the sentence of 'Class struggle is the life itself,' I line up Poulantzas, Thompson and Wood one after another. One of them is the representative of structural Marxism while others represent a historical materialist approach. They possess two different politics that expel each other harshly while positioning themselves within Marxism. 'The struggle' between structural Marxism and historical, humanist, and political Marxism has been under way since the second half of the 20th century. Although they have fundamental divergences regarding class-subject conception and conception of history, I think the two approaches converge since they do not confine the class into an economic position and they conceptualize it within the struggle. I may be uttering 'terrifying' things about inner-Marxism debates. Yet, I still say that I did not refrain from using these approaches one after another in the context that 'they find the class within the struggle.'

Classes exist through class struggle. Everything happens as if social classes were the result of an ensemble of structures and of their relations firstly, at the economic level, secondly at the political level, and thirdly at the ideological level (Poulantzas, 1973). In Poulantzas's (1973, p. 86) words, 'Social relations consist of class practices, in which social classes are placed in oppositions: social classes can be conceived only as class practices, these practices existing in oppositions which, in their unity, constitute the field of class struggle.'

Class formations emerge as people gain experience and cope with problems within the process of struggle. Thompson's (1991) conception of class has the capacity to detect class-based movements even in cases in which there are no major class-based revolts. Discovery of class formations and class-consciousness becomes evident through the experiences and practices of people within the struggle. In this way, class formations within the whole social relations, 'emerge and develop as men and women live their productive relations, and experience their determinate situations, with their inherited culture and expectations and as they handle their experiences in cultural ways' (Thompson, 1991, p. 150).

The continuity of the class struggle also emphasizes the continuity of the resistance. Class struggle—and therefore the resistance of the working class—continues at moments when there are no revolutionary insurrections. We can observe class struggle 'on the street' and 'loud and clear' within certain conjunctures—nodal points and moments. The conjuncture is the object of politics (political practice). In other words, the conjuncture is the present moment that is the raw material which is transformed by political practice. As noted by Poulantzas (1973, p. 41), 'The conjuncture is the nodal point where the contradictions of the various levels of a formation are condensed in the complex relations governed by over-determination and by their dislocation and uneven development. This present moment is therefore a conjuncture, a strategic point where the various contradictions fuse in so far as they reflect the articulation specifying a structure in dominance.' In certain conjunctures, one can refer to class positions. Alliances, strategies, and social powers can come into play in class positions. Yet, regarding class positions, class struggle in economic, political, and ideological fields is continuing day by day. 'The marginal conspiracies and plots active at any given moment are also fermenting the great rages of days to come,' says Bensaid (2001). While he perceives the revolution of capital as 'launched into a conquest of the future along the tracks of progress, these revolutions and roaring locomotives of history,' Bensaid adds: 'The stubborn old mole will survive the dashing locomotive.'

Against 'whom' and 'what' is the resistance directed? The separation of the economic and political fields in capitalism is critical to understanding/theorizing the resistance. In circumstances where economic struggle and political contradictions are not differentiated, the state functions as a central and universal enemy of the working class and is the target of mass struggle. Under capitalism, the struggle for economic rights and class struggle may not proceed hand in hand. In fact, the struggle of the working class for its economic rights—the stage called 'economism'—reflects the underdevelopment of class consciousness. Nevertheless, the basic issue here is that both the objects and the field of political struggle in the capitalist production structure change (Wood, 2005).

In his book, *The Making of the English Working Class,* Thompson states that workers, in order to cope with the poor conditions that they are in, tend towards new class-based forms 'that are well-based and self-conscious'; specifically, they take part in educational activities, establish political organizations, and publish periodicals. And yet, Thompson also states that working class intellectual traditions, the form of social life of the working class, and working class solidarity have been maintained.

How is resistance possible? This question can be considered through Gramsci's (1971) concept of 'war of position,' which includes not only acquired gains and the losses, but also the moments in which things gained (or lost) directly contribute to the escalation of conflict.

In recent years, left intellectuals seem to have given up the struggle against capitalism, either embracing capitalism as 'the best option' or seeking small cracks in the armament of capitalism. Resistances, identities, and discourses are conceived as fragmented and dispersed. This conception, rather than seeking power in objective foundations, tends to fall back on the Foucauldian (1979, 1980) sense of power as encompassing everything without a systemic origin. Wood's (2005, p. 17) question to this conception of power is challenging: 'What better escape, in theory, from a confrontation with capitalism, the most totalizing system the world has ever known, than a rejection of totalizing knowledge?'

The effort of understanding and articulating individual and collective resistance as a practice of class struggle necessitates a distance from discussions of 'resistance' in the intersectionality literature. The concept of intersectionality, which is embraced by left intellectuals, conceives of class, gender, and ethnicity as axes of inequality and injustice. It refuses a hierarchical order among those axes (Walby et al., 2012). Intersectionality has recently become an important concept of mainstream labor studies. As Birelma writes, 'Class is certainly not a field which is capable of explaining all atrocities committed by humankind against humankind. Moreover, arguing that class is the central or most important field, if not the only one, would be a farfetched effort that would lead to injustice' (Birelma, 2014, p. 12). When class is reduced to one of numerous parameters that explain social reality within the framework of the positivist epistemology and methods of bourgeois social science, the question of why class is a superior parameter compared to others emerges Yet, what is essential is not pretending to be 'left' while adopting the epistemology and method of bourgeois social sciences. As Benjamin (1969, p. 41) said, one should not 'become the instrument of the dominant class' and share their sins.' Class is a constituting concept of an epistemology and method for conceiving social reality. It is a constituting relation that produces and reproduces the capitalist relations of production and everyday life within the capitalist social formation. Therefore, the main reason for putting the priority on class does not derive from being 'determinist,' 'reductionist,' and 'essentialist'; rather, it derives from adopting a non-bourgeois epistemology that would grasp social reality. Besides, the resistance can only be struggling against injustice and atrocity within a non-bourgeois epistemology.

The Gezi Uprising was the moment when people en masse said 'no' to the silent violence of the AKP. In Chapter 2, *The Gezi Uprising as a Turning Point for Ideological Struggles in Turkey*, Cenk Saraçoğlu and Melih Yeşilbağ develop a theoretical perspective and a methodological framework for understanding and explaining the historical and structural conditions of the Gezi Uprising. Saraçoğlu and Yeşilbağ point out three primary weakness in attempts to understand the uprising: namely, problematic conceptualizations of time and place, ambiguous and loose definitions of the 'middle class' and methodological individualism. The authors then put forward a reading of the uprising as a symptom of the hegemonic project of AKP, what Žižek (1989, p. 17) would perhaps describe as 'a paradoxical element of a social totality which, without ceasing to be its internal constituent, subverts the very universal rational principle of this totality.' Through this interpretation of the uprising, Saraçoğlu and Yeşilbağ show that AKP gradually lost its ability to appropriate the values and concerns that have been long raised by dissident sections of society and left-wing opposition in Turkey and thus had to take refuge—and indeed, reveal its own true identity—in an Islamic conservative vision of society coupled with an authoritarian and repressive state structure. The authors argue that the Gezi uprising was precisely an effort to reverse 'ideological dispossession' together with the 'movement of class' and the 'class movement' duality.

TEKEL (Former Alcohol and Tobacco Monopoly) Resistance was the 'no' of the working class after a long time. In Chapter 3, *The Working Class Back on the Stage: Ashes and Sparkles in the TEKEL Resistance*, Fatih Yaşlı examines the resistance through its competences, possibilities, and potentials. Yaşlı regards the TEKEL Resistance as the reaction of the working class against a neoliberal-conservative regime. The 78-day-long resistance refused polarizations, either religious, cultural, or ethnic, and the agenda was determined by the labor-capital conflict. The most neoliberal government in Turkish history, the AKP is ironically supported by poor people and receives the majority of its votes from this group.

The TEKEL Resistance is of historical importance because workers became aware of the conservative blanket covering neoliberal policies and decided to fight against it. While discussing the TEKEL Resistance, Yaşlı emphasizes that the working class, as the subject of the movement, took part in the movement not with but *despite* their labor unions in most instances. He also explains that socialist organizations re-established their links with the working class during TEKEL Resistance.

Turkish youth have said 'no' to the AKP rule in a way that challenges the dominant discourse casting them as apolitical, passive, and apathetic. In Chapter 4, *The Campus as a Zone of Dissent: The Eggs, the Canteens, and the Laws*, Ezgi Kaya examines the dynamics of youth mobilizing and the 'creative and productive' power of young people who are either workers themselves or who are being educated to join the labor market and feel anxious about their future. Kaya emphasizes that the youth movements have formed the strongest reactions against the AKP government and that they have developed a critical stance against commodification, commercialization, and conservatization. Student protests in Turkey were among the strongest and most effective reactions against the AKP government, both because they were unexpected by AKP officials and because they generated extensive public discussion and support. Kaya underlines the fact that the university student protests must be analyzed both in terms of their internally interconnected dynamics as well as their confrontation with neoliberal processes. Turkish youth experience precarity in the labor market, on the one hand, and a sense of hopelessness regarding their future, on the other. At the outset of the 21st century, argues Kaya, two tendencies are brought forth and clarified in mutual interaction: the wave of re-proletarianization and youth movement.

Local people in valleys all over Anatolia have stated a resounding 'no!' While the construction of Hydroelectric Power Plants (HES) continues to threaten brooks throughout Anatolia, an organization with perhaps the most beautiful of names relentlessly keeps the resistance alive. In Chapter 5, *Sisterhood of the Brooks: Ruralizing the Dissent and the Anti-HES Movement*, Mahmut Hamsici investigates the struggle of those who demand that, 'Water is life, it cannot be sold! Our brooks are free, they will flow freely.' Hamsici narrates his travels across the Black Sea region during the last two months of 2009, documenting his discussions with local people in coffee houses, vineyards, and orchards. He examines the early experiences of hundreds of villagers involved in the anti-HES Movement—the demonstrations, police batons, and detention. He then investigates the three stages of anti-HES struggle—law, science, and the street—as well as the core symbols of the anti-HES movement, such as the yellow scarf, the accordion, the bagpipe, and the kemençe. The anti-HES movement was an opportunity for people to come together en masse, often for the first time, to discuss their common situation and to take decisions about their future in meetings where everyone had the equal right to speak.

The urban poor have also said 'no' to urban regeneration projects and have struggled to maintain their right to housing. In Chapter 6, *The Struggle of the Urban Poor: Urban Regeneration, the Right to Housing and Fraternity*, Fatma Yıldırım and İnci Özgür İlhan document the struggle of the urban poor in Ankara's Dikmen Valley. With nowhere else to go, residents stayed in the valley and fought. Their achievements against the rentier class have fed their efficacy further. As Gecas (2000, p. 94) states, 'participation in political activism may itself increase feelings of personal and collective efficacy if the actions are successful.'

Women too are collectively saying 'no' to the silent violence of the AKP; indeed, they have come to the fore of the resistance. As the feminization of migration (Toksöz, 2007) and the feminization of poverty (Ecevit, 2007) have been discussed at length, it is time for debates around the feminization of resistance. In Chapter 7, *Women's Movement and Resistance: Different Women, Different Activisms*, Ecehan Balta reflects on the inheritance and tensions that comprise women's movements in 21st century Turkey. At a moment when women's movements in the West have lost much of the influence they gained in the 1970s, Turkish women have been creating remarkably active and vibrant movements. After explaining the milestones of the women's movement, Balta discusses both the state's response to the movement and its attitude towards gender equality. She also notes that women's movements in Turkey have traditionally attracted three groups of supporters— Islamist women, Kurdish women, and 'classical' feminist women.

Public employees are also saying 'no' in the face of eroding social rights and shrinking employment opportunities. Education is the field in which regulations towards public employees have been most visible. Transformation in education has the potential to directly influence the public, public employees, and publicity. In Chapter 8, *Public Employees and Practices of Resistance: The Ideology and Politics of Education and Teachers*, Orkun Saip Durmaz discusses the possibilities of this site for resistance against the AKP regime. Durmaz argues that the resistance against education policies should be discussed in three separate contexts: Labor process, syndical organization, and political regime. Based on in-depth interviews and focus-group-discussions with 41 teachers from seven separate institutions, Durmaz reveals that the hegemony of political Islam over education is neither a negligible detail nor as a 'Kemalist obsession' as liberal arguments claim. If there is a need for organizing an inclusive social opposition today, says Durmaz, the opposition should not limit itself to an economic sphere that is locked into labor union level; rather, it should build its ideological-political line by positioning itself against the dominant discourse of the political regime. According to Durmaz, once we refocus the analysis on the practices of the political regime in social life, then the locus of resistance becomes neither the individual nor the labor union, but the social opposition as a whole defined within the highest level of politicization.

Struggle and Counter-Publics: Voices of 'We Have a Dream' from the Street

Working class culture flourishes and develops at the time and in the spaces in which the experience, ability, and practices of social labor power strengthen in the form of counter strategies. At this point, it is worthwhile reflecting on the proletarian public sphere in which the working class can create its own practical political experiences. The proletarian public sphere redefines the notion of the public sphere within the contexts of labor, production, experience, and class struggles (Negt & Kluge, 1993). In proletarian public spheres, the working class can politically express its specific interests through its own forms of publicity. Therefore, examining class relations in or out of the workplace necessitates a reflection on proletarian public spheres, which can be formed and/or not formed through the experience of the working class.

While reflecting on the proletarian public sphere, it should be remembered that neoliberal policies did not only deregulate and regulate economic and political spheres but also destroyed the possibilities of collective class organization and action. Marx defined collective action in his *Economic and Philosophic Manuscripts of 1844* as follows:

> When communist *artisans* associate with one another, theory, propaganda, etc., is their first end. But at the same time, as a result of this association, they acquire a new need—the need for society—and what appears as a means becomes an end. In this practical process the most splendid results are to be observed whenever French socialist workers are seen together. Such things as smoking, drinking, eating, etc., are no longer means of contact or means that bring them together. Association, society and conversation, which again has association as its end, are enough for them; the brotherhood of man is no mere phrase with them, but a fact of life and the nobility of man shines upon us from their work-hardened bodies ([1844], 1998, p. 134).

Neoliberal political and economic policies damaged the working segments of society to the extent that they would not be able to stand side by side and speak to each other any more. These policies left them without a say or possibilities for action. In *Silent Violence*, we emphasized that the working class lost its belief in acting together, expressing that: 'Our words are silently being taken away' (Coşar & Yücesan-Özdemir, 2012). Hence, close attention needs to be paid to the experiences of the working class to reveal both the possibilities for collective action as well as the obstacles that block this energy.

Labor can create counter-publics that go beyond the horizon of bourgeois democracy, as Ali Murat Özdemir demonstrates in Chapter 9. Focusing on the conditions for such organizing, *Counter-Publics and Organized Labor: Beyond the Limits of Bourgeois Democracy* opens with the claim that, 'there is organized helplessness and unorganized demands.' Özdemir assesses the formation of counter-publics against crises that again and again scatter people who cannot be organized and who did not (or cannot) join the capitalist front within their organized helplessness. Özdemir centers on the organizational conditions for resistance against the commodification and primitive accumulation processes that wreck people's lives with such frequency. Within the counter-publics debate, he highlights possibilities for producing socialist social policy demands in a capitalist society.

Counter-publics are generated through local practices. In Chapter 10, *Counter-Publics and Local Practices: The Struggle for Revolutionary-Popular Government*, Ahmet Kerim Gültekin discusses the role of revolutionary-popular local administrations in the people's struggle for democracy. Gültekin emphasizes that the struggle in the field of revolutionary-popular local government is one of the important historical focal points for the recent mass uprising, yet it is also an area of struggle whose importance has mostly been overlooked in the people's struggle for democracy. From an anthropological perspective, Gültekin evaluates the experiences of the Municipality of Mazgirt to expound upon the theoretical and practical knowledge of anti-capitalist, egalitarian, and participative local governments defying neo-liberal depredation. Gültekin argues that the revolutionary-popular local governments implement alternative economic, social, political and cultural policies with the perspective of creating 'sustainable cities/habitats.' Among the common traits of revolutionary-popular local governments are: The access of people and individuals to positions in local government on the basis of their victimized identities (women, children, minority ethnicity, the impoverished etc.); their participation in processes of decision-making, implementation and supervision; and the determining of the local budget within this framework.

Social media can play its part in the formation of counter-publics to the extent that it enables information-sharing communication, organizing, and resisting class practices. Social media has recently become the main target of AKP repression. In Chapter 11, *Counter-Publics and Social Media: Different Channels for Self-Organization and Red-Hackers*, Şafak Etike, discusses the opportunities and restrictions that the Internet offers for class struggle. Etike studies the Turkish hackers group, RedHack, which has recently attracted significant attention and popular support. Etike shows how RedHack succeeded in leading social mobilization in the digital field, by calling to account political elites and demanding change. She analyzes RedHack in terms of its political form and activities and its language. The capability for establishing freedom of expression is certainly an important element of counter-public debates as well. In Chapter 12, *Counter-Publics and Freedom of Expression: New Forms of Journalism in the Digital Environment*, Emek Çaylı argues that despite AKP's repression, violence, and censorship over media and freedom of speech, the Internet enables political activism and political participation through changing journalism practices, civic journalism, online journalism, and data journalism. Çaylı provides an overview of the new journalism practices and forms in Turkey. She also sheds light on the social media campaign titled '*Diren Gazetecilik*' (Resist Journalism), a recent example of Internet use for political activism.

Taken together, this volume hopes to contribute to the resistance and struggles that continue to be fought on the street, as well as on the economic and political terrain.

References

Ansal, H., Küçükçifçi, S., Onaran, Ö. & Orbay, B. Z. (2000). *Türkiye Emek Piyasasının Yapısı ve İşsizlik*. İstanbul: Türkiye Ekonomik ve Toplumsal Tarih Vakfı.

Arın, T. (2002). The poverty of social security: The welfare regime in Turkey. In N. Balkan & S. Savran (Eds.), *The ravages of neoliberalism: Economy, society, and gender in Turkey* (pp. 73-91). New York: Nova.

Bahçe, S., Yücesan-Özdemir, G., Voyvoda, E., Özdemir, A. M., Candan, M. A., & Kurt, İ. H. (2011). *Emek Politikaları: Ne Oluyor, Ne Yapmalı?* Ankara: Belediye-İş.

Balkan, E., Balkan, N. & Öncü, A. (2014). (Eds.). *Neoliberalizm, İslamcı Sermayenin Yükselişi ve AKP*. İstanbul: Yordam.

Benjamin, W. (1969). *Illuminations: Essays and reflections*. Schocken.

Bensaid, D. (2001). *Resistances: Essai de taupologie generale*. Paris: Payard.

Birelma, A. (2013). *Ekmek ve Haysiyet Mücadelesi: Günümüz Türkiyesi'nde Üç İşçi Hareketinin Etnografisi*. İstanbul: İletişim.

Bölükbaşı, T., & Ertugal, E. (2013). Europeanisation of employment policy in Turkey: Tracing domestic change through institutions, ideas, and interests. *South European Society and Politics, 18*(2), 235-257.

Boratav, K. (2014). *Türkiye İktisat Tarihi, 1908-2009*. Ankara: İmge.

Buğra, A. (2001). Political Islam in Turkey in historical context. In N. Balkan & S. Savran (Eds.), *The Politics of permanent crisis: Class, ideology and state in Turkey* (pp. 107-144). New York: Nova Science Publishers.

Çarkoğlu, A. (2007). The nature of left-right ideological self-placement in the Turkish context. *Turkish Studies, 8*(2), 253-271.

Castel, R. (2003). *L'Insécurité sociale. Qu'est-ce qu'être protégé?* Coll. La République des idées, éd. du Seuil.

Coşar, S., & Yeğenoğlu M. (2009). The neoliberal restructuring of Turkey's social security system. *Monthly Review, 60*(11), 34-47.

Coşar, S., & Yücesan-Özdemir, G. (2012). (Eds.). *Silent violence: Neoliberalism, Islamist politics and the AKP years in Turkey*. Ottawa: Red Quill Books.

Ecevit, Y. (2007). Yoksulluğa Karşı feminist strateji İçin'. *Amarji, 6*, 14-17.

Foucault, M. (1979). *Discipline and punish: The birth of the prison*. New York: Vintage Books.

Foucault, M. (1980). *Power/Knowledge*. New York: Pantheon.

Gecas, V. (2000). Value identities, self-motives, and social movements. In S. Stryker, T. J. Owens, & R. W. White (Eds.), *Self, identity, and social movements* (pp. 93-110). Minneapolis: University of Minnesota Press.

Gramsci, A. (1971). *Selections from prison notebooks*. New York: International Publishers.

İnal, K., & Akkaymak, G. (2012). (Eds.). *Neoliberal transformation of education in Turkey: Political and ideological analysis of educational reforms in the age of the AKP*. New York: Palgrave Macmillan.

Kemal, O. (2007). *72. Koğuş*. İstanbul: Everest.

Marx, K. ([1844], 1988). *The economic and philosophic manuscripts of 1844*. Prometheus Books.

Marx, K. ([1852], 1994). *The eighteenth brumaire of Louis Bonaparte*. Penguin Books.

Negt, O., & Kluge, A. (1993). *Public sphere and experience: Towards an analysis of bourgeois and proletarian public sphere*. University of Minnesota Press.

O'Neill, J. (2001). *Piyasa: Etik, bilgi, politika*. (çev. Şen Süer Kaya). İstanbul: Ayrıntı Yayınları.

Ollman, B. (1993). *Dialectical investigations*. Routledge.

Özdemir, A. M. (2012). Fragments of changes in the legal system in the AKP years: The development and reproduction of market friendly law. In S. Coşar, S. & G. Yücesan-Özdemir (Eds.), *Silent violence: Neoliberalism, Islamist politics and the AKP Years in Turkey* (pp. 43-46). Ottawa: Red Quill Books.

Özdemir, A. M., & Yücesan-Özdemir, G. (2006). Labour law reform in Turkey in the 2000s: The devil is not in detail but in the legal texts too. *Economic and Industrial Democracy, 27*(2), 311-331.

Özdemir, A. M., & Yücesan-Özdemir, G. (2008). Opening Pandora's box: Social security reform in Turkey under AKP rule. *South East Europe Review, 9*(3), 469-483.

Özdemir, A. M., & Yücesan-Özdemir, G. (2009). What is wrong with collective labour law in Turkey? *International Union Rights, 16*(2), 20-22.

Özdemir, A. M., & Yücesan-Özdemir, G. (2011). Labour, law, and society in Turkey: The new labour act in a wider context. *Critique of Political Economy, 1*, 64-87.

Özdemir, A. M., Erel, D., & Yücesan-Özdemir, G. (2004). Rethinking informal labour market in Turkey: A possible politics for unions. *South East Europe Review, 7*(3), 33-42.

Özuğurlu, M. (2010). Tekel Direnişi: Sınıfsal Mücadeleler Üzerine Anımsamalar. In. G. Bulut (Ed.), *Tekel Direnişinin Işığında Gelenekselden Yeniye İşçi Sınıfı Hareketi* (pp. 40-53). Ankara: Nota Bene.

Özuğurlu, M. (2011). The TEKEL resistance movement: Reminiscences on class struggle. *Capital and Class, 35*(2), 179-187.

Poulantzas, N. (1973). *Political power and social classes*. NLB.

Savran, S. (2010a, January 23). Turkey: The working class (literally) takes the stages. *The Bullet: Socialist Project E-bulletin*, 299.

Savran, S. (2010b, March 16). The 'Sakarya Commune' wins the first Round! *Europe Solidaire Sans Frontières E-bulletin.* Retrieved from http://www.europe-solidaire. orgSayer, A. (2005). *Moral Significance of Class.* London: Routledge.

Süral, N. (2005). Reorganization of working time and modalities of employment under the new Turkish labour act. *Middle Eastern Studies, 41*(3), 407-420.

Thompson, E. P. (1991). *The making of English working class.* Penguin.

Toksöz, G. (2007). *Women's employment situation in Turkey.* Ankara: ILO.

Tuğal, C. (2009). *Passive revolution: Absorbing the Islamic challenge to capitalism.* Stanford University Press.

Tuğal, C. (2013). Resistance everywhere: The Gezi revolt in global perspective. *New Perspectives on Turkey, 49*, 157-172.

Walby, S., Armstrong, J., & Strid, S. (2012). Intersectionality: Multiple inequalities in social theory. *Sociology, 46*(2), 224-240.

World Health Organization. (2006). Turkey: Country cooperation strategy at a glance. Retrieved from http://www.who.int/countryfocus/resources/ccsbrief_turkey_ tur_06_en.pdf

Wood, E. M. (2005). *Capitalism against democracy: Renewing historical materialism.* Cambridge University Press.

Yalman, G. (2012). Politics and discourse under the AKP's rule: The marginalisation of class-based politics, Erdoğanisation and post-secularism. In. S. Coşar & G. Yücesan-Özdemir (Eds.), *Silent violence: Neoliberalism, Islamist politics, and the AKP years in Turkey* (pp. 21-43). Ottawa: Red Quill Books.

Yavuz, H. (2006). (Ed.). *The emergence of a New Turkey: Democracy and the AK Parti.* Salt Lake City: The University of Utah Press.

Yeldan, E. (2010, January 30). TEKEL workers' resistance: Re-awakening of the Proletariat in Turkey. *Sendika.* Retrieved from http://www.sendika.org.

Yeldan, E. (2006). Neoliberal global remedies: From speculative-led growth to IMF-led crisis in Turkey. *Review of Radical Political Economics, 38, 193-213.*

Yücesan-Özdemir, G. (2003). Hidden forms of resistance among the Turkish workers: Hegemonic incorporation or building blocks for the working class struggle? *Capital and Class, 81*, 31-61.

Yücesan-Özdemir, G. (2012). The social policy regime in the AKP years: The Emperor's new clothes. In S. Coşar, S. & G. Yücesan-Özdemir (Eds.), *Silent violence: Neoliberalism, Islamist politics, and the AKP years in Turkey* (pp. 125-133). Ottawa: Red Quill Books.

Zizek, S. (1989). *The Sublime Object of Ideology.* Verso Books.

PART I.
RESISTING
NEOLIBERAL
PUBLICS IN
21st CENTURY
TURKEY

2.
THE GEZI UPRISING AS A TURNING POINT FOR IDEOLOGICAL STRUGGLES IN TURKEY

Cenk Saraçoğlu and Melih Yeşilbağ

At the turn of the century, Perry Anderson (2000) wrote in the *New Left Review* that neoliberalism was the most successful ideology in modern history. Although the boldness of the claim may be called into question, there was substantial ground to think likewise. If there was one thing that epitomized the end of the century, it was the triumph of free market capitalism. Communism, once the arch-enemy, was rendered a matter of a bygone antiquity; organized labor, a shadow of its former self, was either reduced to a negligible actor or no longer a threat to the system; other major potentially anti-systemic forces, such as national liberation movements, landless peasants, or demands for more freedom, were somehow coopted, and large masses that were once sources of discontent had been seduced into the establishment by the gleams of consumerism.

Capitalism seemed, more than ever, invincible, robust, and the promising path to prosperity.

Approximately a decade later, this is no longer the case. In the decade—but especially the years following the 2008 financial meltdown—we have witnessed a loss of faith in neoliberalism. The global shock of 2008 dramatically exposed the unsustainable, fragile—not to mention deeply unequal—character of global capitalism and, in the process, rendered the supposed virtues of free markets suddenly obsolete, the ardent gurus of deregulation apologetic, and the long-repressed themes of class-based politics, redistribution, regulation and even socialism once again relevant for public debate (McNally, 2011). Unlike previous social movements of the last decades, which were isolated to specific regions, this unexpected wave of protests spanned the whole globe, filling the streets of both the developing world and the centers of advanced capitalism. The trembling of the ruling classes was so palpable, that historical parallels were made to the revolutionary days of 1848 (Davis, 2011, p. 7).

The contagious wave of protest made itself strongly felt in a diverse array of settings, from Maghreb to Southern Europe, Latin America to the Balkans, and the Middle East to the USA, where mass movements had become increasingly rare and weak. Progressives are presented with a set of crucial intellectual tasks: to offer a detailed map of this epoch of dissent; to provide an overall assessment of the possibilities and limits of the current situation; and to develop new tactics and strategies—both at the level of theory and praxis. Of course, we cannot attempt such an endeavor in this short chapter; instead, we seek to outline identifiable characteristics of this wave of protests in Turkey to open up both theoretical and methodological paths to better understand the Gezi Uprising.

The first observation to be made is that the wave of protest was constituted by a tremendous variation among social movements. Manifestations of resistance varied in terms of their triggering event, demands, social composition, ideological orientation, and outcomes. The characteristics of the power bloc they were critiquing also differed across cases. A few examples will demonstrate this diversity: The sparking event for the Arab world was the suicide of a street vendor in Tunisia as a protest to entrenched unemployment, insecurity, and poverty; whereas in Southern European countries—such as Italy, Spain, and Greece—it was the heavy toll of the recent austerity measures that brought people in masses to the streets. The US Occupy Movement—captured in the compelling slogan, 'We are the 99 percent'—was a response to the vast income inequalities exacerbated as a result of the crisis. In Turkey, the catalyst for widespread protests was a small-scale opposition to the demolition of Gezi Park; whereas in Brazil, the trigger was a bus fare hike.

Demands were diverse too. In austerity-ridden Europe, these were mainly centered on putting a stop to the punitive measures imposed by the Troika, but they were also directed to protecting social provisions and pushing for a more egalitarian, redistributionist political orientation. In the dictatorships of the Arab world, however, political freedoms and the overthrowing of the regime were the prioritized demands of protesters. In Turkey, political freedoms and secularism were at the forefront.

Another point of variation was the social composition of the protesters. In austerity-struck Greece and Spain, the organized working class, along with students and pensioners, were active participants. In countries demanding greater political freedoms, it was well-educated youth who were at the frontline. While this diversity of participants is certainly an interesting point of comparison, it cannot be the primary analytical entry point for assessing contemporary social movements.

Of course, the political orientations of the protests were also shaped by the characteristics of the power blocs being challenged at the time and the organized groups ready to mobilize a wave of dissent. In Greece, for instance, where central left and right parties were deemed equally responsible for the path towards the crisis, a well-organized radical left dominated the streets, although a neo-fascist movement also managed to organize a certain segment of the discontent. In Italy too, where the radical left was weaker, discontent fed anti-immigrant, racist sentiments. In the countries of the Maghreb, well-organized Islamist movements that had been excluded from the upper echelons of the oligarchic dictatorships gained important ground. In the US, disenchantment with the existing political structures not only created Occupy Wall Street and ignited Black dissidence, but also nurtured the extreme right-wing Tea Party. In Syria and Ukraine, the crisis galvanized already existing ethnic and religious conflicts and created peculiar forms of radical right-wing insurgency—Jihadist in the former and neo-fascist in the latter. In Turkey, the protests represented, among other things, the long-accumulated anger towards the authoritarian and Islamist orientations of the ruling party. In sum, the wave of revolt across the world that emerged after the financial crisis of 2008 was significantly heterogeneous in terms of content, composition, and political and ideological orientation.

The scale of diversity raises a fundamental question: Can we still talk about an underlying structural factor that cuts across all of these cases? Or, as some argue, is it simply Twitter or the 'zeitgeist' that made the wave of revolts contagious? We argue that despite the variation in the themes, slogans, composition, form, and political orientations of the protests, all of these movements are affiliated with the crisis of neoliberalism. We further argue that the heterogeneity of these protests is a reflection of the inherently flexible and varied nature of neoliberalism itself. We will elucidate this argument by clarifying our conceptualization of neoliberalism below.

Actually Existing Neoliberalism
and Variants of Resistance

Part of the difficulty of analyzing neoliberalism is that the term itself has become a buzzword within the literature, with disparate and sometimes conflicting uses and meanings. Specifically, there tends to be two related flaws in the literature that contribute to the confusion. First, there is a tendency to equate the theoretical proposals of key neoliberal thinkers such as Hayek and Friedman with the neoliberal policy practice that has been dominant in the last three decades. Yet, as many scholars have noted, there is a significant discrepancy between the normative prescriptions of orthodox neoliberal theory and the actual deeds of neoliberal power blocs across the world. This is perhaps most manifest in the rhetoric of the 'shrinking state' that persists despite the systemic rise of state interventions in areas such as security, commodification, and market building. Scholars have challenged this conflation of theory and practice by distinguishing between a more ideologically-driven phase of neoliberalism marked by an orthodox interpretation of market-reform (as in the case of the Thatcher and Reagan era) and a more politically-driven phase marked by a more moderate and pragmatic approach aimed at containing the tensions and crisis dynamics that emerged in the previous phase (as in the case of 'Third Way' governments).

The second tendency—and a consequence of the first—is to conceptualize neoliberalism in terms of a rigid and monolithic model that is 'invented' somewhere (say, in the Anglo-Saxon world) and transposed to—or imposed on—the rest of the world without modification. This habit of thinking dismisses the huge variation of neoliberalism across both time and space. By now, the discrepancy between the 'Washington Consensus' (a neoliberalization package imposed on the South by the US) and the domestic policies of Washington is well known.

Our approach is premised on that of Brenner and Theodore's (2002) 'actually existing neoliberalism,' which conceptualizes neoliberalism as an inherently flexible hegemonic project rather than a rigid model with a fixed and predetermined character. By doing so, we emphasize the ability of neoliberalism to self-modify, accommodate, and reproduce itself in remarkably different settings—an ability that explains the endurance of neoliberalism despite a series of serious crises (Cahill, 2010). A corollary of this approach is the recognition that although neoliberalism is mainly about the restoration of the power of capital over labor (Harvey, 2005, p. 16), it can articulate itself within a broad spectrum of ideological tendencies and currents— ranging from left to right, liberal to conservative, secular to religious—as well as a broad spectrum of political regimes—ranging from formal democracies to overt dictatorships.

If there is no single neoliberalism with a fixed, predetermined character, then, similarly, we cannot talk about a single crisis of neoliberalism that necessarily manifests itself as a strict antagonism between the laboring classes and capital. Rather, crises emerge within a specific neoliberal regime in a given capitalist social formation (national setting).[9] The specificities of that regime—namely, the political-ideological strategies of the neoliberal power bloc—shape the main axis of conflict and, consequently, the content and the form of the social movements that arise in response to the crisis. This explains, then, the variation with which we introduced the recent wave of protests. We argue that the more appropriate entry point for analyzing social movements since 2008 is the concrete political-ideological dynamics, namely, the hegemonic project, ideological strategies of the power bloc, and crisis dynamics.

The Gezi uprising in Turkey is an important case through which to see the linkages between the actual and concrete form that neoliberal capital accumulation takes in a particular social formation and the nature of a nation-wide uprising that occurred as a defiance against the power-bloc in that social formation. We begin our analysis with a critique of the quite prevalent intellectual tendency in Turkey to conceive of the Gezi uprising as a 'middle-class' revolt.' This critique will function as a point of departure for an alternative framework for understanding the nature of the Gezi Uprising—one based on its position *vis a vis* the ideological and political specificities of actually existing neoliberalism in Turkey. Our objective in this paper is not only to contribute to ongoing discussions pertaining to the Gezi uprising with a new perspective but also to provide some preliminary assertions as to the methods of evaluating popular uprisings since 2008.

The Gezi Uprising: 'A Middle-Class Revolt'?

One of the most prevalent assertions regarding the character of the Gezi Uprising is that it was a revolt of the 'middle class.' This tendency is replete with theoretical and methodological fallacies and limitations. Appearing in the literature in various forms, this approach relies on a 'loose' and ambiguous understanding of the middle class. Rather than enlisting here all versions of the middle-class analysis, we focus on two that have been widely discussed among

---

9 We use the concept of 'social formation' in this paper as the concrete form that a mode of production takes in a national setting. The capitalist mode of production is universally based on the production relations and the contradiction between labor and capital, but this contradiction could be built on different political and ideological structures depending on the historically specific conditions of each national setting. By 'capitalist social formation' we mean the totality of economic, political, and ideological structures that reproduce the capitalist mode of production in a particular national setting.

Turkish academics and intellectuals: The first offered by Çağlar Keyder and the second by Loic Wacquant.

Çağlar Keyder (2014) interpreted the Gezi uprising as a collective reaction of a 'new middle class' against the paternalistic and authoritarian discourses and policies of the AKP government. In this perspective, the new middle class corresponds to the salaried educated workers who, in comparison with the typical working class profile, expend their mental—rather than physical—labor-power in the work process, enjoy more autonomy in the organization of work conditions, and thus escape the absolute control of capitalists. In this respect, the new middle class does not share the same concerns and forms of consciousness as the classical working class. The most important difference lies within the cultural capital that they have acquired studying abroad in upscale universities throughout the 1990s. From this perspective, the Gezi Uprising is an act of middle class defiance against an authoritarian government whose 'governmentality' and conservative and repressive mentality conflicts with and poses a threat to their values and interests.

In his talk at Boğaziçi University in Istanbul, on January 17, 2014, Loic Wacquant offered a similar perspective by asserting that the Gezi uprising represents the reaction and defiance of the middle class or 'cultural bourgeoisie' against economic capital and political capital. It also manifests the middle class' desire to differentiate itself from lower classes. Wacquant interprets the Gezi uprising as one of the typical examples of a series of recent middle-class revolts in different parts of the world. In short: With the retreat of working class politics in the neoliberal period, the middle class came to the fore as the major representative of opposition and it instilled its own concerns, demands and symbolic world into the recent wave of uprisings. The Turkish middle class has long been contemptuous towards AKP's economic, cultural, and political projects that have occupied and hence limited the major social fields in which the members of this class could (re)produce and enhance their cultural capital. The Gezi Uprising is thus one instance of this universal, middle-class outburst.

We turn now to our critique of these two explanations, which exemplify some of the most common problems in the analysis of the Gezi Uprising. In the process we develop foundational premises for an alternative analytical framework.

The Critique of Middle-Class Oriented Explanations

Analyses like those of Loic Wacquant and Çağlar Keyder focus narrowly on the onset of the Gezi events and are based on the agendas and composition of the early participants who initiated the protests. Accordingly, the protagonists of the Gezi uprising overwhelmingly come from middle-class backgrounds and this background is reflected in the discourses, symbols, and slogans of the resistance.

Yet, precisely because this analysis remains fixated on the starting point of the protests, it excludes the formation process from the analytical frame. The error here is significant when we recognize that the uprising actually spread across Turkey in a short while and underwent internal transformations in the process. A reaction that started as an environmentalist protest against the AKP's decision to transform a public park into a shopping mall took on a countrywide political character crystallized in the slogan '*AKP İstifa*' ('The AKP should resign!'). In this respect, any comprehensive analysis of the Gezi uprising must take into account how it developed across time and location. The Gezi uprising should be treated as a long wave of protests, extending throughout the whole month of June—transforming from a localized moment of resistance into a countrywide anti-government movement.

The middle-class-based explanations rest on a misconception of the 'space' of resistance, limiting the locus of the Gezi uprising to the park itself. After a few days of protests in downtown Istanbul, the movement spread across more than 70 cities in Turkey, and massive demonstrations, clashes, and occupations—no less serious than those in Istanbul—took place in Ankara, Izmir, and Adana. The profile of the participants in demonstrations taking place in the Alevi neighborhoods of Hatay (a Southern province of Turkey, which became a hotspot of the movement) and in the low-income neighborhoods of Ankara and Istanbul did not match the middle class typology that was attached to the character of Gezi protests.

Methodological Individualism and its Predicaments

Middle-class based explanations also rely on a problematic 'methodological individualism' in their epistemology, conceptualization, and analytical framework. By 'methodological individualism' we mean the epistemological position that takes the individual as an autonomous social and political actor making decisions and engaging in social action according to his or her own rationality (Schmid, 2009, pp. 26-27). Methodological individualism takes the 'individual' as the main unit of analysis and point of departure for developing explanations about the dynamics, developments, and character of societal phenomena and processes (Udehn, 2002, pp. 352-353). A great deal of the mainstream literature on social movement and collective behavior has developed models and analyses premised on methodological individualism; an analytical priority is given to the perceived interests and values of the individual participants of a social movement or uprising (Oberschall, 1993, pp. 36-37).

There are several implications of methodological individualism in middle-class based analyses of the Gezi Uprising: these explanations conceive class as the sum of *individuals* occupying identical or similar positions in the layers of social stratification. Class, in this perspective, is a category into which individuals are be placed based on the amount of resources or assets they have in relation to the total material or non-material wealth. For both Wacquant and Keyder, the middle class is conceptualized on the basis of the resources, consumption patterns and educational background of the *individuals* that make up this class. Yet, conceiving of class as a collection of individuals tends to dismiss the social process through which individuals form a social entity that transcends and, to a certain extent, shapes and affects their individualistic perceptions, interests, and consciousness (Thompson, 1966). Wacquant's explanation, for example, assumes that the Gezi protests consist of middle-class individuals or members of the 'cultural bourgeoisie,' who participate in these protests to protect or pursue their individual interests (cultural capital). Wacquant presumes that these initial motivations remain primary throughout the protests, never considering the ways in which they may be transformed through participation in the social movement. The possibility that an uprising or social movement may have an independent dynamic that exerts an influence on the attitudes and consciousness of individuals (Barker et al., 2013) is thus excluded.

The logical outcome of the methodological individualism embedded in these analyses is to reduce the meaning and character of the Gezi uprising to the profile of its individual participants. The middle-class-based explanations, owing to this individualistic perspective, do not only state that the Gezi uprising consisted mainly of middle-class sections of society, which is also a controversial argument (Yörük & Yüksel, 2014), but they also assert that the uprising itself is predominantly middle-class in character. This is an endemic problem for different versions of mainstream social movement theories, which are preoccupied with developing models for explaining the processes and motivations with which individuals take part in a social movement. Operating at the micro or meso-level, these social movement theories abstain from contextualizing a social movement or an uprising within the totality of the social formation in which it occurs (Krinsky, 2013, p. 108). In the Turkish context, this perspective fails to develop a comprehensive explanation in regards to the political character of the whole movement against the AKP government and its effects on the ideological and political structures of the social formation in Turkey. Against this approach, we argue that the class character of the Gezi uprising cannot be simply inferred from the assumed class profile of its individual participants; rather, it should also be examined through the values, principles and concerns that the movement expressed, as well as the character of the power-bloc it opposed.

From this epistemological standpoint, we assert that the character of a social movement—and the questions of how to define and describe what a particular social movement is and how and to what extent it is different from other social movements—is more adequately understood by asking a different set of questions:

Which contradictions and problems of the social formation lead to the outburst of an uprising or the emergence of a social movement? How does this movement or uprising influence the existing structure of social formation and what kind of possibilities does it create for social opposition?

Gezi Uprising as the 'Symptom' of AKP's Hegemonic Project

These questions will guide our efforts to develop an explanation of the Gezi Uprising. As a first gesture towards answering the two interrelated questions above, we would like to propose that the Gezi Uprising be evaluated as a symptom of the hegemonic project that the AKP government has been building and consolidating in Turkey over the last decade. We use the concept of 'symptom' in two ways: First, based on the dictionary definition of the term, we see the Gezi Uprising as a concrete manifestation, sign, or indication of the crisis of the AKP's hegemonic project. Second, we refer to Slovaj Zizek's (1989, p. 23) definition of the term: 'a paradoxical element of a social totality which, without ceasing to be its internal constituent, subverts the very universal rational principle of this totality.' In this line, the Gezi Resistance can be seen as a symptom of the AKP's hegemonic project in terms of being an 'internal and necessary element' of this project and, at the same time, a potentiality and a dynamic to subvert it.

Ideological Dispossessions and the Gezi Uprising

At this point, we need to clarify the nature of the hegemonic project that the AKP attempted to construct in Turkey over the last decade, and then explain how and why the Gezi Uprising appeared as its symptom. Since its rise to power, in an attempt to overcome the deep economic and political crisis that Turkish capitalism generated in the early 2000s, the AKP government devised and exercised various ideological strategies. One of these strategies can be conceptualized as the 'ideological dispossession of the opposition.' Taking its inspiration from David Harvey's (2009) concept of 'accumulation by dispossession,' ideological dispossession refers to the attempt of the political power to appropriate the cries and demands of existing or potential social and political opposition in a country. By integrating them into its own discourse and manipulating them in a way that is compatible with its own power strategies, the power bloc deprive the opposition of its own political discourse.

One of the most distinctive characteristics of the AKP, which differentiates it from other right-wing governments in Turkey, was its systematic attempt to represent some of the political issues and concerns that left-wing opposition brought to the fore throughout the 1980s and 1990s. Among these issues and concerns were the democratic rights and freedoms that the 1980 coup had curtailed, the recognition of the Kurdish identity—which would presumably end the low intensity war with the PKK in the Kurdish region—and the anti-labor nature of neoliberal capital accumulation that deepened poverty and inequality across Turkey.

Especially in its first two terms—between 2002 and 2011—the AKP government attempted to become a 'representative of' the issue of democratization and human rights. It did so by bringing to the fore the concerns in regards to the legacy of 1980 coup and engaging in a fierce critique of some longstanding institutions and ideological positions, which left-wing opposition had long regarded as the major culprit of the so-called 'democratic deficit' in Turkey. The AKP's struggle to restrain the army's political power through significant legal-constitutional changes and lawsuits not only debilitated this party's most challenging political rival, but also enabled it to depict itself as the representative of civilian politics against 'military tutelage.' These operations against the military were coupled with an openly anti-Kemalist discourse that denigrated Kemalism and the early Republican period in Turkey as the historical root-cause of the lack of democracy in the political establishment (Yörük, 2014). The attempt of the AKP to 'represent democracy and rights' continued and was reinforced in 2010 by a constitutional amendment proposal that the AKP presented as a radical step towards the elimination of the ongoing effects of the military-tutelage regimes established in the aftermath of the 1980 coup. Certain segments of the left-wing opposition either failed to develop an alternative discourse about these large-scale changes or embraced all these developments as a positive—albeit insufficient—step towards Turkey's democratization (Yalman, 2014, pp. 30-31). In other words, the left-wing opposition was dispossessed of its own agenda of democratic rights and freedoms and the platform upon which it had based its position and identity throughout the 1980s and 1990s.

A similar process can be also observed regarding the Kurdish question—another political field in which the Turkish Left sharply differentiated itself from the state's official ideology and from right-wing political forces. The AKP government authorized a reformist policy including partial recognition of Kurdish identity that was unprecedented on the part of governing authorities throughout Turkish history. This approach to the Kurdish question is owed to the specificity of AKP's vision of nationalism—itself an unparalleled position in the history of modern Turkey. In AKP's nationalism, Sunni-Muslim values are no longer conceived solely as *one* of the common cultural features of 'Turkishness,' but have become the *core* element defining what the 'nation' is (White, 2012). In other words, Islam is no longer a cultural component of Turkishness, but has rather become an independent identity in itself and is no longer necessarily derived from or instrumentalized for the idea of Turkishness. As long as the nation is defined along the lines of common Muslim cultural values and a shared Ottoman history, the Kurds, as well as other Muslim ethnic groups in Turkey, can be incorporated into the 'nation.' In this way, the Islamic conservative nationalism of the AKP—and the vision of nation emanating from it—allowed the recognition of the Kurds in Turkey as a separate ethnic group and acknowledgement of Kurds' certain cultural rights (Saraçoğlu & Demirkol, 2014). At least at the level of discourse and propaganda, the AKP radically criticized the Kemalist assimilationist and denialist project and overtly recognized the presence of Kurdishness as a separate ethnic group. This is also reflected in the decisions to open a state-sponsored Kurdish TV channel and to recognize Kurdish language courses as elective in state schools—both of which are quite at odds with former right-wing parties. Moreover, these reforms were also followed by a negotiation process between Abdullah Öcalan, the imprisoned leader of the Kurdistan Workers' Party (PKK), and the National Intelligence Organization. Given the fact that the left wing had long called for the recognition of the Kurdish identity and the start of a peace process with the PKK, it found itself dispossessed of one of its traditional political discourses.

Despite its loyalty to neoliberal orthodoxy in macro-economic policies and its adoption of typical neoliberal urban strategies, the AKP government attempted to represent a critique of neoliberalism, addressing themes of social justice and equality—the very strongholds of left-wing opposition. In this vein, the party used unsystematic social aid policies, health reforms, and philanthropic projects of AKP-affiliated municipalities in such a way as to create the image that it diverges from the earlier neoliberal governments (Buğra & Keyder, 2006). AKP employed an intensely critical discourse against other preceding right-wing governments, which were blamed for being corrupt and 'materialist' and for dragging the country into a series of economic crisis. These policies were complemented by an anti-elitist and populist discourse that criticized the Istanbul bourgeoisie as being one of the culprits of Turkey's economic troubles throughout the 1990s. In this respect it can be argued that AKP used its neoliberal populism as an instrument of the critique of neoliberalism itself, a strategy that also invaded a political field that the left-wing opposition had long tried to monopolize (Yücesan-Özdemir, 2012).

We argue that the Gezi Uprising was a 'symptom' of the crisis of AKP's hegemonic project, since it occurred, as we will elucidate below, at a time when this party was no longer able to sustain its strategy of 'ideological dispossession.' Moreover, it was also a symptom of a hegemonic crisis; indeed, the uprising itself, as a social dynamic, accelerated this crisis and further undermined AKP's strategy of representing values such as freedom, equality, and justice. After eliminating its potential political rivals within the state—and especially after its sweeping election victory in 2011—the AKP government started to further centralize its power by increasing the authority of the executive and implementing overt repressive measures to suppress any dissent in society. These measures include direct intervention in the media coverage of political issues, the arrest and prosecution of journalists, and the use of brutal police force to suppress any mass public protest or demonstration. These authoritarian measures were necessary to suppress dissenting voices that problematized the illegalities and conspiracies involved in the judicial process through which the former military officers and bureaucrats were trialed and sentenced (Gürcan & Peker, 2014, p. 81). The government was also required to repress the reactions stemming from the scandalous Roboski massacre in 2011, in which a group of 40 Kurdish villagers were killed as a result of the airstrike of Turkish Armed Forces allegedly aimed at PKK members crossing the Iraqi-Turkish border.

The same measures were also used to prevent the expression of reactions against—and critiques of—AKP's Sunni-oriented expansionist foreign policy strategy in the Middle East. In an attempt to legitimize—and acquire popular support for—these overt authoritarian measures, the AKP further resorted to a religious and conservative discourse that consolidated its support base against its political opponents. These were complemented by 'Prime Minister Erdogan's increasing references to Islamic themes, such as his promise to raise 'pious generations,' the introduction of more Islamic themes—on a formally optional basis—into the school curricula, his statements against abortion, his insulting words about alcohol drinkers and unmarried male and female students sharing the same house (Özbudun, 2014, p. 3).

In addition to this, the AKP had to retreat from the discourses of justice and equality, as it could no longer reproduce its image of 'fixing' certain social problems and inequalities associated with neoliberal economic transformation. Neoliberal urban policies, for example, took the form of a frantic attack on public spaces and poor neighborhoods, which mostly benefited the capital groups linked to AKP and Erdoğan's family. The lower-rank bureaucratic positions and employment opportunities were disproportionally reserved for AKP supporters, increasing the sense of inequality and injustice among different sections of society, including Alevis, secularists, and Kurds. Therefore, for a party that embraced the crudest anti-social urban neoliberal urban policies and channeled the state resources to its own members and supporters, it was impossible to sustain the image of a 'reformist' party attacking the longstanding social inequalities and hierarchies and hence representing the victims of inequality.

In this respect, AKP gradually lost its ability to appropriate the values and concerns that had long been raised by dissident sections of society (and left-wing opposition) and thus had to take refuge in—thereby exposing—its true identity:

that is, an Islamic conservative vision of society coupled with an authoritarian and repressive state structure. In this context, the Gezi resistance erupted and spread across different cities and millions of people, the common front being those alienated by the AKP. The government's attempt to demolish the Gezi Park was not only a triggering factor that transformed this increasing discontent into a mass social movement, but it was also a 'symptom' through which the AKP's true identity could be deciphered and exposed. The AKP's plans to demolish a public park for building a shopping center was yet another manifestation of its neoliberal urban strategy of ensuring capital accumulation by privatizing public spaces. That it insisted on conducting this project through bypassing legal restraints and dismissing and intimidating the opponents of the project was another indication of its overt authoritarian and repressive character.

The Gezi uprising was also a symptom of the crisis of the strategy of ideological dispossession in terms of deepening and further subverting this crisis. From the very onset of the protests, AKP used brutal police force that led to the deaths of nine protestors, labeled the protestors as 'plunderers,' depicted them as the 'deviants' attacking the mosques and established religious values in society, and put pressures on the media to represent the events from AKP's point of view. Such violent reactions and the Islamic language it used to consolidate its supporter base against the protestors stripped the AKP of its capacity to represent the very values that it had once appropriated from the Left (Eken, 2014, p. 428).

In this ideological vacuum, the Gezi protestors became a new political subject representing the values of freedom, justice, and equality. Indeed, this became the unifying ground not only for Gezi protestors, but also for the opponents of the AKP from all different segments of society. As a result, the political meanings associated with these values underwent change; rights and freedoms no longer meant the liberation of 'civilian politics' against military tutelage or the free expression of religiosity against a secular authoritarian regime. After the Gezi protests, 'rights and freedoms' entered the discourse of the opponents of AKP and signified emancipation from the political oppression and cultural imposition of the state (which is almost under the total control of an Islamic conservative party). Equality and justice were no longer a rhetoric that AKP used to differentiate itself from the preceding neoliberal parties. During and after the Gezi protests, these themes became the Gezi protestors' language against AKP's neoliberal urban policies and its use of public resources for the benefit of its own cadres and supporters. In this respect, the Gezi uprising combined the rage against the AKP's neoliberal urban policies with the ideas of freedom, equality, and solidarity and, in the process, instilled a new political content to these issues and concerns. In this respect, it emerged as a dynamic that encapsulates an alternative societal vision, which has the potential to reclaim the values that were once dispossessed and manipulated by the AKP for its own legitimacy and for the sustainability of the existing neoliberal social formation.

The Class Character of the Gezi Uprising

Questions concerning the character of the Gezi uprising and its historical meaning for Turkish politics and society can be answered through the framework we have outlined above. The repercussions of the Gezi uprising for the ideological struggles in Turkey should be seen as a part of what the Gezi uprising is. These ideological implications go beyond the personal 'class' profile, interests, tendencies, and cultural/ethnic background of its participants. Instead, the point of departure for an analysis of the Gezi uprising should be its sources in and effects on the totality of the social formation in Turkey.

Seen from this perspective, the Gezi Uprising is no longer an attempt by the middle class to exhibit its own cultural values or pursue its material interests. Indeed, by reframing 'class character' as the ideological and political opportunities it created for class struggles in Turkish society, we get a very different picture: the Gezi Uprising can be seen as defying some of the most essential features of current neoliberal social order (represented by the AKP), deepening the ideological crisis of the dominant social formation, and carrying the *potential* for an alternative societal transformation. It is not a 'movement of class' per se, as it does not spring from or raise the typical economic demands of the working class, but it is a 'class movement' in terms of positioning itself against and challenging the hegemonic strategies of the capitalist class and the existing power bloc in Turkey, as well as reorienting the course of ideological struggles in Turkey in favor of the working class.

The 'movement of class' and 'class movement' duality that we offer here takes its inspiration from Ernesto Laclau's (1977, p. 107) analytical distinction between two spheres of social struggle: class struggle and popular democratic struggle. Class struggle is predicated upon the contradictions stemming from the mode of production, includes a direct confrontation between capitalists and workers, and is 'expressed on the ideological level in the interpellation of agents as a *class.*' Popular democratic struggles, in contrast, spring from the contradictions stemming from the social formation and interpellate the agents as *people*. In other words, popular democratic struggles develop through the contradiction and confrontation between the 'power bloc' and 'people.' As Laclau (1977, p. 108) puts it, 'the people form an objective determination of the system which is different from the class determination: people are one of the poles of the dominant contradiction in a social formation, that is, a contradiction whose intelligibility depends on the ensemble of political and ideological relations of domination and not just the relations of production. As stated and demonstrated throughout this paper, the Gezi uprising went beyond an environmentalist reaction to the government's neoliberal urban policies, gradually turning into a political and ideological defiance against the AKP's hegemonic project. It included a variety of social groups, including woman, youth, Alevis, socialists, republican Kemalists, and LGBT individuals who were alienated from the AKP's increasingly Sunni-oriented conservative dominance. The core of the uprising was not the struggle between the working class and capitalists per se, but a predominantly ideological confrontation between the power bloc represented by the AKP and the *people*.

Nevertheless, this does not mean that popular democratic struggles have no class content; indeed, 'the level of production relations always maintains the role of determination in the last instance in any social formation.' At this point, Laclau states that 'determination in the last instance' reveals itself in the fact that different classes struggle to articulate the popular-democratic struggles in relation to their own projects by presenting their class objectives as the consummation of popular objectives. In this respect 'popular interpellations' are also an arena of class struggle.[10] Here, Laclau reduces the 'determination' to the willful act of the classes to pioneer and transform the popular democratic struggles. Nevertheless, we can also add to this point that the determination of class contradictions—and hence relations of production—also reveals itself in determining the *character* and *meaning* of these struggles for a given social formation. Whether a 'popular democratic struggle' is progressive or not, for example, depends on its real and possible effects on the course of class struggles in a society.

A social movement and a popular democratic struggle acquire a progressive character to the extent that they contribute to opening up new opportunities for the working class against capitalism and strengthen the possibility of building a more egalitarian society that would transcend the forms of oppression crystallized in a capitalist social formation. In this respect, a popular movement's capacity to instigate a progressive transformation in a society depends on its capacity to impact the contradictions at the level of the mode of production and hence to strengthen the position of the working class against capitalism. From this perspective, the Gezi uprising was a 'class movement'; it was not a 'movement of class' since it did not organize and interpellate its participants as a *class* and it did not directly stem from the contradictions at the level of the mode of production. Nevertheless, it was a *class movement* because it posed a political and ideological challenge to the power bloc in a manner that could potentially influence the course of class struggles in Turkey. The contribution of the Gezi uprising to the reversal of 'ideo-

---

10 For a critique and summary of Laclau's position see Mouselis (1978).

logical dispossession,' as stated above, is one of the most significant legacies that this movement left for class struggles in Turkey; it is for this reason that it can be regarded not only as a popular democratic struggle but also as a class movement.

Given the continued power and popularity of the AKP government in Turkish politics in the aftermath of the Gezi uprising, one may ask why this potential did not lead to a drastic and progressive change in Turkish society. As the word 'potential' suggests, the reversal of ideological dispossession could make a concrete impact on class struggles in Turkey if the working class and its political forces could articulate such dispossessed ideological themes in accordance with its own struggle and its emancipatory political project. During and after the Gezi uprising, such an organized political force did not emerge to accomplish this political and ideological task; as a result, the Gezi uprising has not yet yielded a drastic change in the balance of power in Turkish politics. Nevertheless, at the same time, the ideological domain that the AKP had to vacate completely after the Gezi uprising could also not be filled yet by any systemic forces. Nor did the people/power bloc contradiction that crystallized during the Gezi uprising turn into a transformative political project. This situation broadened the arena of class struggle, since, as Laclau (1977, p. 110) states for certain popular democratic struggles, 'it opens the possibility of integrating into a revolutionary and socialist discourse, a multitude of elements and interpellations which have up to now appeared constitutive of bourgeois ideological discourse.' In this respect, it can be expected that the real and concrete effect of the Gezi uprising for class struggles will be more intelligible when such an 'articulation' is achieved by anti-capitalist political forces in Turkey.

Conclusion:

Methodological Suggestions for the Analysis of Post-2008 Social Upheavals

In this paper, we presented a critique of widespread methodological tendencies concerning the Gezi Uprising in Turkey and developed an alternative approach that aims to overcome these shortcomings. We argue that the methodology of our approach might serve as a point of departure for the study of social movements that emerged as a response to the crisis of neoliberalism. We would like to conclude by highlighting the analytical core of our approach.

Our main critique of the existing literature is that the presumed class positions of the individuals that constitute the movement cannot be the entry point for analyzing social movements with respect to their progressive and anti-systemic potentials. We build this critique on several grounds: First, 'measuring' the class position of a social movement is usually undermined by imprecise assumptions, ill-defined categories, and arbitrary break points. This is especially the case with the literature on the 'middle classes,' in which the lack of a shared understanding of the term impairs research and theory. Second, class should not be reduced to 'class positions' defined as clusters of individuals in similar positions on the social ladder. Third and most importantly, this approach isolates class from the fundamentally important ideological/political levels that the given social movement works on. It should be noted that the ideological and political levels are even more important in the neoliberal era. As we discussed in the introduction, neoliberalism—as the hegemonic paradigm of contemporary capitalism—can articulate with, and reproduce itself in, drastically different ideological/political formations, giving way to varied hegemonic projects, axes of political conflict, crisis dynamics, and social movements.

Hence, we suggest a methodology that approaches a given social movement from the totality of the social formation with its economic, political, and ideological levels. In other words, we privilege the social formation in its totality as a methodological entry point. A study of the social formation requires a multi-level framework that evaluates the specific accumulation regime, the power bloc, and the hegemonic project of a given unit. In such a framework, class is neither a separate instance of analysis nor an isolated category that externally impacts other categories of the social. Rather, the notion of class and class struggle is embedded in each and every instance of analysis. Hence, a social movement should first be situated within this totality. Only after completing this task can we comprehensively evaluate a social movement.

We should not be misread as implying that class constituency of a movement does not provide any valuable information. We simply argue that it cannot and should not be *the point of departure* when trying to identify the defining characteristics of a movement. Here, we would like to stress that this is not simply an issue of methodological prudence, but of utmost political significance. To be more precise, we are arguing against a widespread tendency among left scholarship that puts the 'class label' at the heart of the analysis. We believe that this 'class-labeling' tendency is not only a caricature of Marxist class analysis, but is also spectacularly void of any historical sense. Let us elucidate this point: The underlying—but never explicitly stated—assumption of this tendency is that the more a social movement draws its constituencies from poorer/underprivileged/from-below segments of the society, the more progressive/radical/egalitarian it necessarily is. And vice versa. The more a social movement bears middle class elements, the more dubious is its anti-systemic potential. In the best-case scenario, then, we can expect 'petty-bourgeois radicalism.' It is this assumption that has led some on the left to support what turned out to be Neo-Nazis in Ukraine or Jihadists in Syria because they were supposedly working class or coming 'from below.' It is this assumption too that has led others to be skeptical about the masses revolting against an Islamist tyrant in Turkey because they were supposedly 'middle class.' Even a little sense of history would reveal the implications of this spectacular misreading.

The most evident example would be fascism in Germany as a fatally reactionary movement with a huge mass base among the working class. A survey among the Nazis would most probably show the dominance of people from lower echelons of society. Does this make Nazism 'a working-class movement'? Of course not. But we do not have to go this extreme to show the flaws of this reasoning. It is obvious that any successful bourgeois political actor needs to have a base in popular masses. That is what hegemony is about. It is equally true that not all political actors who seek to mobilize the resentments of the masses against the established order are necessarily progressive. That is what ideology is about. Indeed, reactionism in its many variants—including fascism, racism, religious fanaticism, and ethnic nationalism—takes its strength from such resentments.

The existence of middle class elements, however defined, does not necessarily make a movement less radical or progressive. In fact, attributing a 'middle-class character' to a movement does not tell much about it politically. Middle classes have taken dramatically different positions throughout history, to such a degree that it is impossible to talk about a 'middle class movement' as a meaningful category of political characterization. For instance, they have assumed conservative, right wing, pro-dictatorship positions in Argentina (1955-82), Chile (1973) and Venezuela (2002). Yet, they have stood with the laboring classes in support of progressive/radical/socialist agendas in East Asia (1970s-1980s) and in most of Western Europe in the 1970s (to name just a few cases). Even the revolutionary wave of 1848 that perhaps represents the archetype of a working class movement had considerable backing from middle classes. As Therborn (2012) argues, there is nothing inherently democratic or undemocratic about middle classes. Rather than attributing fixed political orientations to the middle classes, it is perhaps a better idea to consider them as an area of political struggle.

Furthermore, any counter-hegemonic project requires a certain degree of support from well-educated urban, professional segments of society. This is even more essential today than the past, since these segments of society do count for a much bigger percentage of the population in general. No social revolution has occurred along the abstract lines of pure capital-labor conflict, in which antagonistic classes appear in themselves like an army to fight one another. Nor is there any reason to believe that class struggle will take this form in the future. Actual revolutions have always been more complex than this through which movements articulating different axes of conflicts with each other have challenged and defeated established orders. The notion of ideological hegemony of the working class, in the sense that representing the interests of the class as the interests of all people, has always been a crucial task in the process of achieving popular hegemony. This will be a key challenge for the social movements that have risen in the aftermath of the 2008 crisis.

References

Anderson, P. (2000). Renewals. *New Left Review*, 1, 1-20.

Barker, C, Cox, L., Krinsky, J. and Nielson, A. G. (2013). Marxism and social movements: An introduction. In C. Barker (Ed.), *Marxism and social movements* (pp. 1-41). Amsterdam: Brill.

Brenner, N., Peck, J., & Theodore, N. (2010). Variegated neoliberalization: Geographies, modalities, pathways. *Global Networks*, *10* (2), 182-222.

Brenner, N., & Theodore, N. (2011). Cities and the geographies of actually existing neoliberalism. *Antipode*, *34* (3), 349-379.

Buğra, A., & Keyder, Ç. (2006). The Turkish welfare regime in transformation. *Journal of European Policy*, *16* (3), 211-228.

Cahill, D. (2010). Actually existing neoliberalism and the global economic crisis. *Labour and Industry*, *20* (3), 298-316.

Davis, M. (2011, November/December). Spring confronts winter. *New Left Review*, *72*, 5-15.

Eken, B. (2014). The politics of the Gezi Park resistance: Against memory and identity. *The South Atlantic Quarterly*, 113 (2), 427-436.

Gürcan, E. C., & Peker, E. (2014). Turkey's Gezi Park demonstrations of 2013: A Marxian analysis of political moment. *Socialism and Democracy*, *28* (1), 78-89.

Harvey, D. (2005). *The new imperialism*. Oxford: Oxford University Press.

Harvey, D. (2009). The new imperialism: Accumulation by dispossession. *Socialist Register*, *40*, 63-87.

Keyder, Ç. (2013). 'Yeni Orta Sınıf', Gezi Park events from sociological and political perspectives. *Türkiye Bilimler Akademisi*. Ankara. Retrieved from http://bilimaka-demisi.org/wp-content/uploads/2013/09/Yeni-Orta-S%C4%B1n%C4%B1f.pdf

Krinsky, J. (2013). Marxism and the politics of possibility: Beyond academic boundaries. In C. Barker (Ed.), *Marxism and social movements* (pp. 103-125). Amsterdam: Brill.

Laclau, E. (1977). *Politics and ideology in Marxist theory.* London: NLB.

McNally, D. (2011). *Global slump: The economics and politics of crisis and resistance*. Oakland: PM Press.

Mouselis, N. (1978). Ideology and class politics: A critique of Ernesto Laclau. *New Left Review*, *1*, 112.

Oberschall, A. (1993). *Social movements: Ideologies, interests, and identities*. New Jersey: Transaction Publishers.

Özbudun, E. (2014). AKP at the crossroads: Erdoğan's majoritarian Drift. *South European Society and Politics*, *19* (2), 155-167.

Saraçoğlu, C., & Demirkol, Ö. (2015). Nationalism and foreign policy discourse under the AKP rule: Geography, history, and national identity. *British Journal of Middle Eastern Studies*, 42 (3), 301-319.

Schmid, H. B. (2009). *Plural action: Essays in philosophy and social science*. Verlag: Springer.

Therborn, G. (2012, November-December). Class in the 21st century. *New Left Review*, *78*, 5-29.

Udehn, L. (2002). *Methodological individualism: Background, history, and meaning*. London: Routledge.

Yalman, G. (2014). AKP İktidarında Söylem ve Siyaset: Neyin Krizi. In S. Coşar & G. Yücesan-Özdemir (Eds.). İktidarın Şiddeti: AKP'li Yıllar, *neoliberalizm ve İslamcı politikalar* (pp. 21-41). İstanbul: Metis.

Yörük, E., & Yüksel, M. (2014, September-October). Class and politics in Turkey's Gezi protests. *New Left Review*, *89*, 103-123.

Yücesan-Özdemir, G (2012). The social policy regime in the AKP years: The Emperor's new clothes. In: S. Coşar & G. Yücesan-Özdemir, G. (Eds.). *Silent violence: Neoliberalism, Islamist politics and the AKP years in Turkey* (pp. 125-153). İstanbul: Metis.

White, J. (2012). *Muslim nationalism and the new Turks*. New Jersey: Princeton University Press.

Yörük, E. (2014). The long summer of Turkey: The Gezi uprising and its historical roots. *South Atlantic Quarterly*, *113* (2), 419-426.

Zizek, S. (1989). *The sublime object of ideology*, London: Verso Books.

3.
THE WORKİNG CLASS BACK ON THE STAGE

Ashes and Sparkles in the TEKEL Resistance

Fatih Yaşlı

T he TEKEL resistance, that started on December 15, 2009 and ended on March 2, 2010 was a response to the privatization of Turkey's state monopoly established in tobacco and alcoholic beverages production. TEKEL resistance had not taken place only because TEKEL is privatized but because the workers were obliged to be redeployed according to 4-C regulation stated by law, which would mean their loss of guaranteed working status. It was the only working class resistance to shake and disturb AKP power during the past 11 years and thus has immense symbolic and historical significance. It is also true that a resistance of this scale has not taken place since 1980. In this chapter, I explore the significance of the TEKEL resistance in relation to the Gezi 2013 civil uprising.

The Gezi resistance was not a working class rebellion; the labor-capital conflict was not its primary determinant. It was more of a sudden outburst against the authoritarian AKP and its overwhelming efforts to impose a conservative life-style on the public. The majority of the participants in the resistance were either university students or newly graduated young people. There was also support from several poor neighborhoods, both in Istanbul and Ankara (a traditional strong-hold of the Left and populated by the Alevi sect). Moreover, while the slogans demanded the government's resignation, they did not explicitly express class-based demands. This does not mean that this uprising had nothing to do with class; if we are to define a 'worker' as a person lacking the means of production and selling his or her labor in return for a wage to survive, then the majority of the people actively participating in the uprising were workers, standing alongside students and young unemployed people. We shall consider university students and newly graduates who are either unemployed or precarious employees.

Given the fact that none of the politicians, theorists, or social scientists foresaw the Gezi resistance, there is now an attempt to understand its roots and points of departure through a reconsideration of working-class protests, feminist movements, urban transformation and environmental protests, and youth rebellions. I argue here that it is worthwhile comparing the TEKEL resistance to the Gezi uprising in terms of the social and symbolic use of specific sites and the creation and defense of a new public space. This chapter is divided into three sections: First, I will discuss the socio-economic program of AKP with particular attention to its promotion of privatization. Second, I will give a short overview of the 78 days that shook Turkey. Finally, I will examine the nature of the TEKEL resistance in terms of its capabilities, possibilities, and potentialities.

The AKP's Way: Justice, Development, and Privatization

On the night of November 3, 2002, when the election results were finally announced, the newly emerging political landscape was astonishing: None of the three political parties constituting the coalition government that had been governing the country for the previous three years—the center-left Democratic Left Party (DSP), the extreme-right Nationalist Movement Party (MHP) and the center-right Motherland Party (ANAP)—managed to secure the 10 percent of votes necessary for parliamentary representation. What had led the citizens of Turkey to give the mandate to govern the country to the newly-founded Justice and Development Party (AKP),[11] while abandoning the three more established political parties?

AKP appeared on the Turkish political landscape as a result of a split within the Virtue Party (FP). FP was the last of the Islamist political parties (gener-

---

11   The Justice and Development Party had been established just 15 months prior, while the three losing parties had been founded three to four decades prior.

ated out of Erbakan's 'National View' movement) found to be unconstitutional and banned for violating the secular articles of the Constitution (Yaşlı, 2004). The split emerging in the party was between the 'traditionalists' (those committed to Political Islam's opposition to the US, Israel and the West) and the 'innovationists' (those representing the IMF and neoliberal policies in conformance with global capitalism and the US) (Yavuz, 2008).

The answer to the question posed above lies in the deep unrest of the 1990s; Turkey experienced crises in both the political and economic spheres, for which the system produced mostly inadequate solutions. The country was politically unstable because of political Islam and the armed struggle of the Kurdish separatist movement. Turkey's economic instability stemmed from capitalism's systemic structural problems. Therefore, the political and economic crisis had led to a deepening political polarization throughout the 1990s: a pro-secular bloc against political Islam and a Turkish nationalist bloc against the ascendancy of Kurdish separatism.

The established order's solution to the crisis was to transfer management of both politics and economics to exceptional and unaccountable institutions and organizations. A great amount of power was handed over to the National Security Council (MGK)—a constitutionally defined institution mainly comprised of members of the army along with a few government officials—for the de facto rule and administration of the country, while the management and command of the economy were handed over to the IMF.[12]

On February 28, 1997, during the National Security Council meeting the soldier members requested that the representatives of the Islamist Welfare Party (RP) and central right True Path Party (DYP) sign a declaration that the fight against political Islam would be the State's priority. Although Necmettin Erbakan—leader of the Welfare Party (RP) and prime minister at the time—had resisted the request during the meeting, he signed a short while after. The decisions taken during the meeting have been supported by a vast media campaign to overthrow the government, followed by mass protest from the people who were uncomfortable with the growing influence of political Islam. Erbakan resigned and attempted to handed over his position to Tansu Çiller, leader of the True Path Party (DYP). The WP-TPP coalition collapsed when Çiller refused to take over the position of Prime Minister. Following a series of coalition attempts, elections were held in 1999 and yet another coalition government was formed between the Democratic Left Party (DSP), the Nationalist Movement Party (MHP), and the

---

12 According to Bedirhanoğlu (2010, p. 51), 'the principle statement regarding AKP would be that AKP was carried to power by both the short term and the long term political and economic crisis caused by neoliberal transformation process.'

Motherland Party (ANAP). For nearly three years, this government of right-nationalist, left-nationalist, and central-right representatives ruled Turkey. During this period, two intense economic crises occurred—in 1999 and 2001 respectively. The government's solution was to invite Kemal Derviş—a Turkish bureaucrat employed by the World Bank—to take a cabinet post and to manage the economy (Zurcher, 2010, p. 430).

In the meantime, the Supreme Court had closed the WP, and administrative officers of the party were banned from politics. Given this process of banning political Islamist parties, former WP members established the Virtue Party (FP), which would split in two to form the AKP. The 'innovative wing' of the FP, led by Prime Minister Tayyip Erdoğan, President Abdullah Gül, and Vice President Bülent Arınç were defeated by Recai Kutan (who was leading the party on behalf of Erbakan) in the party congress. In the process, they had begun to pave the way for a new party.

The Justice and Development Party (AKP) defined itself as 'conservative democratic,' rather than political Islamist, and prepared a party program defending market economics and liberal democracy. AKP's vision is for social life to be determined by religious values but not managed by Islamic rules per se. [13]

Shortly after the foundation of AKP, early elections were announced in Turkey. The leader of the party, Tayyip Erdoğan, acknowledged that the rage among citizens derived from an economic crisis, emphasizing the need for social justice during pre-elections meetings and criticizing the IMF-inspired policies of former governments. The excerpt below—from AKP's declaration for the 2002 elections—outlines the party's critiques of the former governments:

> The stability policies and the bitter measures in the economy caused people to suffer and wasn't enough to place inflation under control. The heavy burden of taxes and the bureaucracy weakened the economy, decreased employment and directed the resources towards incomes of rent, instead of production ... The economic and social costs of the crisis were high, internal and external debt grew in an incredible fashion, hundreds of thousands of businesses closed, millions lost their jobs and the administration of the economy was completely left to the International Monetary Fund and the World Bank. More important than that, our people's trust in the state and the politics has been shaken, their hopes towards the future have been broken ... [The country] is in need of a

---

13 To show that it abandoned political Islam, the AKP invented the term 'conservative democrat.' Indeed, 'with this new definition, AKP considered itself as a counterpart of the Christian Democrats of Europe and even applied to the union which they formed and obtained an observer status' (Uzgel, 2010, p. 22).

political will which will go beyond high rates of inflation and unemployment, constant increases in internal and external debts, instability, dangerous shrinking of the economy, high rates of interest.[14]

When the people voted AKP into power on November 3, 2002, they were reacting against impoverishing neoliberal policies that had endured for years, crisis, political instability, and corruption . AKP has now been the single ruling power for over ten years.[15] While it was originally elected for its 'justice and development' platform, the government has nonetheless applied neoliberal policies in conformance with both global capitalism and Turkey's capitalist system. Even in the AKP'S 2002 elections declaration, we see that while IMF-inspired policies are critiqued, the free-market economy is strongly defended:

The power of entrepreneurship of our people is the most important resource of economic development. The fundamental role of the state in economy is to maintain the conditions of free competition in markets and remove the obstacles before entrepreneurship ... The state, with the help of regulations and controls, will correct the malfunctions of the operations of the free market system, increase productivity and prevent the abuse of the system.

The IMF stand-by agreements began in 1998 by the former governments and they continued until 2008. The most extensive privatizations recorded throughout modern Turkey history have been realized during the AKP's rule. A public reform in conformance with neoliberal governance has been completed and initiatives were taken to make precarious and flexible employment the norm.

The 'Emergency Action Plan' (AEP), declared publicly two weeks after the November 3 elections, is an important document setting out the policies for the next 11 years.[16] It is outlined there that privatization is a prerequisite for a healthy, well-functioning free-market economy and that an immediate privatization process would be implemented according to a new strategy. Capital was to be promoted, land was to be appropriated and given over to investors free of charge and other necessary measures were to be taken for attracting foreign investment. Moreover, in the statement that, 'for our industry to reach an efficient level to compete at international level, it is of utmost importance that export be developed,' the new

---

14 The declaration can be accessed via www.akp.org.tr.
15 Various leftist intellectuals had claimed AKP would create a social-liberal synthesis and follow welfare state policies to eliminate the negative extremes of the liberal market economy. For an early criticism regarding the claims, see Yaşlı (2004).
16 The Emergency Action Plan document can be accessed at http://www.akp.org.tr

government was prioritizing the same model of export-oriented accumulation that had been in place since the *Coup d'état* of September 12, 1980.

To increase the employment rate, the government proposed expanding the infrastructure and construction sectors; specifically, the 'Emergency Action Plan' called for a highway of 15,000 kilometers to be constructed along with a housing campaign. These sectors have indeed been responsible for modest economic gains.

AKP has implemented an austere wave of privatizations on the guidance of the IMF; in the process, many state-owned establishments have been handed over to private capital. As Argın and Bedirhanoğlu (2013) point out:

One of the fundamental differences between AKP power and the previous governments is the high performance recorded regarding the privatization of state enterprises. 8.053 billion dollars have been gained during the 1986-2002 period, whereas AKP governments have reached 35.255 billion dollars between 2003-2012. (p. 76)

It is well known that one of the most important outcomes of privatization is the adoption of flexible and precarious working conditions. Mütevellioğlu (2010) states that:

Privatizations have caused flexible labor market conditions in all countries. Neoliberalism's worldwide employment strategy is to liquidate the rules and regulations organizing the labor and intensify labor exploitation. Flexible employment applications necessitate subcontractual employment where the workers are forced to work at lower wages, [are] deunionised and uninsured. The subcontractor can avoid legal obligations of the social security legislation. (pp. 159-160)

The TEKEL Resistance: The 78 days that Shook Turkey

TEKEL had been introduced two years after the foundation of Republic of Turkey, 1923, following the nationalization of '*La Société de la Régie co-intéressée des Tabacs de l'Empire Ottoman*'—a foreign-owned tobacco producer. The name was changed to the 'Directorate General' in 1946 and to 'Tobacco, Tobacco Products, Salt and Alcoholic Beverages Enterprise' in 1987. In 2002, TEKEL was considered a Governmental Business Enterprise, so it was marked for privatization reforms. In the 1970s, during the ascension of neoliberalism, TEKEL became a target by global and multinational tobacco competitors who critiqued TEKEL's monopoly over tobacco production. Neoliberal policies were implemented by Turgut Özal—the first prime minister of multi-party political life after the 1980 *Coup d'état* and the architecture of neoliberalism in Turkey—and it was inevitable that tobacco production would be reformed.

In 1984, the foreign importation of cigarettes was allowed. Tobacco was released from the state monopoly in 1984 by amending the 1177 no. Tobacco and Tobacco Monopoly law, which led the way to national, local, foreign, and international joint-capital investments in TEKEL. Philip Morris and Sabancı Holding, a local enterprise, founded a cigarette factory with joint capital in 1990. Then, in May, 1991, it was declared that tobacco production would be permitted outside of TEKEL's participation. In 1992, Philsa began production. Opening up the tobacco sector continued after Özal's period. Yet, local tobacco producers in Turkey faced restraints and limitations, while foreign tobacco ventures were increasingly expanded. In February, 2001, the government signed the proposal of the Privatization High Council to fully privatize TEKEL (Aysu, 2010, pp. 192-193).[17]

In January 2002, a bill was voted in parliament to prepare the economic infrastructure for the targeted privatization. İslamoğlu (2002, p. 25) wrote in an essay after the bill had become a law:

The law paves the way for transnational companies and their local partners to realize their projects. First of all, the Asian-type of tobacco production must be limited, so subsidies have been cut and production is subjected to the Regulation Board. It means a decrease in the number of producers from 600.000 to 150.000 (a 40 percent and 50 percent decrease in the Aegean region and the Black Sea region, respectively). Overall, a population of two and a half to three million people would lose their source of income.

According to the law, prices would be set in a contract between the buyer and the producer, which amounted to 'leaving the producer face to face with the buyer's mercy' (İslamoğlu, 2002, pp. 25-26). The conditions to get involved in the tobacco business were put in place to privilege large-scale companies, and an autonomous council, the 'Tobacco, Tobacco Products and Alcoholic Beverages Market Regulation Council,' was established by law (İslamoğlu, 2002, pp. 25-26).

The Privatization High Council decided to restructure TEKEL in March, 2003. TEKEL was divided into two different joint-stock companies, the Cigarettes Industrial Corporation and Business Company and Alcoholic Beverages Industrial Corporation and Business Company. A third company, Marketing and Distributing

---

17   Tobacco's adventure is by no means separate from agriculture's adventure in Turkey. For the neoliberal enclosure surrounding agriculture in Turkey, see Önal, 2012.

Cigarette Business Company, was established for product marketing and distribution. In the same year, the beverages section of TEKEL began to be sold off and transfer was completed in 2008 for a total of 292 million dollars. Production and distribution sections were sold to British American Tobacco in the same year for 1,720 million dollars.

The privatization process had immediate effects on employment. According to the recorded data, the workforce of 30,214 (employed at TEKEL in 2001) declined to 12,000. British American Tobacco cancelled employment contracts with 8248 out of the 10,818 workers after their purchase of TEKEL's cigarettes and tobacco products section. The State, in return, has assigned the workers '4-C' status. This article stated that public services were to be carried out by a) civil servants, b) contract personnel, c) temporary personnel, and d) workers. Temporary personnel referred to those who had been working less than a year,[18] whose wages were determined by contract (Türkmen, 2012, pp. 39-40).

Article 4-C shows that insecure employment became the norm in the public sector, which is directly related to the structural transformation of the state.[19] Along with the readjustments implemented:

> According to 657 State Personnel Law, civil servants' status defined by 4-A have been changed to 'contractual personnel' defined by 4-B and temporary, limited, half-time and personal work contracts have been used, especially in the education and health sectors. Contractual employment has become a norm rather than an exception in the public sector during the period (Kumlu, 2012: p. 88)

According to 4-C the temporary personnel would work for 4 to 10 months with a significantly low wage, get a day-off once a month, be able to get sick-leave for 5 days a year (beyond this, they would not have insurance coverage), and not be permitted to work in any other place. Moreover, extension of the contract term would be decided by the Council of Ministers. Temporary personnel were not allowed to be a member of any trade unions and therefore could not benefit from any collective bargaining agreement (Türkmen, 2012, p. 40).

---

18 Or a seasonal period of time defined by the cabinet, which is itself guided by the Head of State Personnel and Ministry of Finance's assessments.

19 Özuğurlu (2012) states that regulatory state model, which he defines as 'direct sovereignty apparatus of capitalist class' (p. 145) necessitates this transformation. 'Regulatory state is a state model concentrated on the benefits of the ruling class. Subcontract work is the core of the system, precarious and insecure work is the norm. (...) The Ministry of Health data can be consulted to exemplify insecure employment in public sector: 85 percent of total employment is subcontractual based in the ministry, which equals to 116,000 personnel. Only 31 percent of the employees in the Ministry of Education are permanent staff' (Özuğurlu, 2012, p. 145).

The decision to redeploy TEKEL workers in 4-C status is indeed an exceptional practice that is becoming the norm and even expanding in scope:

During TEKEL's privatization process, the Council of Minister's decision on the 21st of December, 2009, regarding no. 2009/15759 formulated the principles for workers who lost their jobs during privatization and were to be redeployed according to 4/C status. The resolution leaves the workers deprived of their employee rights, equal wage for equal job, job insurance, the right to rest and the freedom of association. Only the work places, number of personnel and contract terms are defined, whereas the definition of the service is not discussed. More than 10,000 people working in the public sector for many years have been subordinated to this article and an exceptional practice had been broadened illegitimately. (Kumlu, 2012, p. 90).

The consequences for those workers redeployed as temporary personnel is expressed as:

Provisionally it has important impacts on waged labor. The fact that 'temporary personnel is employed according to a contract and not defined as a labor worker' leaves them out of the range of rights and assurances protected by the Constitution, laws and regulations. Not being defined as a labor worker and being bound to work within the wage limitations fixed by the government makes them deprived of the right to strike and benefits of labor agreements. These rights are protected by international conventions (Kumlu, 2012, p. 89).

It would be meaningful to end this section with the words of a TEKEL worker:

4/C is exactly an imposition of slavery. They used to sell African people and cut their ears to put on earrings. Those people were forced to work day and night. 4/C is the same thing. We would start to work at 8 am yet it is indefinite when we would leave, since the employer holds the right to make us work for 12 hours a day. There is only a 2-day allowance to go to hospital, provided that one works for one month in advance. After two days we have to pay from our own pockets. 4/C means being a slave of the manager in charge. They can fire you with a signature because a union cannot protect you (Türkmen, 2012, p. 98).

The state declared that the workers dismissed from TEKEL must pass to 4-C status by March 1, 2010. However, the workers did not accept the proposal and instead demanded to be transferred to other public positions, carrying the same employee rights and benefits. The demonstrations were first held in the cities where the workers lived and worked and then headed towards Ankara. On December 4, 2009, the TEKEL workers in Izmir occupied the union building to which they were registered to protest the union officials' lack of an action plan against the state measures. In Diyarbakır, another city well known for its tobacco production, the workers marched towards the Governor's Office, blocking traffic from the main street. The police attacked the protestors and two workers were injured. Two others were taken into custody.

Along with their families, workers protested the Prime Minister's inauguration speech in Istanbul on December 5, 2009, Erdoğan continued his speech with his uncompromising attitude:

> I beg your pardon, but we cannot keep you employed in your current jobs. Your union representatives will explain this to you in detail. Do not provoke this gathering. Their perception is like this, they believe that the state's assets are vast, like a sea, and one would be a pig not to benefit from it. We have left the times behind us when money was earned by just lying down, doing nothing. (Bulut, 2010, pp. 301-302)

TEKEL demonstrations have followed one after the other throughout the country in different cities and the union decided to organize a mass meeting in front of AKP's Head Office building in Ankara on December 15, 2009. Arriving from all over Turkey by buses (of which there were 106 in total), workers marched to AKP's Head Office. The police built a barricade nearby the building to stop the workers. There was a negotiation held between the union representatives and the governor and, as a result, workers were allowed to spend the night in the Ataturk Sports Saloon. They were not allowed to march towards the head office building on the following day, and Abdi İpekçi Park was offered to them as an alternative place for their demonstrations and protests. They spent the night of December 16 and December 17 in the park. During the day of December 17, although parliamentary members from the main opposition party were visiting the TEKEL workers to show solidarity, the police attacked and dispersed them. Thirty people, including the union leader, were taken into custody. A group of workers then succeeded to overcome the barricade and attempted to block Atatürk Boulevard from traffic, although they were removed shortly after and 18 more workers were taken into custody. After this attack, the workers decided to gather in front of Türk-İş (Confederation of Turkish Trade Unions) building, of which their union was a member.

On December 18, AKP's Deputy Chairman Abdulkadir Aksu was spotted across from the Türk-İş building trapped among the workers before being rescued by the police. On December 19, women wearing white shrouds (symbolizing death) marched and raised their voices against their 4-C status. They wrote a letter and sent it out to the president, as well as the wives of the prime minister, and parliamentary members:

> We have been continuing our protests on Ankara streets for days now. Our children are waiting for us at home in hunger and thirst. We do not aim to earn money lying on our backs. We have been serving the state for years, we have given our labor, we have produced and the country has gained money. We want to start working again but with our dignity. Listen to us as a woman and a mother. Do not let us be condemned by 4-C misery (Bulut, 2010, pp. 308-309).

The resistance continued on December 22. According to Türk-İş authorities, there were 7200 workers in Ankara. On the same day, the Finance Minister Mehmet Şimşek announced that there would not be any amendments made for the workers' deployment to 4/C status, saying that 'there is a logic behind privatization implementations and it would not be right to act against the logic' (Kumlu, 2012, p.86). On December 23, Türk-İş Board of Presidents had a meeting and decided to continue the protests, declaring that December 25 would be a 'protest day in solidarity with TEKEL workers.' DISK (Progressive Trade Unions of Turkey) and KESK (Confederation of Public Sector Trade Unions) also supported the demonstration. On December 27, Erdoğan's speech concisely stated the government's perception of workers and privatization. Defining TEKEL workers as a burden on the back of the society and blaming them for sitting around and being unproductive in empty tobacco warehouses, he reasserted that the government would not 'dole out money to workers for not producing anything.' In the meantime, the union decided on work stoppages to be implemented on January 8, 15, and 22, supported by press releases in front of AKP's provincial buildings (Bulut, 2010, pp. 311-313; Türkmen, 2012, p. 44).

TEKEL workers celebrated the New Year alongside the public and several celebrities who visited in the name of solidarity in front of the Türk-İş building. On January 1, 2010, Minister of Labor and Social Security, Ömer Çelik, addressed TEKEL workers, stating that they would be given new rights, and asked them to return their homes. Yet the minister added that 'there are hundred thousand of people eager to work instead of them.' In response, the workers and the union reiterated that they did not accept the degraded 4-C status. The union head stated:

> We neither accept nor ask for charity from anyone. God's curse is upon those who formulated. Our union will make referendums in each TEKEL establish-

ment. We declare to Turkey that if the result comes out as 'yes', 12.000 TEKEL workers will put on their shrouds with there spouses (Bulut, 2013, pp. 315-316).

A referendum was held and 9628 out of 9683 voted to continue protesting. On January 7, the union leader proposed a new strategy for the resistance. Workers clothed with shrouds would march in roads on January 14 from all around Turkey. There would be a sit-in protest for three days, starting on January 15, which would then be followed, if necessary, by a three-day hunger strike. If the demands would not be heard and accepted, warned Türkel, the hunger strike would begin. On January 8, a group of workers attempted to tie themselves to AKP Head Office building with chains and 41 workers were taken to custody. Türk-İş decided to organize a mass meeting in Ankara on January 16, called 'Democracy and rights Meeting for Bread, Peace and Freedom.' On January 13th, TEKEL workers occupied a ferry in Izmir, the third biggest city in Turkey. By January 14, workers from all over the country started their journey to Ankara with their blankets. Eleven buses headed to Ankara were stopped by police in Izmir, but they managed to cut of the traffic on İzmir-Ankara highway and then continued on their way. Citing general security concerns, the Governor's Office postponed the mass rally until the following day (January 17) (Bulut, 2010, pp. 318-319; Türkmen, 2012, p. 44).

Due to the decision of the union on January 7, quite a number of workers preferred to stay in Ankara until the meeting. The workers, supported by their families, started a sit-in protest in front of the Türk-İş building, and during those three days, they pitched tents made out of nylon canvas. Some of the workers fell sick as a consequence of cold weather conditions. Eleven of them were hospitalized and 84 received treatment by medical personnel. On January 17, nearly 100,000 people had gathered together, which is definitely one of the largest working-class meetings of the past few years. On January 19, 140 workers began a hunger strike. Meanwhile the number of tents was increasing and people were frequently visiting the workers to show their support and solidarity. Labor and public sector unions' confederations sent their support to TEKEL workers on January 21. The Türk-İş leader's meeting with the deputy prime minister was followed by the decision to hunger strike decision and a general strike was provisionally called if the government refused to compromise. On January 22, Prime Minister Erdoğan once again expressed his attitude towards TEKEL workers:

I hereby warn TEKEL workers. Their attempt to pursue hunger strike is clearly an act of agitation. Do not be fooled by the opposition's filthy games. Do not fall into traps of marginal groups. There are currently 18 000 people working in 4-C status. Are they less a citizen than you? In private sector, they fire such lazy people, they pay your compensation and send you away. (Bulut, 2010, pp. 321-322).

On January 23, the Governor's Office demanded the 40-day protest to be stopped immediately . The written notice sent to the union claimed that the workers were disturbing the environment and the craftsmen nearby. In return, the union stated that they had been exercising their democratic rights and the claims were unacceptable. On January 26, as the time granted to the government was to run out, they were given an appointment to meet with the prime minister on January 28. The meeting resulted in no gains for the workers. The union representatives once again demanded 'the workers to be transferred to other public establishments carrying their employee rights' and the Prime Minister Erdoğan did not accept the terms, restating that 4-C would be valid but suggesting that some ameliorations could be made. The chairman of the union commented that, '4-C conditions refer to slavery order of 200 years back. We, TEKEL workers, do not accept to work in these conditions.' Erdoğan was uncompromising, saying that 'we do not owe our presence in power to TEKEL workers' and added that 'whoever applies for 4-C will benefit from it in a month, yet if they do not accept it, no rights will be reserved for them.' Erdoğan also implied that the police would remove the tents, adding 'we will keep our patience until the end of the month' (Bulut, 2010, p. 322).

The ministers and Türk-İş president met together once again on February 1st. The government offered an amelioration of the rights, which was rejected by the union and workers. The confederations held an emergency meeting and decided on a general strike. A one-day work stoppage was planned on February 4. Erdoğan immediately threatened the workers:

There are 10 850 workers in TEKEL for whom we pay 40 million TL each month. The protests have been transformed into an anti-government campaign. The marginal groups are abusing the workers. I tell you, my brothers, you are being used. Keep in mind that there are over 3 million unemployed and minimum waged workers willing to work instead of you. (Bulut, 2010, p. 328).

Participation in the general strike of February 4 was below expectations. Some confederations backed away just minutes before the protest. Neither the airport workers nor the municipality workers in big cities participated, so the transportation was not disrupted. On the same day, the government released a decree making it possible for 4-C workers to receive severance pay. A second group of 17 workers started a hunger strike on February 5, which was supported by a mass rally on the following day. Representatives from the government and the workers got together several times during the following days, yet there was no positive outcome. A massive gathering took place in Ankara on February 20 and nearly 30,000 people spent the night with the workers in the tents.

Türk-İş announced a two-hour work stoppage for February 27 and a mass press release to be held on February 25. The workers understood that the union was inadequate and unwilling to support them, so they protested the union management. The Tek Gıda-İş leader resigned when slogans were raised against him. On February 25, a TEKEL worker called Hamdullah Uysal was killed by a car on his way to mosque for Morning Prayer. The tension built up when the police prevented the funeral to be held in front of Türk-İş building. The workers shouted out their slogans in rage: 'Killer state, murderer AKP, murderer Tayyip' in front of the police barricade. When a group of TEKEL workers attempted to occupy AKP's city building, the police intervened and 19 workers were taken into custody. An important development took place on March 1st when the supreme administrative court granted a 30-day stay of execution for TEKEL workers to be redeployed to 4-C status. The court's decision meant that TEKEL workers would be granted loss of employment insurance. The workers resisting against 4-C would be paid equal to double the minimum wage for a period of eight months. On March 2, the union declared an intermission for 15 to 20 days, and the tents were pulled of immediately. Even though protests continue to be organized in different cities, the resistance had de-facto ended when the resistance site was evacuated. When the workers came to Ankara once again after a month, the police blocked the area surrounding Türk-İş building and prevented the workers' entrance. Severe clashes took places for two days and the union postponed the demonstrations. The union's attitude meant betrayal to the resistance. It was evident that the workers were let down and would have to fend for themselves.

The TEKEL Resistance: Potentialities, Capabilities, and Possibilities

TEKEL resistance could not prevent the workers from being deployed to 4-C status, yet it definitely succeeded in influencing the workers' class movement and social struggle. For the first time under AKP rule, a working class protest had achieved a political agenda.

The ineffectiveness of the prior period should be briefly summarized: The *coup d'état* of September 12, 1980, eliminated and dissolved all organized political bodies and structures of the working class in society. Leaders of the working class have either been prisoned or murdered. The first demonstrations after the coup were organized in the spring of 1989 by public employees, gaining the name 'the spring protests' in Turkey's working class history. From

November 30, 1990, to February 6, 1991, mine workers' demonstrations took place, with 70,000 participating.

However, the working class and labor movements failed to intervene in politics in accordance with their own demands and benefits during the tumultuous 1990s. The continuing clashes between the armed Kurdish movement and the state yielded to an upsurge of nationalism. On the other hand, political Islam gained ground and grew stronger, leading the way to tensions between the laic-secular camp and conservative-religious camp within the society. Thus, the polarization within the country was based on ethical and cultural—rather than class—differences.

AKP's rise to power occurred at the end of 2002, when the worldwide economic crisis and recession ended and a new wave of economic expansion arose. The wave of economic expansion brought financial capital to Turkey between 2003 and 2008, which led to economic growth. Boratav (2010) assesses the situation by saying 'it is difficult to design more ideal conditions for a change of power in a country peripherally located in the imperialistic system than 2002.'

AKP brought into office a mission to re-establish the legitimacy of the system and to resolve the economic and political crisis that had prevailed throughout the 1990s and threatened to continue into the 2000s. They put their support behind deepening neoliberal policies, while trying to minimize the negative social consequences.

AKP managed to fog the class characteristic of power and this is why the lower class members support them:

AKP used the Housing Development Administration of Turkey (TOKİ) as a perfect tool for establishing hegemony throughout the seven years in power. According to official data, TOKİ has constructed 394,804 buildings between 2003-2009 and 341,796 of them have been sold to lower and middle income groups of people based on long-term payment plans. The importance of making nearly 400,000 families owners of their own houses can not be overseen in a society such as Turkey, where it is of utmost importance to own a house ... In 2008 alone, the AKP government has distributed 1,951,240 tons of coal to 2,084,681 families to provide their heating, and 1,951,420 students were paid within range of 20 and 45 liras on monthly basis. During the same year, 213.7 million liras worth of food aid had been given (Yaşlı & Sümer, 2010, pp. 16-17).

Several other regulations to ease the daily lives of lower income groups should be added to this institutionalized aid mechanism. The AKP had facilitated private hospitals to people holding social security by paying an amount of a contribution fee, millions of green cards were distributed so people could benefit from health services free of charge, a prescribed medicine sale was dispersed to all pharmacies removing limitations (there used to be endless queues in front of hospital pharmacies). and textbooks were distributed to students free of charge in the beginning of education term. These gestures were considered remarkable when compared to the negligence of previous governments, and as a result, the people showed their appreciation at the election booths.

There is also a cultural dimension to AKP's neoliberalism. Relatively poor sections of society show their class-based reactions on a religious base in Turkey. AKP is glorified as a political party combatting the 'order' and the owners of the order, namely the rich elite. The owners of the order belong to the middle and upper classes and they live distinct lives; they do not share the same cultural and moral values as the lower classes. In short, they do not live a religious and conservative lifestyle. People from these classes have internalized modern and secular values. The rage of lower classes towards them targets their clothing, 'immoral' life styles, drinking habits, etc. The rage of lower classes fails to be embodied in a economic-political consciousness.

According to this point of view, higher classes see themselves as the genuine owners of the country and they insult both the poor and the religious. AKP successfully presented itself as coming from the lower-middle classes with the help of the party's cadres. Similar lifestyles were exhibited as they do not drink alcohol, they pray, they feast on Ramadan, and they continuously argue with the alienated and westernized elites. The discourse of Prime Minister Tayyip Erdoğan (and leader of AKP) portrays a fight against the elites and a defense of the lower class. Erdoğan is praised as a leader who successfully brings the state together with the people. The irony is that the most neoliberal government of our history is supported by poor people and receives the majority of their votes. Neoliberalism is fortified by conservatism; neoliberal policies are covered up with conservative culture policies to disguise their goals.

What signifies TEKEL resistance as historically important is the fact that the conservative blanket became visible to a group of workers and they have decided to fight against it probably for the first time ever.

We shall listen to Murat, one of the TEKEL workers from the Bitlis tobacco factory:

From now on I will think thoroughly before doing anything. I will not make any instant decisions. I will not believe in the Muslim groups who manipulate religion. We are all Muslims. I personally practice my prayers five times a day. But I do not believe in those people from now on. Whenever a person reached us saying he is a Muslim, we followed him. We should be more careful about people and who to trust from now on. We are all humans, we should all be treated equally. There should not be favoritism. One should treat his son and a foreigner equally. If they let their relatives, electors and supporters benefit from the wealth of Turkey and exert pressure on the others, we should not believe in those people whatsoever (Türkmen, 2012, pp. 170-171).

The words of Ünsal, a TEKEL worker coming from Muş, are also important for us to see the relations with AKP and the drastic changes after TEKEL resistance:

I will prevent everyone in my family and friends from voting for AKP. When we first came here, to Ankara, we did not expect such support. People have shared their food, clothes, and money with us. Then we have realized the difference. Now the difference between the right and the left is clear. I have always voted for the right up to now but my thoughts are totally different from now on. I have never been interested in politics. I thought that politics began where the truth ends. However, politics will be a part of my life from now on. Even for only to ask payback for our sufferings, we will be involved in politics (Türkmen, 2012, p. 138).

TEKEL resistance has created significant awareness regarding Kurdish issues as well. Primarily because of the fact that an important portion of TEKEL workers are Kurds, Turkish and Kurdish TEKEL workers have collectively asserted an identity beyond ethnical belongings for the first time. The Kurdish and the Turkish workers have overcome the determining influence of nationalism and being a member of the working class became top priority. In the meantime, a common will has been revealed in regard to living together on equal citizenship basis. Abdullah, a Kurdish worker from Siirt, explains:

They have tried to divide us according to our ethnicities. They even tried to make enemies out of brothers. They did not give us the chance to live together for more than 3 days. They did not expect that a man from Diyarbakır could play horon (a traditional folk dance special to Eastern Black Sea region) with another person from Trabzon. Yet they witnessed that we share our food and lived together like a family. So they realized that they cannot divide us. I like the country, it is ours. I have completed my military service and I pay my taxes … We just want a democratic country so we can live on equal terms. Our grand-fathers, ancestors have founded this country. We are all brothers. (Türkmen, 2012, p. 148)

During the 78 days of the TEKEL resistance, neither religious, cultural, nor ethnic polarization emerged. The agenda was determined by the labor-capital conflict. The mainstream media neglected the protests in the beginning, but as time passed, their live broadcasting cars and cameras were all over the streets. The resistance was on the news. People supported and showed solidarity following the media's broadcast. Sakarya Street, where the resistance mainly took place and tents were set, became a place where both socialists and people all came together with the workers. They brought clothes, blankets, and medicine, and they sat down to discuss and drink tea. The area was transformed into a forum and a living space. Carrying out protests with tents is evidently a trademark for the Egyptian rebellion and Occupy Wall Street. Yet TEKEL resistance was prior to both of them and used the tactic of claiming a place (the area surrounding Türk-İş building), occupying it and converting it for public use. This is perhaps the main aspect of the TEKEL struggle that will place it in the history books of collective struggle.

TEKEL resistance has been the most massive and prominent demonstration in Turkey against precarious employment, leading to debates about subcontract work, precarious employees, and deunionization. On the other hand, the resistance revealed that union managements have a parasite character. As the labor force became more radical and gained conscience to progress ahead, union bureaucracy has hindered them. The union management did not support the workers effectively and failed to intervene at proper times. At the end, the union withdrew its support for collective resistance.

Socialist organizations discovered the chance to re-establish their ties with the working class and socialize. Although some of the socialist organizations that are still under the influence of old habits tried 'to transfer consciousness,' most of the socialists have endeavored 'to learn together.' Young members of the leftist organizations have directly witnessed a manifestation of a class struggle and actually became a part of it. On the other hand, although the workers were in contact with young and educated men and women in a common public space, they probably do not share the same cultural codes. Although it would be inaccurate for us to conclude that the workers have defined themselves as socialists at the end of the resistance, it seems highly possible for us to claim that their perceptions of leftists and socialists have changed. One of the workers from Samsun explained:

We have taught and we got taught a lot. I personally learned a lot. We sat down with very young people. I prefer to spend time and talk with young people. I feel happy to see them here. You get very emotional when you see a high school student standing beside you fighting for your future. When they sleep outside, they get very cold. They are probably too shy to get into our tents. We may have acted indifferently as well. We did not properly welcome them into our tents.

Now we go outside and cover them with our blankets. Sometimes we wake them up and offer them to sleep in our tents. We have been educated for sure. (Kumlu, 2012, p. 126)

TEKEL resistance has seriously undermined the ruling party. The AKP's legitimacy has been challenged and its social base has been split. The Vice President of the government, Bülent Arınç, was the guest speaker on a TV program right after the mass demonstration, which took place on January 17. His words below reveal AKP's concerns:

I am not pleased to see that social opposition has grown and been dispersed out on the streets. An administrative party in power would not be content to see that. We do not take the criticism of opposing political parties seriously in the parliament. We just laughed at them because they do not affect us at all. But if the opposition will get out on the streets altogether with our sisters, young people and our own children to campaign against us, I get worried as a politician.

Time verified Bülent Arınç's worries regarding the opposition growing on the streets in three years time. AKP has faced a much bigger and more effective resistance. Overall, we find it meaningful to claim that more comprehensive studies will be completed in the future, which will evaluate TEKEL resistance and the Gezi resistance together to explain and illuminate the latter.

References

Angın, M., & Bedirhanoğlu, P. (2013). AKP Döneminde Türkiye'de Büyük Ölçekli Özelleştirmeler ve Devletin Dönüşümü'. *Praksis*, *30-31*, 77-95.

Aysu, A. (2010). TEKEL ve Tütünün Öyküsü. In G. Bulut (Ed.), *TEKEL Direnişinin Işığında Gelenekselden Yeniye İşçi Sınıfı Hareketi* (pp. 189-199). Ankara: Nota Bene.

Bedirhanoğlu, P. (2010). Türkiye'de Neoliberal Otoriter Devletin AKP'li Yüzü. In İ. Uzgel & B. Duru (Eds.), *AKP Kitabı* (pp. 40-66). Ankara: Phoenix.

Bulut, Ç. (2010). Ülke-Gündem-Direniş. In G. Bulut (Ed.), *TEKEL Direnişinin Işığında Gelenekselden Yeniye İşçi Sınıfı Hareketi* (pp 301-352). Ankara: Nota Bene.

Boratav, K. (2010). AKP'li Yıllarda Türkiye ekonomisi. In İ. Uzgel & B. Duru (Eds.), *AKP kitabı* (pp. 463-473). Ankara: Phoenix.

Boratav, K. (2012). *Türkiye ekonomisi*. Ankara: İmge.

Ertuğrul, İ. (2010). AKP ve Özelleştirme. In İ Uzgel & B. Duru (Eds.), *AKP kitabı* (pp. 522-559). Ankara: Phoenix.

İslamoğlu, H. (2002). Yeni Düzenlemeler ve Ekonomi Politik: IMF kaynaklı Kurumsal Reformlar ve Tütün Yasası. *Birikim*, *158*, 20-27.

Kumlu, A. (2012). *Neoliberal Çağda İşçi Sınıfının Konumu ve Sınıf Hareketi: 4/C ve TEKEL Direnişi Örneği* (unpublished doctoral dissertation). Ankara Üniversitesi.

Mütevellioğlu, N. (2010). Özelleştirmelerin Krizine Karşı Toplumsal Olanı Savunmak. In G. Bulut (Ed.), *TEKEL Direnişinin Işığında Gelenekselden Yeniye İşçi Sınıfı Hareketi* (pp. 149-173). Ankara: Nota Bene.

Oğuz, Ş. (2011). TEKEL Direnişinin Işığında Güvencesiz Çalışma/Yaşama: Proleteryadan 'Prekarya'ya mı?' *Mülkiye, 271,* 7-24.

Önal, N. E. (2012). *Anadolu Tarımının 150 Yıllık Öyküsü.* İstanbul: Yazılama.

Özuğurlu, S. (2012). Düzenleyici Devlet Modelinde İstihdam Rejimi: Güvencesizlik. In Ö. Göztepe (Ed.), *Güvencesizleştirme: Süreç, Yanılgı, Olanak* (pp. 143-147). Ankara: Nota Bene.

Sönmez, M. (2010). Milli Görüş'ten Neoliberalizme ve Krize AKP'nin Ekonomi İcraatı: 2002-2009. In Ç. Sümer & F. Yaşlı (Eds.), *Hegemonyadan Diktatoryaya AKP ve Liberal-Muhafazakâr İttifak* (pp. 263-285). Ankara: Tan Kitabevi.

Sümer, Ç., & Yaşlı. F. (2010). Liberal-Muhafazakâr İttifak Üzerine Notlar. In Ç. Sümer & F. Yaşlı (Eds.), *Hegemonyadan Diktatoryaya AKP ve Liberal-Muhafazakâr İttifak* (pp. 9-29). Ankara: Tan Kitabevi.

Tuğal, C. (2011). *Pasif Devrim İslami Muhalefetin Düzenle Bütünleşmesi.* İstanbul: Koç Üniversitesi Yayınları.

Türkmen, N. (2012). *Eylemden Öğrenmek, TEKEL Direnişi ve Sınıf Bilinci.* İstanbul: İletişim.

Uzgel, İ. (2010). AKP: Neoliberal Dönüşümün Yeni Aktörü. In İ. Uzgel & B. Duru (Eds.), *AKP Kitabı* (pp. 11-40). Ankara: Phoenix.

Yaşlı, F. (2004). AKP, Muhafazakâr Demokrasi ve Yeni Sağ. *Birikim, 180,* 39-46.

Yavuz, H. (2008). *Modernleşen Müslümanlar, Nurcular, Nakşîler, Milli Görüş ve AKP.* İstanbul: Kitap.

Yıldırım, D. (2010). AKP ve neoliberal popülizm. In İ. Uzgel & B. Duru (Eds.), *AKP kitabı* (pp. 66-108). Ankara: Phoenix.

Zürcher, E. (2010). *Modernleşen Türkiye'nin Tarihi* (Y. Saner, Trans.). İstanbul: İletişim.

4.
THE CAMPUS AS A ZONE OF DISSENT

The Eggs, the Canteens, and the Laws

Ezgi Kaya

Up until the Gezi protests in June 2013, it was a commonly held and expressed opinion that young people in Turkey were politically apathetic, indifferent, and inactive. Hence, when the reaction of the young people against the destruction of the Gezi Park rapidly turned into a politicized critique of the AKP government, it came as a surprise for most people. Gezi protests were associated either with an 'awakening of the youth' or the realization that the youth in Turkey had never been *entirely* apathetic. However, both responses falsely assume young people were more or less politically apathetic at some point. In fact, there was an ongoing prior process of acute politicization of youth, which became openly apparent for many only as a result of the Gezi protests. Despite the overall appearance of the youth as inactive and indifferent, it became evident through the Gezi process that some fish had already been swimming against the stream and when the right current hit, they were the ones who made the leap.

Looking at the ongoing student protests and struggles that became especially visible since 2010 provides us with clues to the origins of the politicization of youth. In fact, I believe that it is necessary to interpret the actions of youth during the Gezi uprising as part of a process that has been active during the last years of the AKP rule. In what follows, I will share the notable instances of these processes of student protest, which were among the strongest reactions towards the AKP government, both because they were unexpected by the AKP officials and because they brought forth an extensive public discussion in which the students had many supporters. I will analyze these instances of protest in a manner that sheds light on both their interconnectedness as well as the dynamics of their confrontation with large-scale processes of neoliberalization. Before doing so, I will address how the discourse of an apathetic youth—dominant in the period following the 1980s—has been taken up, debated, and challenged.

Debating Apathy among University Students

It has been a widespread and well-voiced argument in Turkey that young people have become politically apathetic since 1980s. This has been attributed either to the structural and political pressures over university education and the erosion of political culture in the universities due to the military coup of 1980, or to the neoliberalization process that picked up pace after the coup and the subsequent transformation it brought to both the form of university education and the student profile that enrolled in universities (Lüküslü, 2013, pp. 14, 122). Both associations have occasionally been taken to the extreme, painting a gloomy picture of the state of student mobilization in Turkey. In this section, I will focus on how the student movement that preceded the 1980s has been analyzed and how post-1980s youth have been distinguished from the youth of the '60s and '70s.

Turkey has had her share of student movements and protests in the wake of 1968, which continued in the following decade as well. The '60s and '70s in Turkey were politically turbulent years that anticipated the military coup in 1980. In particular, the '60s and '70s generation of university students participated in political action ranging from university-based protests to armed struggle. The political activity of student youth brought forward an anti-imperialist leftist movement that culminated in Marxist political organizations. Throughout the '70s, this movement was confronted by anti-communist organizations and went through an era of violence and bloodshed between students with left and right leanings.[20]

---

20 See Bali (2010) and Alper (2009) for a detailed account of the history of political and student movements in Turkey. University students had been politicized to a great extent in these decades, especially in response to the infiltration of Western political and economic agents into Turkish politics and economics. Among the notable instances of student protests of these decades that have since gained symbolic meaning are the student march on the deployment of the U.S. 6th Fleet in 1969 and the burning of the car of the U.S. Ambassador Robert Kommer during his visit to the Middle East Technical University in 1969.

The history of the student movement of the '60s and '70s, which was cut short by the military coup in 1980, has been evaluated from a number of perspectives: It has been narrated as a cautionary tale against politically polarized student action, as a story of the historic peak of student political action, opposition, and struggle, or as an example of an ideal era of student politicization and involvement in social struggles of the time. While the student movement was idealized and romanticized to a great extent by the leftist tradition, the conservatives and the right wing denounced it for having provoked a military coup. However, a debate has recently emerged in academic circles on how to evaluate these movements outside the confines of these binary interpretations.

Discussions about how to interpret the seemingly stark differences between the politicized youth of '60s and '70s and the contemporary apathetic youth and whether the current apathy is a result of a process of social and political repression or a result of some current socio-cultural and political conditions have already been kindled. It is commonly proclaimed that the definition and the connotations of 'being young' have changed in the post-1980 period, yet there is a diversity of opinions about what such a change entails. Some emphasize that youth have always carried historical baggage in Turkey, starting from the early years of Republic up to the 1980s. This historical baggage takes different forms, such as 'a myth that ascribes responsibility to youth for the well-being of the country' (Lüküslü, 2013), 'a national force of struggle for revolution' (Ahıska, 1999) or 'a privileged semi-intellectual group fighting for the rights of their people' (Benlisoy, 2011). What such different interpretations share is the claim that the post-1980 period breaks with these youth ascriptions and that youth have been, in a sense, 'left on their own' for good or bad. Hence, despite the negative connotations of politically apathetic youth, the parties in such a debate also perceive a potential for the creation of a young generation liberated from the historical baggage of the past and free to follow its own course brought forward by the post-1980 period.

The student movements of the '60s and '70s can be analyzed from one perspective as part of a 'youth myth' generated to encourage young people to take responsibility for the 'benefit of the country' and to construct themselves as a political category. From this perspective, this youth myth served the reproduction of elitism and authoritarianism in the statist tradition in Turkey (Lüküslü, 2013). According to this perspective, the room for individual action and liberation was limited in the student movements of '60s and '70s and the main ambition of the students who participated in the political activity of these decades was 'saving their people,' rather than attaining a course of individual emancipation. Hence, this perspective suggests that the student leaders of the '60s and '70s thought of themselves as already-emancipated agents that would enable the liberation of the poor, disadvantaged, and uneducated segments of society through their own political struggle, reproducing both an elitist perspective that asserted themselves as natural leaders and the people as mere followers and an authoritarian perspective that esteemed in-group discipline and the repression of dissent for a unified front in the struggle for political ends (Lüküslü, 2013, pp. 97-98). The post-1980 generation of youth, in contrast, was completely focused on individual benefit and wellbeing to the extent of excluding any concern for community and society as a whole. However, this perspective interprets this apathy and lack of political concern and affiliation in post-1980s youth as a rejection of the elitist and authoritarian tendencies of the preceding generations and perceives them as subjects of a process of 'necessary conformism': despite having problems with the political situation in Turkey, they fall into apathy due to the lack of acceptable—that is, individualizing and liberating—courses of political action (Lüküslü, 2013, p. 193). Hence, this process could also be interpreted as the subjectivization of youth (Neyzi, 2001).

This perspective challenges the widespread convention of portraying post-1980s youth as disregarding and ignoring political problems of the day for the sake of their individual wellbeing and comfort and invites us to dig deeper into the underlying reasons for the apparent apathy. Yet, while this perspective aims to play a disillusioning role in the analysis of student movement of '60s and '70s, it creates other illusions both about the '60s and '70s youth and about the post-1980s youth that tend to reaffirm the very points it initially attempts to clarify. Most importantly, it takes for granted the seemingly clean break between the politicized youth of the '60s and '70s and the apathy of the contemporary youth. I believe that this assumption leads to two problems in the analysis of student and youth movements. First, it obscures the underlying currents of student political action, which, despite failing to create a social and political rift in society and being unable to incorporate a high number of students, nevertheless existed and provided spaces for students to express their concerns and interests. Second, it neglects the necessary analysis of certain underlying social processes that re-shaped contemporary youth movements. To gain an understanding of what would drive the political activity of today's youth, it is crucial to recognize that the processes that provided the motive for crushing the previous political mobilization of the '60s and '70s youth in the form of a military coup are the same processes that call for the students' political involvement and action today. The military coup of September 12, 1980, was carried out in the context of neoliberal reforms that had been initiated with the economic decision package of January 24, 1980.[21] The latter provided the state with the ability to control and reshape the labor market in accordance with the

---

21 See Çoşar (2012).

interests of capital, without regard to or interference from labor representatives.[22] These decisions have formed the basis of a neoliberal transformation of the social system in Turkey, the results of which eventually constituted the core concerns of student opposition.

Commodification, Commercialization, Conservatization: Three Nemeses to Student Opposition

The AKP government rule from 2003 to today can be described as the consolidation period of neoliberal capitalism in Turkey, in which neoliberal policies of the most violent and corroding kind were implemented in not only economic, but also social and political life. It is possible to see the instances of commoditizing and commercializing relations in almost all of the main areas of social life in which the state had previously carried responsibility, such as healthcare system, social policies, labor regulations and workers' rights, and education. Although these processes were already at work in universities since the 1990s, they were consolidated during the AKP period. Moreover, as the student opposition to these measures intensified during this time, government responses became increasingly violent.

The processes that directed the students towards defending the campus first and foremost against neoliberalism can be summarized as the commodification of student life and the commercialization of campus activities.[23] As these processes picked up pace during the AKP period, the students became more and more integrated into social life in a twofold manner: First, the student was transformed into an immediate member of the cheap labor force, in addition to having been a future member of a qualified and skilled labor force. Second, the student became the intended target of different kinds of commercial activities that took place directly within the university or accessed the student through in-campus activities, transforming the students into actual consumers within their daily activities (Deniz, 2014, p. 286ff).

The commodification of student life involves the absorption of both educational and social aspects of student life into the market. The educational system in universities has increasingly been incorporated into market relations in two primary ways: first, an overarching number of private universities funded by the foundations directly affiliated with corporations have been established in

---

22 See Boratav (2009), Zürcher (2004) and Feroz (1993).

23 For examples of struggle against neoliberal education policies in other countries, see Jones (2012).

which the educational functions of the universities were directly commoditized (Birler, 2012, pp. 144-147). Second, even the state-funded universities have been coming up with ways to transform the results of study and research activities into commodities that can be directly translated into value in the market (Özuğurlu, 1999, pp. 101, 106). The collaboration between business corporations and universities has resulted in research facilities within campuses being directly occupied by firms. There has also been an increase in paid programs opened by state-funded universities. Hence, in some of its functions and to a certain extent, the university has been imitating a corporate firm.

This commodification of university education has brought forward a twofold commodification process in student life as well: First, the student becomes part of the workforce *during* his or her university education. Especially in privately funded universities, students—and graduate students in particular—work in the university facilities or on research projects in exchange for partial or full scholarships for tuition or minor fees (Benlisoy, 2011, p. 130). Second, the students are compelled to work outside the university to fund their own studies or pay for life expenses, even if they are in a state-funded university. The public life of students on university campuses is already under the controlling hand of capital through 'career days,' alumni talks, and on-campus recruitment by company executives (Benlisoy, 2011, pp. 137-138). Moreover, the job market for students generally consists of low-paid, temporary, and precarious jobs. Hence, the student is transformed into an actual member of the informal workforce before s/he even graduates and the university is transformed into a workstation for the students in return for the privilege of receiving an education. Student precariousness is intensified by having to work while studying (Benlisoy, 2011, p. 126). Rather than receiving education as a fundamental right once they are enrolled in a university, the students more and more realize that if they want to hold on to their education, they also need to hold on to the jobs that fund their education (either those directly provided by the university or those obtained in other sectors).

The accompanying process of commercialization in the university reorganizes a number of daily in-campus activities as commercial activities that the students have to pay for; in the case of privately funded schools, students are immediately transformed into customers by virtue of their student identity.[24] Many universities collaborate with banks through ID cards for students' payment of in-campus expenses. Besides this direct incorporation of the student into the consumer role by way of being a student, an increasing number of companies have

---

24 Up to 2003, the ID cards of Boğaziçi University students were double-sided: one face of the card served as university ID and the other face as an ATM card for a debit account that was automatically opened for each student who enrolled in the university. Other universities such as Dokuz Eylül University in İzmir and Ankara University followed the trend as well.

installed branches in universities, directly offering a variety of consumer goods to students. Consequently, students are confronted with consumer culture as they go about their everyday activities on campus. In effect, the university is transformed into a mall.

These processes of commodification and commercialization have been the target of student actions throughout the 1990s in the form of canteen boycotts and protests against increasing tuition fees and YÖK (*Yükseköğretim Kurulu –* The Board of Higher Education: a central state board which enables the state to have direct control over universities) (Mater, 1996). However, what is particular to the AKP period is that student protests have singled out the political party in power as their ultimate nemesis. As will be seen in the following sections, the most widespread and influential student protests were sparked by opposition to a political persona affiliated with AKP. Indeed, an important third measure that has inflamed students' opposition to AKP is the party's openly expressed vision of constructing a *conservative* youth. Prime Minister Recep Tayyip Erdoğan has frequently insisted on the party's goal of raising 'pious generations,' claiming that the alternative was 'substance abusers, rebelling against their elders, having no spiritual or national values.' He also stated that they were 'against parents who want to raise their offspring as atheists.'[25] Another direct discursive attack on university students by the prime minister came when he publically expressed his disapproval for male and female students living on the same premises and then went on to underhandedly associate student houses with criminal activities, saying that security forces are receiving intelligence about them and the state is going to intervene.[26] Erdoğan's statement sparked a harsh public debate bringing university students who were living in student housing face to face not only with the reality of security forces, but also with parents and family members who (perhaps out of intimidation) used this opportunity to express their own disapproval and reluctance for these living arrangements. Despite these pressures, students held many protests in different universities against Erdoğan's statement and were supported by a number of civil society organizations participating in solidarity protests.

The AKP's vision of youth conservatization, combined with its neoliberal agenda, acted as a catalyst to bring together the students' struggle against commercialization and commodification, on the one hand, and their political objections to

---

25 See 'CHP head accused of int'l smear campaign,' February 8, 2012, Retrieved from http://www.hurriyetdailynews.com/chp-head-accused-of-intl-smearcampaign.aspx?pageID=238&nID=13263&NewsCatID=338 and 'E-education project kicks off in Turkey,' February 7, 2012, Retrieved from http://www.hurriyetdailynews.com/e-education-project-kicks-off-in-turkey.aspx?pageID=238&nID=13170&NewsCatID=341

26 See 'Turkish government to act on accommodation housing female and male students', November 5, 2013, Retrieved from http://www.hurriyetdailynews.com/turkish-government-to-act-on-homes-housing-both-female-and-male-students.aspx?pageID=549&nID=57392&NewsCatID=338

the government, on the other. As a result, specific forms of student mobilization were generated, incorporating and even fusing together elements of resistance against all three processes. In the following examples of student mobilization, it is not possible to discern which elements respond to commodification from those that respond to political conservatism. Even though the student movement does not appear as a monolithic opposition bloc, it incorporates responses to the three dimensions of AKP's agenda in a unified, integrated manner. I argue that this is precisely the characteristic that lends power to contemporary student opposition.

Students' Protests against AKP's Neoliberal Agenda From the Snowflake, into the Avalanche: Berna and Ferhat

As campus life becomes ever more commoditized and commercialized, and as students are increasingly transformed into low-paid workers, subject to the imperatives of the labor market, resistance should come as no surprise. 'Free education' has been a primary demand of leftist student movements in universities for some time.[27]Leftist students began increasing their protests against the commercialization of education through private universities and the semester fees in state universities. On March 14, 2010, during a meeting about Romanian citizens in which Prime Minister Tayyip Erdoğan participated, students from the leftist organization Youth Federation opened a banner saying 'Parasız eğitim istiyoruz, alacağız' (We want free education. We will get it). The students were forcibly removed from the meeting hall by the Prime Minister's bodyguards and detained by the police. Two students among them, Berna Yılmaz, 22, from Ankara University and Ferhat Tüzer, also 22, from Trakya University, were arrested on March 17. In the trial that followed, they were accused of being involved in an armed terrorist organization and faced with a possible jail sentence of 15 years. The incidents that were shown as evidence in the trial were all peaceful protests. The trial lasted 19 months before Berna and Ferhat were freed.[28] Their long period of detention became a symbol in itself for the atrocities of law in Turkey during the AKP government; however, more importantly, their detention ignited a wave of protests among students in different universities, which carried on low-scale for a considerable length of time. Those protests were almost never on a mass scale or high on the public agenda, but they contributed to the formation of a critical collective attitude in student movements against the AKP government's treatment of student

---

27 See Interviews with Student Collectives (2011).
28 See 'Students sentenced to eight years for banner in Turkey,' June 8, 2012, Retrieved from http://www.hurriyetdailynews.com/students-sentenced-to-eight-years-for-banner-in-turkey.aspx?pageID=238&nid=22632

protests, and this became a strong factor in the various protests leading up to the Gezi uprising. In that respect, the injustice dealt to Berna Yılmaz and Ferhat Tüzer in response to their demand for free education served as the snowflake that would turn into an avalanche of student protests and mobilizations against AKP in the following months.

'Welcome to the Collective Egg Festival'

On December 4, 2010, a student protest against Erdoğan's meeting with university rectors in Istanbul was forcibly repressed. A number of students had been beaten and wounded by the police or detained.[29] The government would later defend the police attack, accusing the students of acting in accordance with a hidden agenda.[30] Students were very angry and reactive towards the government. On December 8, 2010, AKP deputy Burhan Kuzu and the opposition party (CHP) deputy Süheyl Batum were to give talks at Ankara University, in the Department of Political Science (Cebeci Campus), where students are known to have dissenting political affiliations. Süheyl Batum, who was first to speak, received loud protests from the students and was unable to complete his talk. Burhan Kuzu, arriving after Batum's departure and not being informed of the protests, ascended the platform as planned. To his surprise, students began throwing eggs at him, some of which hit right on target, and opened an appropriately worded banner: 'Welcome to the Collective Egg Festival.' Kuzu was escorted out of the hall after calling for the resignation of the faculty dean and the rector, and the police entered the university and attacked the protesting students with tear gas.[31] Both Kuzu and Prime Minister Recep Tayyip Erdoğan lashed out at the students in an insulting manner, accusing them of having ties with illegal organizations (Tahincioğlu and Göktaş, 2013).

'ODTÜ Has Risen'

On December 18, 2012, Prime Minister Recep Tayyip Erdoğan was expected at ODTÜ (the Middle East Technical University, METU) for the celebration of a research project of TÜBİTAK (*Türkiye Bilimsel ve Teknolojik Araştırma*

---

29 See 'Police beating draws ire of Turkey's main opposition,' December 5, 2010, Retrieved from http://www.hurriyetdailynews.com/default.aspx?pageid=438&n=police-exerts-violence-against-student-protesters-2010-12-05

30 See "Students faked police beatings' says Turkish Minister,' December 21, 2010, Retrieved from http://www.hurriyetdailynews.com/students-faked-police-beatings-says-turkish-minister.aspx-?pageID=438&n=students-throw-themselves-to-ground-to-make-news-2010-12-21

31 See 'University students protest members of Turkey's ruling, opposition parties,' December 8, 2010, Retrieved from http://www.hurriyetdailynews.com/university-students-protest-members-of-turkeys-ruling-opposition-parties.aspx?pageID=438&n=students-protest-akp-chp-members-2010-12-08

Kurumu—The Scientific and Technological Research Council of Turkey). A group of students wanted to march to the TÜBİTAK building inside the university to protest Erdoğan. Before the students could even approach the building, the police force that had accompanied Erdoğan to the campus began attacking the protesters with tear gas. However, instead of dispersing the students, the attack actually provoked more students to join the protest. When students with no initial intention of protesting the prime minister heard about the attack, they came to support their peers and to protest against police violence. Within a short time, thousands had gathered. In turn, the police strengthened the attack and the incident turned into a battle ground; students tried to defend their ground with stones and fireworks against the police who attacked them with sticks, plastic bullets, and tear gas. In fact, so much tear gas was used that visibility was impaired in the main road beside the university entrance, and the campus itself was hidden under a cloud of tear gas. The police attacks did not subside until long after Erdoğan left the campus. When the police finally left the campus, they left behind a large number of students wounded, beaten, and traumatized by the effects of the tear gas.

The effects of the ODTÜ protests lasted for a few days. First, ODTÜ students themselves did not allow the incident to simply pass. Protests inside the campus continued for days. Thousands of ODTÜ students marched to the university stadium and wrote 'ODTÜ AYAKTA' (ODTÜ HAS RISEN) on the field by forming letters standing up (an act reminiscent of an ODTÜ tradition of writing 'DEVRİM' (REVOLUTION) on the field during spring festival). An open class was held, in which professors gave short lectures about democracy, government pressures and the unacceptability of police violence. Importantly, the students also received support from the academic staff. Right after the incident, the academic organizations released press statements that they were aligned with students and criticized the police violence.[32] However, the reactions to police violence were not all of this kind. Rectors from other universities all around Turkey released a joint press statement, justifying the police violence by saying that it protected the government officials from student violence and criticizing the students for being disrespectful to the democratic process.[33] This led to a new surge of dissent in universities all around Turkey; students critiqued their rectors and voiced support for ODTÜ students. In Istanbul's Galatasaray University, the students occupied the rectorate hall and would not leave until the rector withdrew his signature in

---

32 See 'Academicians launch campaign against PM, University Presidents,' December 26, 2012, Retrieved from http://www.bianet.org/english/youth/143088-academicians-launch-campaign-against-pm-university-presidents

33 See 'Universities release joint statements blaming students for Odtü clashes,' December 25, 2012, Retrieved from http://www.hurriyetdailynews.com/universities-release-joint-statements-blaming-students-for-odtu-clashes-.aspx?pageID=238&nID=37600&NewsCatID=339

the press note.[34] The protests died down eventually; however, the feeling they left behind was one of hope and solidarity.

AKP's Response: Manipulative Legal Strategies Against Student Opposition

The protests against AKP officials and the students who criticized them publicly did not go unpunished. As the number of protests against AKP increased, the students began to face dangers more extreme and longer term than sporadic police violence. Following several protests, a number of students who were already spotted and noticed in other protests were detained by the police and a few of them were put on trial. The trials had a common factual basis: Those students who had joined the protests, who were perceived to be politically active, and who had already been affiliated with dissenting political organizations, were selected, arrested, and accused of being members of armed terrorist organizations. This charge was based on flimsy evidence, such as joining marches and protests, being in possession of Marxist classics or even owning banners and posters of political organizations (Tahincioğlu; Göktaş, 2013, p. 149). All of them were acquitted once trials were held; however, the long terms of detention that preceded the trials were supposed to act as actual and sufficient punishment for the dissenting students. On the other hand, these long periods of detention also endangered the students' university progress. Many students who were detained were unable to attend their exams and dismissed from their universities on the basis of taking a long absence without excuse. Many of them had to postpone their graduation as they could not complete the required amount of courses, which extended and deepened their already precarious conditions of life. It is not possible to address the issue of jailed students within the confines of this paper, as it has become a complex problem with too many grievances involved; it will suffice to say for now that the prosecuted students were not arrested and detained for joining a single protest but because they were already involved in political organizations and activities: their detention was meant to have a cautionary effect on other students. Moreover, the prosecution of students extends well beyond a specific response to protests; a number of students have been taken into custody and arrested in connection with other problematic trial processes in Turkey. Unfortunately, an account and analysis of these processes are beyond the scope of this chapter.[35]

---

34 See 'Turkish PM accuses CHP of abusing student protests,' December 28, 2012, Retrieved from (http://www.hurriyetdailynews.com/turkish-pm-accuses-chp-of-abusing-student-   protests.aspx-?pageID=238&nID=37829&NewsCatID=338)

35 There has also been a number of students arrested in connection with the cases of Ergenekon, KCK (Kurdistan Communities Union) and Devrimci Karargah (Revolutionary Headquarters), whose trial

Students' Response to In-Campus Neoliberalism – Creating Zones of Dissent: Occupy the Cafes!

The student protests mentioned until now have all taken on a form of refusal—a way of disagreeing and making that disagreement known through political processes. However, students understood that action of a different kind was also needed to displace the neoliberal relations encompassing university and campus life. In Ulrike Meinhof's (2011) view, the protesting students have made it known that they are refusing to go along anymore; however, the transformation of a protest into resistance requires 'making sure everybody else stops going along as well' (239). A moment of such transformation is evident in the recent opposition of Turkish university students.

The actual place that was transformed into a locus of resistance against commodification and commercialization was the university canteen. The small canteens and cafes in university buildings are usually owned by the university but leased to private individuals or small firms that run the place, provide the goods, and collect the profits. These canteens usually have cheaper prices than the other chain stores located on campus and are thus often preferred by students from low-income backgrounds who are barely able to fund their own education. However, taking advantage of the fact that they are the sole option for cheap food on campus for low-income students who do not have the time or ability to cook for themselves, the canteens raised their prices. This pursuit of more profit can be interpreted as a direct effect of the transformation of the university into a locus of profitmaking and the transformation, in turn, of the student into an actual consumer. It is not surprising that by observing the students shopping from the more high-end stores located on campus, the canteen owners saw a potential for further profit. As a result, the prices in canteens were raised gradually, until the students felt its pressure in their own financial conditions. At that point, the prices in canteens became a direct problem of everyday life for the students, leading to an opposition aimed at the functioning of the cafes.

The student opposition to food prices in university revealed itself in two forms: First, the students took issue with the first locus of commercialization—the chain stores themselves—and protested against the installment of more branches on campus; Second, the cafes with high prices were boycotted and the students began to organize alternative spaces and practices for cheaper food on campus.

---

processes were laden with injustices, unjustified extended periods of detention, and weak legal bases. The students were arrested in connection with various individual terrorist organization allegiances through flimsy and fabricated evidence and the excessive sentences they confront constitute a significance problem in Turkey.

There had already been instances of protests against the installment of food chains on campuses in the past years. A well-known example is the protests against McDonald's in the METU campus, which went on for four years, from 1997 to 2001. The students protested the newly installed branch of McDonald's on the METU campus for both economic reasons—the prices were too high for the students—and symbolic reasons—McDonald's was seen as a symbol of American imperialism by a portion of the students. McDonald's stayed in business for four years in METU; however, as the protests and the calls for boycott permeated the student body, in 2001, it shut down because of low profit margins and lack of customers.[36]

Ten years later, the students in Boğaziçi University tried the same strategy against the installment of Starbucks on the campus. The protests went on for two months in front of the store; however, they had no effect. Starbucks carried out business as usual while the students protested outside. Seeing that their protests were ineffective, the students came up with a different strategy. On December 6, 2011, the protesting students directly went into the Starbucks shop on campus and announced that they would not be leaving. They did not only refuse to leave but they also decided to make use of the place themselves. While Starbucks kept on operating on one side of the counter, the occupying students began to run their own food court in the sitting area. They made tea and sandwiches and omelets and gave them out to other students who came in to support them. The activities the students organized on the Starbucks premises were labeled as a 'festival.'[37] There were songs, movie screenings, and performances. Professors gave their support to the occupying students in the form of talks, debates, and open courses. The students stayed on the Starbucks premises until the rector of the university agreed to listen and respond to their demands himself. Even then, the students refused to send a delegate to the rectorate. They demanded the rector come and speak in the presence of all the students who joined the occupation. They demanded the closing of the Starbucks store on campus, the installment of a café that would be run by the students in its place, and a reduction in the prices of the servings in the dining hall of the university.[38] The rector talked to the students about their demands and brought them in front of the university board. After an occupation of 80 days, the students left the Starbucks. Their demands were not entirely met by the board, as Starbucks kept operating on the campus; however,

---

36 See 'ODTÜ'de McDonald's protestosu [McDonald's protest in ODTÜ],' May 23, 2001, Retrieved from http://hurarsiv.hurriyet.com.tr/goster/ShowNew.aspx?id=-244627, and 'Solun Yapamadığını Ekonomik Kriz Yaptı [What the Left could not achieve was done by economic crises]', December 17, 2001, Retrieved from http://arama.hurriyet.com.tr/arsivnews.aspx?id=43197
37 See 'University students occupy Starbucks shop', December 8, 2011, Retrieved from http://www.hurriyetdailynews.com/university-students-occupy-starbucks-shop.aspx?pageID=238&nID=8757&NewsCatID=341
38 See the demand list at http://starbuckssenligi.blogspot.com.tr/

the occupation had provided an invaluable experience of resistance and dissent for others to look upon. Following the Starbucks occupation at Boğaziçi University, the creation of an alternative food zone became a popular method at other universities and high schools for taking action against the commodification of food and the high prices in student canteens. One such example was given by students in the METU English Preparation Class, Geological Engineering and Civil Engineering who organized occupations in the student canteens in their own department buildings. In each department building, the students set up tables, 'solidarity canteens,' from which students gave out tea and sandwiches for free. In all three departments, the canteen leasers agreed to reduce prices after a couple of weeks of boycotting.[39]

Another example of canteen boycotts took place at Edirne's Trakya University, where the canteens were gradually being transformed into cafes. The remaining canteens had also been raising prices, while the quality of the food was constantly declining. The dining hall in the university took payment only through the 'campus card,' which was essentially a bank debit card. As a response to these developments, the students first organized a 'teahouse' as an alternative to the canteens in April 2012, giving out the food they prepared themselves for a couple of hours a day. In addition to the reduction of prices in the canteens, the students also demanded that the canteens be transformed back into a shared public space, where they would be able to socialize, organize, and do as they saw fit, rather than be limited to private establishments of the leased cafes. Despite pressures from the dean's office, the rectorate, and the private security guards, the teahouses remained active for nine months. After a march to rectorate hall on December 2, the rector accepted the demands of the students for the prices to be reduced and the spaces to be re-allocated for student activities in faculty buildings.[40]

Conclusion:

Campus-Based Struggle for the Right to Dissent and the Reclamation of the Possibility of Counter-Publics

As the accounts of such protests and demonstrations show, the student movement in Turkey cannot be termed nonexistent, nor should the students be labeled 'apathetic.' However, one can still argue that the mere existence of these instances of outspoken dissent and protest is not sufficient for claiming that the

---

39 See 'ODTÜ için Boykot Vakti [Boycott time for ODTÜ],' January 3, 2012, Retrieved from http://baskaldiraninsan.com/2012/01/03/odtu-icin-boykot-vakti/
40 See 'Trakya'da Kantin Baharı [Canteen spring in Trakya University],' January 9, 2013, Retrieved from http://www.sendika.org/2013/01/trakyada-kantin-bahari/

university youth are still politically active and that the extent and intensity of these protests are parochial among university youth. I wish to make two points regarding this suggestion: The first speaks to the effect of political student and youth organizing over the course of these protests and the second concerns the response of 'unpoliticized' youth to increasing political and social pressures. The pressure I am referring to does not merely include the exclusionary political discourse of the government towards students, but it also incorporates the economic and social pressures experienced by students as a result of neoliberal reforms in the university system. Despite the fact that these protests are still limited in scope and effect, an increasing number of students feel sympathy and solidarity with their discourses and demands, creating a potential for further politicization.

The literature on youth discussed earlier opened up the assumed political apathy of the youth to discussion, while denouncing political student movements of the past as restricting individual autonomy through collective organizational patterns and behavior. However, in each of the instances of student protests mentioned above, the initial spark either involved a call from political student organizations on campus or it was immediately supported by them.

Rather than harshly denouncing the '60s and '70s student movement as elitist and naively celebrating contemporary youth as chasing individuality and liberty in the course of becoming a subject (Lüküslü, 2013), it is possible to understand and contextualize these two eras of youth attitudes within a transformation of potential class positions among university students. The youth of the '60s and '70s had become students in universities with the confidence that once they received university education, they would be able to conduct their own lives above a certain life standard—an expectation that rendered them quite privileged compared to the lower segments of the population who had not had access to such an opportunity. The university youth knew for a fact that through education, it had become possible for them to rise above their initial class backgrounds and achieve better, more secure, and privileged life conditions. Once their privileged position was recognized, with the addition of a Marxist outlook to life, it was understandable that their main concern in political action was directed not to their own lives but towards the lives of other, less privileged segments of society. Hence, it is possible to say that the potential class position of the '60s and '70s university youth led them to position themselves as 'the intellectual dissenting and struggling for the benefit of the people' (Benlisoy, 2011, p. 122). In contrast, the contemporary university youth occupy a different potential class position, partly due to their limited future prospects and partly due to the alteration in the class origins of average university youth.[41] A certain portion of contemporary university

---

41 As access to university education has become further and further limited for children from working

youth is not at all secure regarding its future position in society and is troubled by the idea that it will not be possible to overcome its current precarious, untenable socioeconomic position at the end of its period of education. Hence, its primary point of concern and affiliation in politics becomes oriented to the agents and processes it holds responsible for the current precarity of its own positions. In such a context, it does not make sense to expect a form of outgoing political involvement similar to that of the past decades, nor is there justification for disregarding student actions and attitudes as not sufficiently political or as narrowly concerned with individuality over the collective. I believe it would be more meaningful to say that student politics in the post-1980s period of neoliberal expansion has taken on a different form than it did in the '60s and '70s. Since the AKP began consolidating and deepening the neoliberalization process in so many parts of social life, the university students were directly and personally confronted with the effects of these measures in their immediate experience of on-campus life. As a result, the campus itself became a political territory. Student politics principally sought to reclaim the campus from neoliberal forces, while concerns for broader political processes were incorporated into the student movement through the mediation of on-campus politics.[42]

The instances of student protests mentioned above can be better comprehended through this context. From this perspective, we can identify the opening up of new counter-publics for resisting extensions of neoliberalism into the university campus. Neoliberalism operates through reformulating the public sphere in accordance with its own needs and standards. The AKP government has taken up the same drive to transform the public sphere in line with its own politico-economic project; indeed, the conservative tendencies of AKP policies were one of the main reasons behind the Gezi protests. The emerging student movement in universities, best understood as a response to this transformation at the hand of AKP, seems to have a dual character: It both reacts against the political agents of this neoliberal transformation and seeks to establish alternative publics against neoliberal extensions into the campus.

---

class families, there is also a significant number of students who have better future prospects due to the social situation of their families. However, one of the most dedicated policies of the AKP government was the establishment of state universities in almost all cities, leading to an increase in the numbers of universities and university students (Günay & Günay, 2011; Altınsoy, 2011). Hence, on the one hand, quality university education is more generally received by children of upper class families; on the other hand, this does not decrease the number of students from lower class families receiving university education.

42 I am grateful to my colleague Gökhan Bulut for bringing to my attention this distinction between the off-campus political leanings and ambitions of the '60s and '70s student movements and the on-campus political leanings and ambitions of contemporary student movements.

The first kind of protest is directed against the agents currently responsible for the execution of neoliberal agendas. Protests of this kind, involving the tossing of eggs or battles with the police on campus, may be misread as fragmented instances of student mobilization that fail to achieve anything in the aftermath of the action. However, I believe such an outlook takes these protests out of the context of a struggle with neoliberalism and makes the mistake of treating them as individual cases of political reaction against AKP. They should rather be analyzed in connection with one another and in the context of the contradictory processes of neoliberalism.

What may seem as a mere protest of specific student groups against the presence of Burhan Kuzu or Tayyip Erdoğan on the campus can in fact be understood as a politicized response within the struggle against neoliberalism, rather than a single and sporadic reaction against figures of state authority. AKP serves as the current executive agent of neoliberalism in Turkey with a specific agenda for establishing a neoliberal regime. The students have come to be among those in the most vulnerable and precarious positions in neoliberal society. Hence, the protests against government officials or the prime minister can be considered as the immediate political aspect of an ongoing process of resistance and struggle, elucidated in a particular moment of confrontation. In the person of Burhan Kuzu or Recep Tayyip Erdoğan, it is the political aspect of neoliberalism that the students are protesting. Thus, the political significance of these protests can only be given meaning when they are understood in light of the larger processes of commodification and commercialization in universities. This is why such protests remain a moment of victory in the minds of those who have participated in them, despite the fact that they lacked immediate political consequences.

The prosecution of the students is also to be understood in this context. It was startling for some to see the harshness of the AKP's reaction to the protesting students, the amount of police violence, and the extent of legal repercussions dealt out to them. Why was a harsh and violent response used against a few protesting students? In fact, the AKP's response to the student protests was indicative of its fear of bursting the bubble of neoliberalism. Through students' confrontation with imposed precarity and commercialization, universities emerged as spheres in which the sutured parts of neoliberalism hung by fewer and weaker threads. It became possible to see through the façade of free and liberated education through a direct confrontation with these processes. The AKP, ever wary of the spheres in which the sutures of its neoliberal agenda did not hold tight and have an immanent potential of ripping, took harsh measures against the student protests to prevent exactly this revelation of the real mechanisms and outcomes of its agenda.

The canteen occupations and the Starbucks protest, on the other hand, constitute another aspect of the students' struggle against neoliberalism. Such forms of protests demonstrate that this struggle is not merely reactive and does not simply remain at the level of problematizing the political rule of AKP while failing to notice the social and economic relations and mechanisms behind it. In fact, protests of this form reveal that it is neoliberalism, and not merely AKP, that is the primary target of student opposition.. When considered as different parts of a seemingly sparse process of opposition, the protests against the prime minister and the AKP officials serve as an immediate response to immediate political decisions and agenda, while protests against Starbucks, McDonald's or canteen prices function as more direct form of response against the spatial dynamics of the neoliberalization process. The students are trying to reclaim the spaces central to their social life on campus from the neoliberal transformation of the university. This reclamation is indicative of another process that accompanies it, namely, the first steps of creating a counter-public sphere on campus. The students who boycotted the canteens or occupied Starbucks did not merely restrict themselves to a disruption of the commercial activities taking place on the premises. In fact, new practices set in place by students in the canteen or in Starbucks are far more important than simply disrupting business as usual. The students' activities in the canteen provided them with the main tenets of a new struggle against neoliberalism on campus, namely the values of sharing rather than selling and solidarity rather than competition. Through these counteractive public practices, students were able to jump out of their roles as student-as-consumer and student-as-cheap labor force, if only momentarily. This provided the student movement as a whole with a valuable realization that another way of experiencing life as a student is still possible.

References

Ahıska, M. (1999, Summer). 'Genç Olamayan Gençler' Üzerine Bir Deneme. *Defter, 37*, 11-19.

Ahmad, F. (1993). *The making of modern Turkey*. Routledge.

Altınsoy, S. (2011). 'A Review of University Facilities in Turkey', CELE Exchange, Centre for Effective Learning Environments, 2011/06, OECD Publishing. http://dx.doi.org/10.1787/5kg5c8cch88p-en

Bali, R. (2010). *Turkey in the 1960s and 1970s*. İstanbul: Libra.

Benlisoy, F. (2011). Neoliberal kapitalizm Devrinde Gençlik Muhalefetinin İmkan ve Açmazları. In D. Öz, F. D. Atbaşı, & Y. Bürkev (Eds.), *Gerçek, Yıkıcı ve Yaratıcı: Dünyada ve Türkiye'de Üniversite, Eğitim ve Gençlik Mücadeleleri* (pp. 117-151). Ankara: Nota Bene.

Birler, Ö. (2012). Neoliberalization and foundation universities in Turkey. In K. İnal & G. Gürkaynak (Eds.), *Neoliberal transformation of education in Turkey: Political and ideological analysis of educational reforms in the age of AKP* (pp. 139-151). Palgrave Macmillan.

Boratav, K. (2014). *Türkiye İktisat Tarihi, 1908-2009.* Ankara: İmge.

Çoşar, S. (2012). The AKP's hold on power: Neoliberalism meets the Turkish-Islamic synthesis. S. Coşar & G. Yücesan-Özdemir (Eds.), *Silent violence: Neoliberalism, Islamist politics, and the AKP years in Turkey* (pp. 67-93). Ottawa: Red Quill Books.

Deniz, A. Ç. (2014). Öğrenci İşi': Üniversite Öğrencilerinin Gündelik Hayatı, İstanbul Örneği. İstanbul: İletişim Yayınları.

Emin, A. (2009). *Student movement in Turkey from a global perspective, 1960-1971* (unpublished doctoral dissertation). Boğaziçi Üniversitesi.

Günay, D. & Günay, A. (2011). Quantitative developments in Turkish higher education since 1933. *Journal of Higher Education and Science, 1* (1), 1-22.

Jones, K. (2011). Avrupa'ya Musallat Olan Hayaletler: Eğitimde neoliberal reform ve Onun Düşmanları, Fransa, İtalya, İngiltere. In D. Öz, F. D. Atbaşı, & Y. Bürkev (Eds.), *Gerçek, Yıkıcı ve Yaratıcı: Dünyada ve Türkiye'de Üniversite, Eğitim ve Gençlik Mücadeleleri* (pp. 87-117). Ankara: Nota Bene.

Kolektifler ile Söyleşi. (2011). Üniversitenin İçinden Yükselen Özne: Gençlik Hareketi. In D. Öz, F. D. Atbaşı, & Y. Bürkev (Eds.), *Gerçek, Yıkıcı ve Yaratıcı: Dünyada ve Türkiye'de Üniversite, Eğitim ve Gençlik Mücadeleleri* (pp. 261-271). Ankara: Nota Bene.

Lüküslü, D. (2013). *Türkiye'de 'Gençlik Miti': 1980 Sonrası Türkiye Gençliği.* İstanbul: İletişim.

Mater, N. (1996, March 5). Protests underline crisis of affordability. *IPSnews.* Retrieved from http://www.ipsnews.net/1996/03/turkey-education-protests-underline-crisis-of-affordability/

Meinhof, U. (2011). From protest to resistance (1968). In *Everybody talks about the weather... We don't: The writings of Ulrike Meinhof* (pp. 239-244). Seven Stories Press.

Neyzi, L. (2001). Object or subject? The paradox of 'youth' in Turkey. *International Journal of Middle East Studies, 33,* 411–432.

Özuğurlu, M. (1999). Üniversite-sanayi işbirliği programı üzerine bir eleştiri, *Kültür ve İletişim.*1, 3-7

Tahincioğlu, G., & Göktaş, K. (2013). *'Bu Öğrencilere Bu İşi mi Öğrettiler?': Öğrenci Muhalefeti ve Baskılar.* İstanbul: İletişim.

Zürcher, E. (2004). *Turkey: A modern history.* I.B. Tauris.

5.
SISTERHOOD OF THE BROOKS

Ruralizing Dissent and the Anti-HES Movement

Mahmut Hamsici

Water is life. It cannot be sold! Our brooks are free, they will flow freely.

Platform of Sisterhood of the Brooks

In 2014, valleys all over Anatolia have turned into construction sites. Trucks and caterpillars are rattling and construction of hydroelectric power plants (HES) is continuing constantly. Local people are in a legal and on-site struggle against HES projects. The government is trying to repel citizens from legal acquisitions through new legal regulations. In some places, people are facing harsh interventions by gendarmerie and private security guards. These changes did not come out of the blue. Prime Minister Recep Tayyip Erdoğan summarized his opinion of the regulations of energy and water resources in his address to his Justice and Development Party's (AKP) parliamentary group back in July of 2008: 'The mentality of 'Water flows, Turk watches' is changing. We are introducing the mentality of 'Water flows, Turk builds.'[43] On September 8, 2008, Environment and Forestry Minister Veysel Eroğlu said this at the opening of the Sustainable Water Management Conference, organized by the Association of Turkish Industrialists and Businessmen (TÜSİAD): 'There's about \$50 billion investment potential in water; \$25 billion for hydroelectric power plants, \$20 billion for irrigation investments and about \$5 billion for potable water supply. The private sector's participation would be felicitous.'[44]

According to the information released by the General Directorate of State Hydraulic Works (DSİ), 1,738 HES projects are under way as of March 2010, of which 172 were complete and 148 were in process.[45] These numbers are constantly changing in practice. When the information coming from the field is compiled, the targeted number of HES projects reaches to 2,000 (Kocabıçak, 2009). A new reality is in place in Turkey: Giant corporations and international organizations that regard natural resources, particularly water, as a field of profit, especially since the crisis of the 1970s, are commercializing water and water basins (Maude, 2009; Poblete, 2007); the government runs the state like a company, selling water resources to private companies for periods of up to 49 years, even though it has been elected for four years, and responds to people's legal claims with new regulations; large and small domestic capital owners, the majority of which are pro-AKP and act as a government agency, control run-of-the-river hydroelectric plants as a new area of capital accumulation (Öztürk, 2010); and new 'security' forces do not hesitate to intervene when people object to these policies (Ercan, 2009). On the one side are gathered all of these forces; on the other side are those segments of people who defend their living spaces against the interests of a small minority (Kocabıçak, 2009). It is that simple.

In this chapter, I carry out an environmental impact assessment, not of state institutions but from the perspective of citizens. In doing so, I expose the 'ecocide' (a term created by Indian author and activist Arundhati Roy (2009)) that has been committed. I shed light on the main motives behind hydropower plants while sharing local people's experiences of struggle against these plants. I hit the road to make on-site observations of HES resistances and traveled across the Black Sea region from Kastamonu (in the center-west) to Artvin (in the east).

All of the brooks and valleys of Black Sea region are under attack by HES projects; among them are the brooks of Ordu, Giresun, Trabzon and Rize and the valleys of Salarha, Çağlayan, Senoz, İkizdere, Fırtına, Kelebekler, Macahel

---

43 'Su Akar, Türk Bakar Sözünü Türk Yapar'a Dönüştüreceğiz.' Retrieved from http://arsiv.sabah.com.tr/2008/07/21/eko106.html
44 'Türkiye'de Su Yönetimi: Sorunlar ve Öneriler', http://www.tusiad.org.tr/_rsc/shared/file/su-yonetimi.pdf
45 'Hidroelektrik Santral Projeleri Listesi', http://www2.dsi.gov.tr/skatablo/Tablo3.htm

and Pishala. Passing through several residential areas and valleys that are under attack, we conversed with local people in coffee houses, vineyards, and orchards around the region. Talking with local people in the Black Sea region was often easy; they seem to be used to outsiders, precisely because of the presence of HES projects. Nevertheless, we sometimes confronted obstacles to free conversation with locals. While we were resting and chatting with people near the mosque in a village in Pishala Valley, an old woman approached us, lifted her cane threateningly, and asked: 'Who is this, one of those HES-builders?' I replied, 'No ma'am, I'm a journalist,' 'Then, that's fine' she said and took a seat near us. During our conversations and meetings, I lent an ear to their experiences on HES projects, and I endeavored to make their voices heard in my study.

Collectivization of Anti-HES Movement: Sisterhood of the Brooks Platform

Turkey experienced significant changes in the energy sector in 1980s. Adopted in 1984, law No. 3096 enabled authorization of enterprises other than the Turkish Electricity Administration (TEK), a state-owned enterprise, to produce, transmit, distribute, and trade electricity. Dating back to 1997, law No. 4283 on 'Establishing and Operating Electric Power Plants and Sale of Energy through the Build-Operate-Transfer Model' brought into being a model enabling private enterprises to establish and operate power plants. The state would thereafter buy the generated energy according to this model. Yet, private enterprises were allowed to establish only thermal power plants, while hydraulic, geothermal, and nuclear and other renewable energy areas were left out of the scope of that law. In 2001, law No. 4628 on 'Electricity Market,' was adopted to outline a set of basic principles in the energy sector. According to this law, the Energy Market Regulatory Authority (EPDK) was established to 'create a competitive energy market and ensure an independent regulation and control over the market.' This law smoothed the way for private sector investments in all areas of energy. On June 26, 2003, a 'regulation on signing of the right of water usage agreement for carrying out production activity in electricity market' was issued. Under the aegis of these laws and regulations, private entities began researching the possibility of energy production through the methods of transfer water from one basin to another (Yılmaz, 2009).

In different localities of the Black Sea region, platforms, forums and councils against HES projects were established. Collectivization of the resistance against HES projects paved the way for communication between villages that used to be rather inward-oriented and disconnected from one another. For example, villages settled many decades ago along the Aksu Brook had always been introverted with minimal contact with adjacent peoples; these included the villages of Abkhaz, of Rize-origin people, of Trabzon-origin people, and of Ordu-origin people. Remarkably, for the first time in their history, these villagers collectively organized with their neighbors to protect their water. As a result of these meetings and reciprocal village visits, unprecedented bridges have now been built between communities.

Collectivization of the anti-HES movement is based upon cooperation of different political parties and movements. From the very beginning, the anti-HES movement was conducted by the Tonya Sisterhood of the Brooks Platform in Trabzon's Tonya district. The platform has a kind of 'sui-generis' structuring: It works as a kind of umbrella organization above distinct political parties, such that Kemalists, Islamists, socialists and nationalists are all under the same roof. A senior member of the platform explains the diversity of participation:

We had an old slogan: Common attitude against common enemy. Now this slogan came true in Tonya. There's a common enemy: those who sell and buy water. Now we, as residents of Tonya, have a common attitude against this. We are getting wet under the same rain, we are buying bread from the same bakery, we are mourning in the same funeral and we are cheering in the same wedding. Can there be anything more natural than us being together? There's a rain and we have to get under the umbrella. Now we are under this umbrella. A movement began in Tonya and we are saying, 'It will never be the same again in Tonya.' We hope that people somewhere else who have political contrasts can also strike a common attitude for their soil.

Platforms that remain isolated within their region recognized what was going on in other places of Turkey and made efforts to establish cooperation. Anti-HES groups discovered other groups suffering from the same troubles and started to participate in their demonstrations. An activist from Loç Valley tells of how his group participated in a protest against the World Water Forum:

We had to make our voice heard. All right, but we were the people who never participated in a protest or rally! We learned on the web that there was a place called Munzur and they would make a statement to the press in Sütlüce. We contacted them and asked, 'Can we walk together with you?' Our aim was to help everybody who is in trouble. We thought, 'If we help them, they will help us too.' We went to Sütlüce. For God's sake, everywhere was full of police officers. Some of our friends said 'Maybe we should go back before it's too late.' But we didn't go back, we hit the road with a flourish of trumpets and slogans. We came to the AKP building. The press left those from Munzur and paid attention to us. Then, when we appeared on newspapers and TVs and when police did not beat us, we took courage. As soon as we were seen in public, people started to recognize us. Then they started to invite us to their own platforms. Then, on April 25, 2010, we realized that we were organizing a rally in Kadıköy to say stop to energy production that destroys life and we were one of the five hosts!

This collectivization of resistances created an organization with perhaps the most beautiful of names: 'The Sisterhood of the Brooks Platform.' This is composed of local platforms that are against selling and marketing the brooks, establishing hydroelectric plants on them, and the destruction of nature. The chairman of the Executive Board of the Platform, who is a retired teacher, states:

Sisterhood of the Brooks is local people. We, as the platform, are traveling to these regions because of calls from local people. People are working voluntarily here. We are not outsiders, we are local people. The Environment and Forestry Minister says 'natural gas lobbies are backing them.' I am traveling everywhere by spending my own money. I am spending my family's daily bread. No lobby is supporting us. Sisterhood of the Brooks has no business with lobbies. They founded lots of environmental organizations in order to divide the struggle. We are the people; if they have the money, then we have the heart and labor. Sisterhood of the Brooks draws its strength from the people and does not lean its back on oil companies, the European Union or [famous speculator George] Soros. Water is not a mere human right, we object to that as well. Water is the right of all living beings and non-living things. We will use water only as we need. We do not look to the water from the money point of view, we deem it as life. Water is the right of the ecosystem. Trout in the brook, frogs and creepy crawlies, all should make use of water. Brooks are like blood flowing in human's veins. We as Sisterhood of the Brooks, do not question water of life. We say 'what flows in the brook is already water of life.'

Firsts in the Anti-HES Movement: 'Soldiers of the Company'

With the anti-HES movement, hundreds of villagers got acquainted with demonstrations, police batons, detentions, and prison for the first time in their lives. A villager from Fırtına Valley of Rize describes the situation of villagers who took a stand against the state for the first time:

We are like Indians at the moment. The state is the USA and we are Indians. People here do not have a considerable income. They are selling tea there, which is not compensation for the pain they suffer. The state comes here, takes your water, your neighborhood and everything away. For some reason, there's an outrageous allergy against the Black Sea region.

Some encountered security forces for the first time in the context of the anti-HES movement. A villager from Loç Valley of Kastamonu describes it as follows:

We traveled from İstanbul to Kastamonu by minibuses and cars to make a press statement in June 2010. Undercover cops chased us along the way. We made the safest journey on that night, as police officers later said! Police officers in every province that we passed chased us until we got out of the borders of that province. We entered Kastamonu in the company of a police motorcade. It seemed to us as if we were terrorists, but on the other hand, we understood that the government is aware of our rebellion.

We heard about the discomfort with the gendarmerie in another house. 'We have never encountered gendarmerie throughout our life. But now they always call the gendarmerie,' a villager from Loç Valley said. A 43-year-old woman from Loç Valley told us that she saw gendarmerie officers in her village for the first time and described Loç Valley from her point of view:

Schools were closed on Friday and I came here at night. I have an eight-year-old daughter and she was longing to swim in the creek. Children are generally told 'if you study your lessons, you will be rewarded with a bike,' but we say 'if you study your lessons, we will go to the village.' This is a reward for our children. My daughter is constantly asking 'Why don't we go swimming in the creek, did somebody take it away?' since we come. Now we have to buy water in our own village. They are giving truckloads of trees that they chopped down from our village to people who did not object to [the building the HES]. Our people of Black Sea region do not know how to demand. You know, people say, 'Paris, Paris' [to describe a beautiful place]. Paris is here for me. If my daughter did not go to school in İstanbul, I would not go back.

While we were making an interview, a gendarmerie officer popped in and asked what we were doing and whether we have the required permission for it or not. When they left, a youngster told us of his dialogue with children outside. One of children asked 'Brother, who are they?' 'They are soldiers,' the youngster replied. Then the child posed another question that caused the older ones to ponder the distinction between 'private' and 'public': 'Are they soldiers of the company?' This childish question is worth reflection.

Many people in the Black Sea region are annoyed with the attitude and behavior of company officials. Tractors, loaded with vegetables, shuttle in and out of Amasya's Umutlu village square, where vegetable farming is the main source of income. Boxes of eggplants and onions are scaled and loaded onto the trucks to be taken to the city center. Villagers who provide irrigation for their gardens with water from the Yeşilırmak River believe that the HES project will clear away their source of income. The village chief is annoyed with both the HES project and 'the attitude and behavior' of company officials.

> When they first came, they said 'We will do a feasibility study and we will build it if it's suitable.' They are deceiving people. And they act recklessly. First we said, 'we will not let you work here unless you inform us about your project.' 'We will do what we want to, who are you to stop us?' they said and acted recklessly. And we as the citizens intervened and kicked them out. We filed a lawsuit against the project. They would cut people's water of life here, if they succeeded. We made a stand against it in our way. We are against the HES and we will fight against it.

Another 'first' experience within the resistance process was that brothers become Cain and Abel because of the HES projects. A villager in Loç Valley said: 'Brothers become Cain and Abel here. The older brother supports the building of power plant, he was given something. But the younger brother objects since he loves the nature and his hometown. It's just a matter of time before people slaughter each other.' A villager from Rize's Salarha Valley expresses his opinion on this issue as follows:

> Though nobody lays stress on it, many close relatives, friends, and neighbors are at odds with each other because of these HES projects. In many briefing meetings, furious debates are sparked and seeds of discord and enmity are sown among people. The Greatest civilizations had been established near water resources throughout history. If we take it in micro scale, brooks influenced the development of villages. Villagers who identify themselves with the brook learned how to swim in that brook. They sit, make friends, sing songs and fall in love near that brook.

Symbols and Language of the Anti-HES Movement: Yellow Scarf, Accordion, Bagpipe, Kemençe

Items intrinsic to everyday life and culture have become symbols of the anti-HES resistances in different regions and neighborhoods of the Black Sea region. In every environmental demonstration around Kastamonu province, we saw people with yellow scarves wrapped around their necks. They also waved yellow scarves like a flag while they chanted slogans. A scarf, yellow colored, has geometric figures or flower patterns on it. A Yellow scarf is one of central cultural motifs in Kastamonu. But the yellow scarf became the trademark of the citizen movement against the HES projects.

Brooks in the Black Sea region are themselves decisive and deep voices of the anti-HES struggle. While I was watching the brook in Fırtına Valley in Rize, a citizen reminded me of an important tip about the region where Laz people live:

> There is the culture of people who have been living on this territory for centuries. This water is the very subject of this culture. The vanishing of the water would lead to vanishing of the culture. They are doing the same as they did in Munzur and Hasankeyf. One of the reasons that our Black Sea people are speaking loud is these brooks in fact.

Collectivization of the resistance against the HES projects brings different villages and different societies together. As mentioned above, Aksu Brook in Düzce is noteworthy on this point. All different ethnic and cultural identities around Aksu Brook united for the struggle. Thus, hands playing accordion, kemençe, bagpipe, and drum joined for the first time in the struggle for their rights.

Resistance Methods of Anti-HES Movement: Law, Science, and Street

In the course of our research across the Black Sea region, we noticed three struggle methods against HES projects. The first takes place on the legal field; lawsuits are currently being filed against HES projects. Before diving into the details of these battles, it is worth noting that legal experts argue that HES projects' are in contradiction with national and international legal and administrative regulations. According to many experts, HES projects are first and foremost against the Constitution of Turkey. According to Article 17 of the Constitution, everyone has the right to life, the right to protect and improve his/her corporeal and spiritual existence, and the right to live in a healthy and balanced environment. According to Article 56, it is the duty of the State and the citizens to improve and protect the natural environment and to prevent environmental pollution. In addition, Article 28 of the Turkish Environmental Law states that the person who pollutes or damages the environment is liable for damages caused by pollution and deformation even if he or she is not at fault. In this paragraph, objective liability is regulated. The second paragraph of article 28 is about reserving the compensation liability in Civil Law. According to article 28/2, the compensation liability of the polluter due to general rules of Civil Law is also reserved. The third paragraph of article 28 is about statute of limitations. According to article 28/3, the compensation claims due to the environmental damage may occur up to five years after the aggrieved person learns of the damage.

Legal experts also suggest that HES projects are against conventions and treaties that Turkey is party to. Among these treaties and conventions are the UN Convention on Biological Diversity, the Bern Convention on the Conservation of European Wildlife and Natural Habitats, the Convention on International Trade in Endangered Species of Wild Fauna and Flora (CITES), the UNESCO Convention Concerning the Protection of the World Cultural and Natural Heritage (HES projects specifically in Hasankeyf, Munzur, İkizdere, Fırtına, Allianoi are allegedly against this convention), and the Ramsar Convention on Wetlands of International Importance (Yılmaz, 2009).

Secondly, HES projects are open to debate in science circles. An official recites the activities of the İkizdere Association of Rize as follows:

İkizdere realized the truth better because of the scientific and legal struggle of the İkizdere Association. Local people comprehended how the HES projects damage nature thanks to the drafted reports, academic congresses, published books, and statements, and they built up strength behind the İkizdere Association. We tried to keep the issue on the agenda with press statements, rallies, marches, and many other activities. We attempted to keep people focused on this issue constantly. Our congresses, which were attended by many rectors, deans, and scientists from universities, were especially effective. And our banquettes in İstanbul and İkizdere were morale-boosters for our people and consolidated our unity and solidarity.

Thirdly, they hit the streets to voice their demands. Here is the experience of Fırtına Valley:

You start the struggle and you do whatever is needed for it. We went beyond the limits of the law, which is very rare. But I can't tell you all of them. For example, you lie down in front of the Caterpillar to stop it, or when dynamite would be blown up, you go and sit there. Then the man in charge alerts you. But maybe the other man is deaf, he does not hear! In fact, you can hear, but you do what you do to stop them. You should not let them operate. They should shiver when they see you. They should say to themselves 'Alas! There they are again.' Let's assume that they blew up the dynamite, one would drop dead! So you should risk something. Otherwise, struggle is not possible only with speaking. We attended that Water Council meeting. We said 'Let's walk straight down to the hotel and get covered with mud. And let people see us like that.' Then they might say 'These people certainly have a problem, so that they wallowed in the mud.' That's it. That's the matter, that's the exact matter.

The issue of the struggle's legitimacy and the fact that it exceeds the limits of the law is also being discussed. An activist from Fırtına Valley said:

Movements attract people, but only if you are able to explain there's a benefit for people in these movements. This is a certain part of the struggle. My friends and I still can't explain it exactly to our people. Our people are faithful to the state. Particularly here in Hemşin region, people are peculiarly faithful to the state. We can't overcome it. We can't convince people 'The state is unfair to us here.' We don't tell them to rebel against the state but we can't convince them that there's something unfair in what the state or government are doing. If somebody stabs a knife in you, you prick him with a needle in return. But pricking with a needle is a crime according to our legislation. But stabbing a knife in us is not a crime. Why? Because he stabs a knife in us by permission of the state. But you are using the needle by your own will, so your action is a crime.

Without a doubt, the legal struggle and the social movement are the matters in question. An official from Erzurum's Çamlıkaya Valley explained 'the social movement' as follows:

Frankly speaking, legal means are somewhat degenerated. Somewhere in [Aegean town of] Muğla, a construction was halted by court decision, but they started to work again by saying 'There are some mistakes, we will correct them.' Then they cut down 200 to 300 trees in one night although they were taken under protection. Then citizens see in the morning that it's not like they were told before. Starting from that date, they began keeping guard of the trees. So that's what happens!

Another significant characteristic of the anti-HES movements are their direct democracy practices. Activities conducted against HES projects along Aksu Brook in Düzce can be summarized as 'silent but profound.' The Gölyaka-Hendek Union for Protection of Aksu Brook was founded in the spring 2010. Regular meetings are being held with representatives from each village, who take decisions on what to do and review what they did against HES projects. A tough legal battle is going on; at the same time, struggle on the ground is not neglected. Booths were set up to promote the anti-HES struggle, a petition was started demanding a halt to HES projects, and mass protests were held. During a meeting of the Union that we also attended, representatives who have different political opinions and ethnic origins had discussions within a culture of democracy. They reviewed the previous week's affairs and planned what they would do in the next week. At the end of the meeting, they decided to buy notice boards to inform people about HES projects and news stories and to hang them in coffee shops. They also decided to visit local press representatives in Düzce to inform them about their activities.

Social media is also an important medium for organizing the anti-HES movement. Founders of the Association of Protection of Ecological Life in Solaklı Valley were not able to come together for a long time since the Valley encompasses several districts in Trabzon province. Eventually, they were able to come together thanks to a Facebook group called 'Let the Solaklı Brook flow freely.'

Convincing people is also crucial for organizing the resistance. An activist from Fırtına Valley stated:

> To win the struggle, you have to draw a roadmap in your mind. How would it be if we did it like this or that. You should discuss it among yourselves. This is a committee. Let's say you formed a committee composed of 10 to 20 people. This committee should come up with new ideas. When you form the group, one thing leads to another. Why? Because there's something prepared. You have a group to struggle. You can go everywhere with your group; there's a self-sacrificing group. People, who drop everything, travel with you and struggle shoulder to shoulder with you ... We wanted to hold a protest march here. Sometimes lack of experience is a very bad thing. We don't have a leader, someone who says 'you should do this and that for the struggle.' And we decided to hold a march in Çamlıhemşin. We elected an old man as the head of the committee. But some said to that old man, 'You would not get anything by hitting the streets and you will tarnish the reputation of Çamlıhemşin.' They said so-called provocateurs would get on the stage, they would provoke us, and then a quarrel would erupt and so on and so forth ... What happened? They barred our march. How? Since my friends and I did not know anything at the time. But thank God we are not like that today.

Another activist from Fırtına Valley emphasizes that one should tirelessly and persistently explain to people the reason for the struggle to convince them:

What will you do and how—you should explain all this to people. Take a power plant that would be built in this region. You should portray what would this plant bring and take away if it's built in the region. You make calls to people: 'There will be a meeting on that date, please attend.' But our people are not so sensitive on these matters. Then you should go to them. You should say 'We will visit this man's house and that man's shop this night and another shop tomorrow night.' What will you do? You will stroll around. You will explain to them. But you will not be able to tell them. They will not accept you. But you will explain to them again. They will kick you out of their house, but you will explain to them again and again.

Activists often underlined that those who are organizing the resistance should keep out of financial matters. An activist from Fırtına Valley speaks about this issue:

While you are in a struggle, you should be far away from financial matters. This is fundamental. If you are inclined to financial benefits, you can't take part in a struggle. Why? Wherever financial matters arise, nothing is rational. Money helps people to put bread on the table, but it doesn't make a human a human. Money is a tool for us to have bread and butter, to have clothes, and to have a roof over our head. A human being is insatiable. We took the road for the struggle. Some say we were hungry. Yes, we were, but what should we do? It doesn't matter if we are hungry for three or five days. I was a shepherd for years and I often strolled around hungry. Indeed, it's not that hard. On one occasion, the undertaker hosted a dinner here. I didn't even attend that dinner. Why? Maybe I would have enjoyed that dinner and been mesmerized because of it. Our village chief, who took part in the struggle before, attended that dinner and on the following day he came and told us: 'We were misinformed, the power plant have several benefits.'

Solidarity and unity are also important matters for organizing the resistance. One activist from Fırtına Valley recalls: 'We have always kept our unity and solidarity. We were always together. We fought shoulder to shoulder. At the end of a protest, none of my friends said 'Count me out.' When one of our friends was called to give testimony, he said 'Yes, I was there.' Maybe he wasn't there at that moment, but he said 'I was there.'

To organize an effective resistance, one must think carefully about the location and come up with a strategy. In Ardanuç district of Artvin province, the Ardanuç Water Council was formed against the HES projects and later changed its name to the Platform for the Sisterhood of the Brooks in Ardanuç. A representative from the platform said that they ruminated on how they could inform people around the region about their struggle; eventually they started to attend Friday prayers in village mosques all year round:

> Villages here are far from each other and it's difficult to gather everybody together. For this reason we decided to conduct meetings in mosques. I was very excited the first time. I wasn't able to sleep the previous night. A memorial service was being held on that day. The village chief said 'You will start after the memorial service and speak until Friday prayers.' Then we started to speak. When the time is up, I said 'Let me not speak too long, you will perform Friday prayers.' 'Please go on, we can perform prayers a little bit later' they said in response. They were all ears while I was speaking. Then throughout the winter, we visited villages no matter how much it rained or shined. Our meetings were announced from the loudspeakers of the mosques beforehand. And we were conducting at least two meetings every Friday—one before the prayers and another after the prayers. And we were learning in the meantime while we were talking to people. We were both speaking and showing people through the computer the current situation of places where HES projects were built, such as Murgul Kabaca Valley.

Pioneers of the Anti-HES Movement: Women

Kocabıçak (2009) tells the stories of women who are resisting across the country in his article, 'Women's battles for water against the process of the commercialization of water.' It was remarkable that many of the men we spoke to in the Black Sea region were more moderate, while women were more outspoken. Among some of the remarks I often heard from men and women in this region were: 'Women of this region are actually [like] men,' 'the Interior ministers of our home are women,' 'We don't waste time trying to convince men, we just finish up.'

Women in the Abkhaz villages in Aksu Valley are quite active. A women's committee was founded within the Union for the Protection of the Aksu Brook. Founders of the women's committee are women from Abkhaz villages. An activist from the women's committee said that they were having hard times because there was no contact between separate villages, and women outside Abkhaz society did not participate in social and public life. She said: 'We are taking two steps further and ten steps backwards. Just when we make contact with somebody, they hold back. We are inexperienced, but we will learn. Look here, there's no women at this meeting; but they promised they would attend the next meeting.'

A woman from a village in Giresun explains why she took part in the struggle:

When the water is gone, our lives are gone. How can we live here when the water is gone? 'Our water is our honor,' we said. How will I irrigate my property and where will my cows drink water? We can't go; but they will go. We will not give our water. What can we do without a grain mill? Nobody knows when this grain mill was built. I can give my life, but I don't give my water. A village gave its water, but now they can't find water to drink. We will continue to resist and we will not give our water. I was also at that march. I participated in such a rally for the first time in my life. But I'll participate if it takes place again.

All women who we spoke to across the Black Sea region said exactly the same thing: 'We are ready for a fight!' However, a woman, who had previously taken the floor at a rally in the Tonya district of Trabzon province, spoke bitterly as she lifted up the spud she held in her hand:

We are against giving away our brooks. They drop litter to the brook, then it rains, washes, and it gets clear. If they do that, our water will recede and we will run out of water and flies will come. If we, about 100 women of this village stand up, we can drive them into the brook. Believe me, we can. Our women of Tonya can do it. If you twist the lion's tail, you will bitterly regret it. Our women carry guns, like bandits. They'd better hold back, otherwise we would beat and hang them on the trees. And we don't include men in the fight.

Women in the Fındıklı district of Rize province established a 'private security system' against companies conducting HES projects in their valley. Whenever they see a vehicle carrying 'outsider' license plate, a series of phone calls begin and eventually, they stop the vehicle and ask people inside the vehicle why they are here. A woman from the Arslandere village in Fındıklı explained their system: 'We keep watching and when we see a vehicle, we call each other and we stop them here. They can't drive beyond. My grandfather, grandmother grew up near this brook. God bestowed this nature to us. Why would we sell it?' Company officials were previously coming by vehicles with license plates starting with 06, which is Ankara's code. After these village 'stoppings,' they began driving rented vehicles carrying license plates starting with 61, which is Trabzon's code. However, they still cannot escape women's notice. A women activist from Arslandere village said, 'If they come again, we will turn them back with eggs on their heads.'

Conclusion

Environmental movements in Turkey primarily arose in the early 1980s. The most significant movements were the ones formed by urban middle classes who approach environmental issues in good faith without touching upon the political sphere. In addition, 'flower-power groups' (as critics call them) launched their activities as large capital groups and the government was tolerant of them. Nevertheless, the destruction of forests, rivers, lakes, air, and mines—due to neoliberal policies—led to dissent by sufferers of this destruction and the direction of environmental movements changed. When these movements gained strength and civil society organizations, sponsored by large capital groups, became institutionalized, Turkey became acquainted with people's resistance. This was a turning point for environmental movements.

When today's movements are examined, one notices a new type of social movement—that of the oppressed defending their living space against pillage across Anatolia. Local communities such as those resisting nuclear power plants in Sinop and Mersin, those objecting to the thermal power plants in Kahramanmaraş and Bartın, those protesting against cyanide gold mining in Çanakkale, and those struggling to shut down the gold mine in Eşme district of Uşak province—all have become important constituents of social movements in Turkey. In this respect, people who are resisting against HES projects, and whose stories have been told in this chapter, are some of the most important constituents of these movements.

Those who struggled against HES projects for water and the right to a livable environment not only raise their objections to impoverishing and dispossessioning neoliberal policies, but also they come up with responses and visions about what kind of country they wish to live in. Is the infringement of their right to clean water the only reason for their anger and their readiness to sacrifice their life? Responses suggest that, above all, citizens are resentful towards the companies and the state because they do not respect citizens. They cannot stomach the fact that their opinion on an issue, which directly concerns their life, is not regarded as relevant and that they do not have the right to speak or participate in the process. They cannot stand the violence that they are subjected to when they object to the projects. In other words, people are primarily conducting a struggle to be respected. They demand the right to speak on the issues that directly concern their life. This demand, perhaps unwittingly, makes them long for a true, direct democracy. And they lay the foundation of that democracy through their activities. In many places, people come together en masse for the first time, and they discuss and take decisions on their future in meetings where everyone has an equal right to speak.

Women, who are the indisputable pioneers of the anti-HES movements, are more and more participating in the alternative public sphere created in many places, despite men's rather restraining attitude. While the prejudgment that 'the state does everything right'—prevalent for centuries—is in question for the first time in some regions, villagers have begun to realize that the old order is no longer. There is no Turkish social state to speak of, and without a good struggle, it will never be put in place again. People encounter big companies and realize that they are not at all pleased to meet their acquaintance. Yet, given the national private sector investment in HES projects, the discourse that 'all of these are the plans of foreign capital and states' is not true in this case and thus remains inadequate as an analytical device. Although it has not yet been reflected in political choices, discontent toward the AKP government is increasing day by day.

Citizens' opportunities to protect their rights by legal means have been vanishing constantly. The government is blocking all legal solution by abolishing administrative courts' expediency powers with the new Constitution and by adopting the Law on Protection of Natural and Biological Diversity, which bars protection of brooks by having the basin declared as a 'National Preservation Site' as it happened in Fındıklı and İkizdere. This circumstance increases the need for on-field struggle against HES projects.

Citizens' voices are not heard in mainstream media unless violent incidents take place or particularly interesting protests are held; they therefore find ways of creating their own media apparatuses. Young people in particular are forming new communication networks by using the Internet. Footage of a demonstration, which is not broadcasted on national TV channels, can be reached by thousands of people through websites, blogs, and social media. Local newspapers, radio, and TV channels are becoming important communication tools for the struggle. A movement of the people's media, in which citizens produce their own news, has been gradually developing.

The bridges of the sisterhood (brotherhood/fraternity) are being built through the brooks at a time when ethnic, religious, sectarian, and regional divisions among Turkish society incite discrimination and prejudice. Aksu Brook in Düzce brings the Black Sea region-origin people and Circassians together for the first time in 100 years. Yörüks of Antalya gather together with the Alevis of the region in the same meeting hall; they discuss their problems and decide on acting shoulder to shoulder. The Munzur river flows from Dersim in Eastern Anatolia to Loç Valley, joining Kurdish people and Kastamonu-origin people behind the same banner in the field of struggle: 'We are at the starting line; they shall be ready for our surprises.'

References

Maude, B. (2009). *Blue covenant: The global water crisis and the coming battle for the right to water*. New Press.

Çepel, N. (1992). *Ekolojik Sorunlar ve Çözümleri*. İstanbul: Tübitak.

Çoruh, M. (2009). *Kusursuz Enerji Planı: İnanılmaz Bir Melanetin Öyküsü*. İstanbul: İhlas.

Öztürk, Ö. (2010). *Türkiye'de Büyük Sermaye Grupları: Finans Kapitalin Oluşumu ve Gelişimi*. İstanbul: Sosyal Araştırmalar Vakfı.

Pearce, F. (2007). *When the rivers run dry*. Beacon Press.

Roy A. (2009). *Listening to grasshoppers: Field notes on democracy*. Haymarket Books.

Vandaba, S. (2007). *Su Savaşları: Özelleştirme, Kirlenme ve Kar*. İstanbul: bgst Yayınları.

Yılmaz, G. (2009). *Suyun Metalaşması: Kıtlığın Nedeni Kıtlığa Çare Olabilir mi?* İstanbul: Sosyal Araştırmalar Vakfı.

Boratav, K. (2006). 'Su Kavgaları: Sır Türkiye'de mi?' *Cumhuriyet*, 5 Nisan.

Ercan M. (2009). Küresel Isınma ve Karbon Ekonomisi-1. *Radikal*, 23 Eylül

Horuş M. (2007). Yağmur Duası. *Almanak 2006*. İstanbul: Sosyal Araştırmalar Vakfı.

Minibaş, T. (2007). Suyun Ekonomi Politiğİ. *Almanak 2006*. İstanbul: Sosyal Araştırmalar Vakfı.

Öngür T. (2009). Su Kültürünü Öldürüyorlar: Celladın Alkışlandığı Yer. *İktisat Dergisi*, 508-510.

Kocabıçak E. (2009). Suyun Ticarileştirilmesi Sürecinde Kadınların Su Savaşları. *İktisat Dergisi*, 508-510.

Poblete, D. S. (2007). *Neoliberalizm ve Su. Almanak 2006*. İstanbul: Sosyal Araştırmalar Vakfı.

6.
THE STRUGGLE OF THE URBAN POOR

Urban Regeneration, the Right to Housing, and Fraternity

Fatma Yıldırım and İnci Özgür İlhan

The neoliberal Islamic conservative party, AKP, which has been governing Turkey for the last decade, followed a specific urban and environmental policy on the accumulation of capital. In this context, urban regeneration has been proposed as a solution to the social, hygienic, and aesthetic problems of cities. This typically involves the destruction of the local socio-cultural environment and gentrification—the displacement of the urban poor from their neighborhoods and the attraction of prestigious newcomers through new spatial design and inflated property prices (Fullilove, 2001; Ergin, 2006; Çoban and Duru, 2009; Queirós, 2013). Although couched in a language of regeneration, this process is more about activating the real estate market and generating profit (Smith, 2002). During the 2000s, many urban regeneration projects were initiated in cities throughout Turkey by governmental or municipal agents in collaboration with the private sector (Dündar, 2001; Ergin, 2006). In the same period, one can also find examples of construction projects aiming to make buildings resistant to natural disasters and to conserve cultural and natural assets (Hague, 2012).

Urban regeneration entails large-scale construction projects involving thousands of people and their social environment. In addition to being forced to live in changing physical and social conditions that they would never choose for themselves, dislocated poor families have had to go into long-term debt to buy new houses (Karaman, 2013). Both the social and psychological aspects of urban regeneration have been neglected by those participating in these projects, especially the Turkish government. This is true despite the fact that projects are so widespread and so radically implemented that the scale of demographic and social change is enormous.

This chapter draws on research conducted in the Dikmen Valley where an intensive 'regeneration' project is underway. Initially, we planned to conduct a survey on the negative psychosocial health impact of this project. We decided that we needed to speak to people about the specific impacts on their community, so we arranged both individual and group interviews. In the process, we discovered that our interviewees were more optimistic than we had anticipated. We thus decided to reorient our study around participants' general assessments of these projects, rather than concentrating solely on the negative psychological states of depression and anxiety. It is important to keep in mind that participants were not merely passive spectators, but active subjects in the processes taking place around them. With this in mind, we explore interviewees' self-efficacy and the community's collective efficacy.

Our two-month field survey was conducted in March and April of 2007—one month after the first demolition of homes in the Dikmen Valley—and a second survey was conducted in October. The results of our study will be presented here in three sections: First, we will shed light on the Dikmen Valley Urban Transformation Project and present our observations about both individual and community reactions to the demolition. Second, we will present the findings of our October survey, which provided an overall description of the community's socio-demographic profile and an assessment of the presence and severity of depression and anxiety symptoms, as well as levels of self-efficacy. Third, we will integrate our observations and findings, offering tentative conclusions about the psychosocial impacts of the demolition project on the people of the Dikmen Valley.

Dikmen Valley's Urban Transformation Project and the Demolition of 2007

Ankara is one of the cities that received a significant number of rural migrants as a result of state agricultural reforms in the 1950s and 1980s. Urbanization in Turkey took place in a much different way from the Western world because of the lack of industrial development. Employment opportunities in the city were few (Kıray, 2003) and housing was scarce at the time of the migrants' arrival. In the absence of an official housing policy or plan, migrants built their own houses on vacant public land. These squatter houses, or 'gecekondu' (meaning 'built overnight'), emerged rapidly, creating poor neighborhoods on the outskirts of the cities. Gecekondu soon became the typical housing pattern of the urban poor in Turkey (Mahmud & Duyar-Kienast, 2001). These neighborhoods were recognized as legitimate by the government and municipalities provided infrastructure facilities to the gecekondu districts.

Gecekondus were built as one or two-storeyed houses, often with a garden. The vegetable garden and fruit trees enabled a degree of self-sufficiency and nutrition for the poor. The garden also had a symbolic meaning for the newcomer, maintaining the link to earth and nature that had been cultivated in his village. It was not unusual to add rooms to the original building as the family expanded through new marriages. The homes were shaped and modified according to the needs and preferences of the family and, in this way, the dwellers had a sense of inner control over their near environment. According to social psychologist, Fritz Heider, an inner sense of control is a basic need of the human being (as cited in Kağıtçıbaşı, 2010). One's sense of belonging, safety, and attachment to place are other important dimensions of the relationship between subject and space.

Place determines the quantity and quality of relations and social networks. The structure of the gecekondu neighborhoods promotes frequent social interactions compared to apartment buildings. A considerable amount of daily life occurs outdoors and one can always see chatting neighbors and children playing outside. Familiarity of this kind encourages closer and deeper relations among residents (Kağıtçıbaşı, 2010) and a greater sense of safety compared with big apartments. Gecekondus are usually built in collaboration with neighbors, embracing a collective culture and solidarity that provides significant coping mechanisms to the urban poor (Erman, 1997). In contrast, the vertical construction of large apartment buildings could not possibly cultivate this sense of community, nor could it provide any of the benefits obtained from living in an open space. Dikmen Valley is one of neighborhoods with this housing pattern.

After the 1989 municipal elections, the Greater Municipality of Ankara (GMA) introduced the Dikmen Valley Project (DVP) as a big urban regeneration project. At that time, the number of squatter houses was around 4000 in the whole project area (Günay as cited in Uzun, 2005). Originally it was a sample project designed to take into consideration Dikmen Valley as both a natural site to be preserved and an urban area to be rehabilitated.

In the beginning, public meetings and decision-committee meetings were held with the aim of facilitating public participation in the project. However these participation mechanisms did not work. The GMA changed hands after 1994 elections. Dikmen Valley, having significant land value, attracted the new rightist GMA. The participatory character of the project was totally lost in the process, and the focus shifted to distributing the profits that would be generated by the project (Türker-Devecigil, 2005). With the DVP, big firms were to reconstruct and transform the gecekondu neighborhood into a prestigious area with luxury housing and offices (Dündar, 2001; Türker-Devecigil, 2005). The project was planned for five implementation zones successively; the first three steps (zones) of the project are now completed. Real estate was bought up by the middle class and residents vacated to neighborhoods with more affordable living costs (Uzun, 2005). The implementation of the project in the forth and the fifth zones was suspended due to residents' opposition in 2006.

Dikmen Valley was included in the GMA project as two of five zones to be regenerated. But it is here that the GMA met significant resistance. The GMA did not take over the responsibility of building new houses for former residents; instead, the latter were invited to buy vacant land with neither infrastructure nor transportation facilities in an area very far from the city. Residents were expected to construct their own houses with their own resources. These conditions were very far from being suitable or affordable for the majority, although a few residents of Dikmen Valley accepted the offer of the GMA. They moved out and became tenants in other neighborhoods.

The history of gecekondu construction in the Dikmen Valley dates back to the 1970s. Dikmen Valley (comprising the forth and fifth zones) contains gecekondu houses scattered on two small hills along the bed of a stream. It is also a green area with old trees and gardens. Although originally it was a remote gecekondu neighborhood outside the city, it became surrounded by luxurious houses and apartments as the city expanded. The exchange value of the land increased and this attracted a rentier class. Meanwhile, rights holders in the DV Project started a legal defense process. Without waiting for the judgment of the court, the GMA forces attempted to pull down the houses suddenly at three o'clock in the morning, on February 1st, 2007,[46] while everyone was sleeping in their beds and the valley was covered with snow. A huge demolition team of 5300 policemen and municipal personnel, 100 ambulances, 84 trucks, 44 demolition graders, and 40 fire engines entered the valley (Almufti-Karadağ & Buğralılar, 2008). Residents of Dikmen Valley resisted and managed to stop this attempt. At that time, there were around 1083 houses in the region, 1063 of which were officially unregistered.

Here are two examples of residents' experiences of the police attack and the demolition. Mr. A was 55 years old and was living with his wife and three sons. On the night of the demolition attack, he was at home with his mother, who was

---

46 'Dikmen Direnişi 1 Yaşında', http://www.sendika.org/2007/02/dikmen-direnisi-1-yasinda/

older than 80 years and living in the same house. Having had a cerebrovascular attack, his mother was not mobile, so she put her leg out of the window to show her condition to the destruction team and to prevent the demolition of the building. This women passed away a few months after the attack and Mr. A became an activist in the resistance movement.

Mrs. B (50 years of age) was living with her husband, who had had both of his legs amputated above the knees. Her husband was alone at home when the authorities came for demolition, and he could not get out of the house because of the stairs. She built a ramp in front of the house for her husband to go out easily using the wheel chair after the attack in case another were to occur.

Successive and smaller attacks followed the first one. This struggle between the GMA and Dikmen Valley has continued, and the GMA managed to pull down only three houses up to now. The whole event seemed to be experienced as an acute trauma as well as a continuous experience of anxiety because of the ongoing risk of another attack. The GMA intermittently announced that the Valley people should leave their houses, as they would begin demolition soon. In this way, the threat of losing one's home has become a continuous source of stress. As residents shared:

When I hear a noise at night, I think that they've came for demolition and I wake up my wife.

Earthquakes destroy houses and kill people. Indeed there is a continuous earth-quake in Dikmen Valley.

The Struggle in Dikmen Valley

Government forces swore and humiliated the Valley people during and after the attack. The Valley people were angered when they became aware of the incon-sistencies in the government's housing policy and have since lost trust in the authorities. One resident said, in astonishment and anger, that he was previously a hard-working and obedient worker in the GMA—in his words, the 'right hand of İ. Melih Gökçek (the mayor of Ankara),' but now Gökçek was trying to pull down his house.

When the first rumors about the transformation project and a possible attack reached the Dikmen Valley, three women from the neighborhood discussed how to defend their houses. They began to deliver pamphlets to the Dikmen Valley residents and tried to persuade them to defend their houses altogether. First they received no support from others, even their husbands, but they persisted in their effort to persuade the people of the valley. After seeing their determination, the number of people joining them increased day by day. They soon attracted many others in the valley. Here is the story of one of those three women:

Mrs. C was forty years old, married, and had three daughters. She has been working as a maidservant and her husband as a hairdresser. She was from a village in central Turkey and had moved to Ankara with her husband and his family seventeen years ago, after they had married. At the beginning, she and her husband were living in the same house with her husband's family, but she and her husband built their new gecekondu next to her mother-in-law's when her first daughter was five years old.

She was one of the first three activist women in the valley. On the day of the demolition attack, she was arrested without being aware of what was going on. She still tells her story of arrest with surprise, and she recalls being very worried about her children after the attack. She said: 'We did not know how to stop the demolition of our houses, we did not know how to struggle. We were just ordinary people.' After telling their story of struggle, she added: 'So, I can think reasonably, I will do what I should do.' She said that she became more self-confident and believed that she was doing the right thing once they began to receive the support of others. She said that previously, social movements did not mean anything to her and she avoided a protesting crowd that she met on her way, but now she would support any demonstration demanding people's rights.

This was the transformation story of an ordinary woman in Dikmen Valley. The lives of many other women in Dikmen Valley underwent a similar change. Housewives got out of their houses and met other women and men in their neighborhood. Even women from rather conservative families started to greet men on the street. Besides getting to know each other, Dikmen Valley people attended meetings, held with their own resources, to discuss and decide about solutions for their common neighborhood problems. Of course, resistance against demolition was the major topic of these meetings.

In fact, struggle in Dikmen Valley had started before the GMA attack in February 2007 and it has been gradually growing. When municipal services were withdrawn, the Valley people began to endure daily hardships, such as having to navigate roads of mud and dirt and having to maintain the garbage system by themselves. They gathered scrap material and built a playground for their children. Besides actively resisting every attack in the street, they established 'the Right to Housing Office.' Their legal struggle against the demolition plans of the GMA continued to advance; they followed the legal process and archived court documents pertaining to all the right-holders and paper news about the Dikmen Valley in this common office in the neighborhood. The importance of this office in this struggle is perhaps best revealed by the fact that it suffered a suspicious fire and all the documents were burned. Nevertheless, it was rebuilt.

Residents also used the open space in front of the office to gather for their meetings during the summer and established a library next door. They organized occasional events like photography exhibitions and other meetings in the space and musicians were invited to give voluntary open-air concerts. They also received support from non-governmental organizations, such as ATO (Ankara Medical Chamber), TMMOB (Turkish Engineers' and Architects' Association), KESK (The Confederation of Public Workers' Unions), **DİSK (Confederation of Revolutionary Trade Unions of Turkey)**, ÇHD (Progressive Lawyers Association). They organized panels and seminars with volunteers from universities and students gave lessons to the women and children of Dikmen Valley without any charge.

It was the Dikmen Valley people's common decision not to leave their houses and resist that actually changed the way they used space and socialized with one another. Most importantly, they continued to express their determination and solidarity:

'People have to defend their houses, because there is nowhere they can go.'

'I have a child of thirteen. If they come again, I will take my child to a safe place and I will go on resisting.'

'When you are alone, you can leave here and go to the most remote place in Ankara, however, we won't. We take decisions altogether here. We created this neighborhood and we constructed the fraternity here altogether. We are a community here.'

Their resistance has led them to a transformation in their view of the world and life itself:

Thank God I do not have the deed for my house; otherwise I would not be able to see this resistance. It gives me pleasure as if it is worship. Now I think that this struggle is a human duty.

There are two categories of people: oppressed people on one side and the oppressing ones on the other. We are oppressed people. I did not join any non-governmental organization until now, but I will from now on. We went to Istanbul to support people's struggle to defend their homes; I saw that they are just like us.

Before the resistance, there were social subgroups, which were formed according to the town of origin, religious sect, or political orientation. Their common goal of defending their houses brought them together. Everyone got to know each other better and the social network of relations has become more expansive and diverse. For example, one resident said that he had not previously made a habit of greeting some of his neighbors, but now he feels closer to them than his own relatives who had left the valley after signing the contract with the GMA. Another woman said:

> I used not to go near a man, particularly in this place; but now we are coming together like sisters and brothers. This struggle has brought us together like a fist.

In this way, gender roles are being transformed. Women who were living in a conservative family context and previously had to request their husbands' permission to go out were now leaving him at home with the housework and attending meetings outside. As one resident said:

I had never cooked at home. But now I am cooking and surprising my wife.

The trauma experienced by the Dikmen Valley population led to a loss of trust in the government, a change in the level of awareness and meaning. This should be taken as a change in an individual's view of the protective and authoritarian role of the government. These were experiences and feelings shared frequently in interviews. On the other hand, a psychosocial transformation was observed related to the strengthening of social interconnectedness, collective mobilization of social resources in dealing with problems, and fraternity and solidarity.

A Psycho-social Analysis of the Dikmen Valley Struggle

Self-efficacy, a term used in Social Cognitive Theory, refers to one's belief in his/her ability to start, to continue, and to complete an action in a way that would have an impact on his/her environment (Bandura, 1994). It involves a realistic sense of competence and motivation in one's planning and a belief in one's capacity to organize an action. It is also the major determinant of achievement. Bandura (1994) defined the self-efficacy construct as a significant predictor of human behavior. Self-efficacy does not correspond to level of skill, but depends on an individual's appraisal of his/her resources. A person with sufficient skills for coping with a situation and a low level of self-efficacy would not reveal his/her relevant skills. Self-efficacy requires initiative, persistence, and effort. The concept of self-efficacy includes such elements as planning an action, awareness, and organization of the required skills and the level of motivation after reviewing the potential gains and difficulties of a given situation. In his analysis of performing an action, Bandura takes motivation as central to efficacy belief; additionally, an appropriate state of mood and positive feelings and thought processes would form the basis of beginning an action. Expectations about the outcome of an action form the motivation, while the cognitive appraisal of the given circumstances, organizing and planning of that action, comes after. Cognitive processing is analyzed here as weighing and integrating predictive factors, testing and revision of one's judgments against immediate and distant results of one's actions and remembering previous experiences.

Previous successful experiences, examples of the achievements of others with similar personal characteristics, positive feedback from one's environment, and a positive mood support one's belief in his/her self-efficacy. When an action results in failure, people with a high level of belief in their self-efficacy do not relate the failure to their own deficiency, but to the methods and strategies they used. According to Bandura (1997), the most significant characteristic that distinguishes individuals with a low level of self-efficacy from those with a high level is that the latter would recover faster following a failure, insist on their action, and not give up.

General self-efficacy has been found to be related to mental wellbeing (Magaletta & Oliver, 1999). Self-efficacy provides a sense of control over one's life and vice versa. This would preclude ambiguity, which is the major cause of anxiety. Self-efficacy also requires a sense of personal worth, which provides a high mood instead of a depressive psychological state. Bandura (1999) says: 'Those who have a high sense of efficacy visualize success scenarios that provide positive guides and supports for performance. Those who doubt their efficacy visualize failure scenarios and dwell on the many things that can go wrong.' A high level of self-efficacy facilitates the experience of success and well being and in particular, personal development and further development of one's skills.

Beyond self efficacy, collective efficacy has been defined as a group's shared belief in its conjoint capabilities to organize and execute the courses of action required to produce given levels of attainments (Bandura, 1997, 1999). Here the construct of self-efficacy is extended to groups and communities. Self-efficacy is closely related with collective efficacy as a group's level of collective efficacy depends on its individual member's level of self-efficacy. The interrelation of self-efficacy and collective action seems to be a reciprocal dynamic process (Kiecolt, 2000). To join a larger group and contribute to its action as an active member requires a sufficient level of self-efficacy. Collective efficacy has been taken as a major psychological motivational force underlying social changes by collective action of communities. Bandura (1999) enthusiastically says: 'Realists may adapt well to existing realities. But those with a tenacious self-efficacy are likely to change those realities.'

Closely related with collective efficacy, is 'political efficacy,' which Bandura defines as people's beliefs that they can influence the political system (Bandura, 1997):

The responsiveness or changeableness of the governmental system is neither a fixed characteristic nor independent of personal efficacy. Influential constituents shape the form   of governmental functioning and to whom the office-holders are most responsive. Human behavior is governed largely by beliefs about personal efficacy and the controllability of social systems rather than simply by their objective properties. Thus, individuals who believe themselves to be inefficacious effect little change even in social systems that provide many potential opportunities. Conversely, those who have a firm belief in their efficacy, through ingenuity and perseverance, figure out ways to exercise some measure of control over social systems containing limited opportunities and many constraints.

So, objective conditions of contradictions between social groups are essential, but not sufficient in the development of social movements. A high level of efficacy beliefs in a community is crucial for effective resistance against inequality.

Survey Methods, Participants, and Discussion of Findings

A field survey was held within a year of the first attack in Dikmen Valley from the psychological and mental well-being perspective. This study enabled descriptions of the socio-demographic profile of the community, assessment of the presence and severity of depression and anxiety symptoms, and the general self-efficacy levels of the Dikmen Valley population, and a comparison of the findings from the Dikmen Valley with that of another neighborhood in Ankara. Saimekadın was chosen as the comparison group having similar socio-demographic features (Table 6.1). Saimekadın neighborhood is composed of a population living in gecekondu houses near the city center but has not been included in any urban transformation project. They did not face any risk of losing their houses and constructing their new houses was up to their will in making individual contracts with construction companies.

The study sample was drawn from the population residing in the forth and fifth implementation areas of the DVP. Initially, a sample of 73 individuals was estimated as the sample size to be recruited from the neighborhood based on an expected prevalence of depression as 5 percent and a 95 percent confidence. Taking the design effect as 2 and considering probable losses, a total of 208 individuals were targeted from each neighborhood—104 households from each. Sampling in the Dikmen Valley was problematic because of the missing addresses, as a considerable number of families had already left. The remaining addresses were reviewed with the help of a list from the Right to Housing Office and the field was overviewed. Using systematic random sampling, a total of 106 households were surveyed in the Dikmen Valley. The survey was completed in Dikmen Valley in October 2007. It was targeted to individuals above 17 years of age living in the address. 63.1 percent of the household in the Dikmen Valley participated in the survey. Thus the whole sample consisted of 220 individuals from Dikmen Valley. Data from 201 individuals from Dikmen Valley have been found to be valid.

The mean age of the DV sample was 39.7±14.5 years. The distribution of demographic characteristics of the sample by neighborhood is shown in the Table 6.1. Mean monthly income levels of the DV were 803.1±424.4 TL (472.4±249.7 Euros) (converting Turkish Liras to Euros according to exchange rates at study time). The DV sample has been living in Ankara for 25.0±10.7 years on average.

Table 6.1. Demographic Features of the Dikmen Valley and Comparison Samples

	Dikmen Valley		Comparison Sample		χ^2	p
Gender						
Female	126	62.7	111	62.4	0.004	0.948
Male	75	37.3	67	37.6		
Education						
Illiterate	22	14.1	17	10.7	2.293	0.514
1-8 years	88	56.4	97	61.0		
9-11 years	31	19.9	35	22.0		
11 years or more	15	9.6	10	6.3		
Marital status						
Single	39	19.5	21	11.8	9.058	0.011
Married	149	74.5	133	74.7		
Divorced/Widowed	12	6.0	24	13.6		
Employment						
Unemployed	104	56.5	89	58.2	1.246	0.742
Employed	56	30.4	49	32.0		
Retired	3	1.6	3	2.0		
Retired-still working	21	11.4	12	7.8		

The Beck Depression Scale (BDI): Hisli (1989) conducted the Turkish adaptation of this scale, which was developed by Beck (1961) for assessment of somatic, emotional, cognitive and motivational symptoms of depression. It is a self-rating scale, which consists of 20 items. The scoring for each item ranges between 0 and 4 and total score is between 0 and 63. Scores higher than or equal to 21 indicate presence of moderate or severe depression (Hisli 1989).

The Spielberger Trait Anxiety Inventory (STAI): The Trait Anxiety Scale, which includes items on how an individual feels in general, was developed by Spielberger et al. (1970) and adapted to Turkish by Öner and Le Compte (1985). It is a self-rating scale, which consists of 20 items. An increase in the score indicates an increase in the level of general anxiety level. The possible maximum total score is 80.

The General Self Efficacy Scale-Turkish version (GSE-T) reflects the belief that one can control challenging environmental demands by means of taking adaptive action. The General Self-Efficacy Scale was originally developed by Sherer et al. (1982) and it was adapted into the Turkish language by Yıldırım and Özgür İlhan (2010). This version of the scale has been found to be a reliable and valid instrument in measuring general self-efficacy.

Table 6.2. Comparison of the Psychological Test Scores of the Dikmen Valley and Comparison Samples

		mean ± standard deviation	t	p
BDI	Dikmen sample	20.8 ± 11.6		
	Comparison sample	14.7 ± 10.3	5.428	0.000
STAI	Dikmen sample	47.6 ± 10.4		
	Comparison sample	44.4 ±9.4	3.173	0.002
GSE-T	Dikmen sample	60.3 ± 10.4		
	Comparison sample	59.9 ±9.5	0.373	0.709

Table 6.3. Comparison of GSE-T scores of the Dikmen Valley and Comparison Samples Controlling for BDI and STAI Scores

	GSE-T score	mean	95 percent CI	F	p
BDI score controlled	Dikmen sample	61.3	60.0-62.6		
	Comparison sample	58.9	57.5-60.3	5.763	0.017
STAI score controlled	Dikmen	61.1	59.9-62.3		
	Comparison sample	59.1	57.8-60.4	3.173	0.026

CI: confidence interval

The demolition attempt in Dikmen Valley in February, 2007, induced depressive and anxiety symptoms in the Dikmen population apparently as a result of its direct consequences. The relationship between depression and anxiety with threat of losing one's home, being left by neighbors, and the appearance of debris in place of the left houses, as well as withdrawal of municipal services and other public services (such as postal delivery), were closely observable. Thus, it has been shown that both depression and anxiety scores of the Dikmen Valley sample were significantly high. This finding is not surprising. Erman (1997) observed the sadness and grief of the displaced and relocated urban poor in her study of another UTP in Ankara. Erman (2009) performed a field study on effects of the Northern Ankara Entrance Urban Transformation Project in people's lives in the framework of the displacement and forced relocation of the urban poor. The study demonstrated that the urban transformation practices, without taking into consideration social and psychological aspects, showed more negative impact than positive. The relocated individuals reported both economic and social difficulties in their resettlement in apartments. They fell into debt for the coming 15 years. They expressed the difficulties of having to adapt to new economic challenges, such as apartment rent and fees, new heating systems, and even losing one's job due to transportation problems. The relocated interviewees, particularly women, expressed that they missed close and warm relationships with their old neighbors, the feeling of safety and freedom, their garden, and even the birds in their former neighborhoods. In the same study, 72.5 percent of respondents said that they would continue to live in their gecekondu if it were up to them.

Anxiety and depression are closely related feelings. However, anxiety is a psychological state that is related to possibilities and the future, whereas depression is related to the past, one's losses, and the persons or things one has left behind. For the Valley people, the ambiguous future and the threat of losing one's home created an understandable anxiety. It was also traumatic. The past was full of memories of the old neighbors and ruined houses, which were once full of life with familiar faces—a thoroughly depressing landscape of recollection. What is worth noting here is how this group of people coped with this anxiety and depression.

The most striking finding of the study is the high level of general self-efficacy of the Dikmen sample in spite of the negative psychological experiences. Perceived self-efficacy is defined and studied as the main predictor of psychological change and behavior (Bandura, 1994). The Dikmen Valley population had no other chance than to defend their houses and housing rights, as they had nowhere to go because of poverty. They determined this common goal and realized that they had to handle the situation using their own resources, without depending on any other agent. The whole process after the traumatic attack seemed to increase the level of self-efficacy in Dikmen.

Self-efficacy is inversely related to depression and anxiety (Bandura, 1997; Pinquart et al., 2004). The high level of depression and anxiety and high self-efficacy of the Dikmen (after depression and anxiety scores were controlled in the statistical analysis) indicates the likely presence of the two separate groups in the Dikmen sample, one being rather depressive and anxious and the other having a high level of general self-efficacy without much psychological distress. From our perspective, individuals in contact with the Right to Housing Office had a higher level of general self-efficacy than the rest in Dikmen. VanEijk (2010) has emphasized the importance of neighborhood settings, which facilitate routine encounters between people in forming local social networks, especially in poor neighborhoods, thus empowering resource-poor people. The Right to Housing Office was such a setting for the Dikmen Valley People, facilitating gatherings and discussions on their common issues and providing a space for socializing. Its main function was to offer a common space for people to meet and communicate with each other and to widen one's social network. All these activities apparently facilitate collective action and consequent achievement seems to be a protective factor against depression and anxiety. Ahern and Galea (2011) found that a high level of neighborhood collective efficacy was associated with a lower prevalence of major depression, particularly among older adults in 59 community districts in New York. The association between social integration (Seeman, 1996) or social network (Pinquart & Sörensen, 2000) and mental health and well being has already been established. Collective efficacy was found to be closely related with social well being (Keyes, 1998), physical health (Browning & Cagney, 2002), and inversely related with substance abuse, violence, and crime (Sampson et al., 1997; Morenoff et al., 2001) in urban studies. High levels of self- and collective efficacy most probably are protective factors in Dikmen Valley in terms of psychosocial urban problems, such as substance abuse, as well.

Methodologically, collective efficacy has not been taken as a simple sum of individual levels of self-efficacy. Still, measurement of collective efficacy level also involves individual self-efficacy scores, as one is related to the other (Gecas, 2000; Fernández-Ballesteros et al., 2002). Thus, the high level of the general self-efficacy of Dikmen Valley population and individual and group interviewees indicates a high level of collective efficacy.

Conclusion

There are two alternative reactions for even the simplest organism in nature in case of danger: fight or flight. Dikmen Valley people had nowhere to go, so, they had to fight and they did so successfully. The Dikmen Valley people defended their houses with a survival reflex. And yet, participating in the struggle has enhanced their community life and raised their consciousness. They realized their efficacy and power to change as they saw the result of every successful step in their struggle.

With respect to the resistance and struggle in Dikmen Valley, the dimension of the social context that must be stressed is not structural, but it is the dynamic collective nature of the social network organized by the Dikmen Valley community against the psychological mass trauma and persistent pressures. Their achievements against the rentiers fed their sense of efficacy further. As Gecas (2000) states, 'participation in political activism may itself increase feelings of personal and collective efficacy if the actions are successful.'

Five hundred and fifty households in Dikmen Valley have been resisting. They also visit other gecekondu neighborhoods included in urban transformation project areas and share their experiences through panels and other meetings. They explain that municipal agencies would not dare to dislocate other people from their neighborhoods because of their unfortunate experiences in Dikmen Valley. They have been in close contact with other local social movements, which they inspired, such as '2-B resistance' in Antalya (a struggle against destruction of forests on lands that the government wants to develop). As one of the key persons in Dikmen Valley resistance believes, every word they speak, every discussion they make for the sake of their struggle, and every action has a meaning in the resistance history of the proletariat.

Residents keep holding their regular meetings in the Right to Housing Office. The inform each other about the legal process still going on. They organize FestiVadi, an annual festival that lasts one week, to which the entire Valley people and people from other neighborhoods are invited. Artists and academics also participate and support the organization. They continue to organize games, concerts, workshops, and panels.

Erman (2009) stated that in the Northern Ankara Entrance Urban Transformation Project the people attempted to resist the dislocation once and they did not insist on a continuous movement against the municipality. So it remained a small and short-lived social movement without positive results. An extraordinary example of struggle for the right to housing in Turkey was the establishment of the Mayday Neighborhood (BirMayısMahallesi) in İstanbul in 1977, where people built their gecekondus collectively and resisted three waves of demolition without leaving their places and constructed their houses again and again. They also established a democratic government system for themselves. Several socialist groups coming from outside the neighborhood had helped Mayday Neighborhood people during the whole process. The difference in Dikmen Valley Struggle is that although leftist groups and non-governmental organizations supported them from outside, it was Dikmen Valley's own struggle using their own resources. The Dikmen Valley people never allowed the outside socialist groups of political parties to enter the valley using their names. Although the Dikmen Valley Struggle is not the first in terms of defending the right to housing (Aslan, 2013), it has been the subject of much academic interest and research. What makes it unique is that a very powerful and at the same time aggressive municipality could not succeed to enter Dikmen Valley. So their struggle forms an excellent model with respect to its organization for the proletarian.

Acknowledgments

This study was supported and funded by the Ankara Medical Chamber. The authors would like to thank Salime Tarihçi, Menaf Turan, Nail Dertli, Figen Şahbaz, Eriş Bilaloğlu, Onur Can Taştan, Burhanettin Kaya and Mine Kaya for their suggestions at various phases of the study.

References

Ahern, J., & Galea, S. (2011). Collective efficacy and major depression in urban neighborhoods. *American Journal of Epidemiology, 173*(12), 1453-1462.

Almufti-Karadag, L., & Buğralılar, E. (2008). Dikmen valley: A story of resistance from Turkey. *Monthly Review*. Retrieved from http://mrzine.monthlyreview.org/2008/kb091108.html

Aslan, S. (2013). *1 Mayıs Mahallesi: 1980 Öncesi Toplumsal Mücadeleler ve Kent.* Istanbul: İletişim.

Bandura, A. (1994). Self-efficacy. In V. S. Ramachaudran (Ed.), *Encyclopedia of human behavior* (pp. 71-81). New York: Academic Press.

Bandura, A. (1997). *Self-efficacy: The exercise of control.* New York: Freeman.

Bandura, A. (1999). *Self-efficacy in changing societies.* Cambridge University Press.

Beck, A. T. (1961). An inventory for measuring depression. *Archives of General Psychiatry, 4*, 561– 571.

Blackman, T., & Harvey, J. (2001). Housing renewal and mental health: A case study. *Journal of Mental Health, 10*(5), 571–583.

Browning, C.R., & Cagney, K.A. (2002). Neighborhood structural disadvantage, collective efficacy and self-rated physical health in an urban setting. *Journal of Health and Social Behavior, 43*, 383-399.

Çoban, A., & Duru, B. (2009). Emek Ekseninde AKP İktidarının Çevre ve Kent Politikaları. **İktisat Dergisi**, *508*, 57-68.

Dündar, Ö. (2001). Models of urban transformation: Informal housing in Ankara. *Cities, 18*(6), 391-401.

Ergin, N. B. (2006). *Grassroots resistance against urban renewal: The case of Güzeltepe, Istanbul* (unpublished master's thesis). Middle East Technical University.

Erman, T. (1997). Squatter (gecekondu) housing versus apartment housing: Turkish rural to urban migrant residents' perspectives. *Habitat International, 28*(1), 91-106.

Erman, T. (2009). Kuzey Ankara Girişi Kentsel Dönüşüm Projesi ve Yerinden Edilme: Deneyimler, Söylemler, Uygulamalar. *6. Ulusal Sosyoloji Kongresi Bildiri Kitabı.* Adnan Menderes Üniversitesi.

Fernández-Ballesteros, R., Díez-Nicolás, J., & Caprara, G.V. (2002). Determinants and structural relation of personal efficacy to collective efficacy. *Applied Psychology: An International Review, 51*(1), 107-125.

Fullilove, M. T. (2001). Root shock: The consequences of African American dispossession. *Journal of Urban Health: Bulletin of the New York Academy of Medicine, 78*(1), 72-80.

Gecas, V. (2000). Value identities, self-motives, and social movements. In S. Stryker, T. J. Owens, & R. W. White (Eds.), *Self, identity and social movements* (pp. 93-109). Minneapolis: University of Minnesota Press.

Hague, C. (2012). Küresel Krizde Kentsel Dönüşümü Yeniden Düşünmek. In D. Özdemir (Ed.), *Kentsel Dönüşümde Politika, Mevzuat, Uygulama: Avrupa Deneyimi, Istanbul Uygulamaları* (pp. 98-106). Ankara: Nobel.

Hisli, N. (1989). Beck Depresyon Envanteri'nin Geçerliği Üzerine Bir Çalışma. *Psikoloji Dergisi, 6*, 118-122.

Kağıtçıbaşı, Ç. (2010). *Günümüzde İnsan ve İnsanlar.* İstanbul: Evrim.

Karaman, O. (2013). Urban renewal in Istanbul: Reconfigured spaces, robotic lives. *International Journal of Urban and Regional Research, 37*(2), 715-733.

Keyes, C. L. M. (1998). Social well-being. *Social Psychology Quarterly, 61*(2), 121-140.

Kiecolt, K. J. (2000). Self-change in social movements. In S. Stryker, T. J. Owens, & R. W. White (Eds.), *Self, identity, and social movements* (pp. 110-131). Minneapolis: University of Minnesota Press.

Kıray, M. B. (2003). *Kentleşme Yazıları.* Ankara: Bağlam.

Magaletta, P. R., & Oliver, J. M. (1999). The hope construct, will and ways: Their relations with self-efficacy, optimism, and general well-being. *Journal of Clinical Psychology, 55*, 539-551.

Mahmud, S., & Duyar-Kienast, U. (2001). Spontaneous settlements in Turkey and Bangladesh: Preconditions of emergence and environmental quality of gecekondu settlements and bustees. *Cities, 18*(4), 271-280.

Morenoff, J. D., Sampson, R. J., & Raudenbush, S. W. (2001). Neighborhood inequality, collective efficacy and the spatial dynamics of urban violence. *Criminology, 39*(3), 517-558.

Öner, N., & Le Compte, A. (1985). *Durumluluk-Sürekli Kaygı Envanteri El Kitabı.* Istanbul: Boğaziçi Üniversitesi Yayınları.

Pinquart, M., & Sörensen, S. (2000). Influences of socioeconomic status, social network, and competence on subjective well-being in later life: a meta-analysis. *Psychology and Aging, 15*(2), 187-22.

Pinquart, M., Silbereisen, R. K., & Juang, L. P. (2004). Moderating effects of adolescents' self-efficacy beliefs on psychological responses to social change. *Journal of Adolescent Research, 19*, 340-359.

Queirós, J. (2013, July 10-12). *Social housing demolition as state-led gentrification in Porto's city centre.* Paper presented at the ISA RC43 Conference, Centre for Urban Studies, the University of Amsterdam.

Sampson, R. J., Raudenbush, S. W., & Earls, F. (1997). Neighborhood collective efficacy: Does it help reduce violence?' *Science, 277*, 918-924.

Seeman, T.E. (1996). Social ties and health: The benefits of social integration. *Annals of Epidemiology, 6*(5), 442-451.

Sherer, M., Maddux, J. E., Mercandante, B., Prentice-Dunn, S., Jacobs, B., & Rogers, R. W. (1982). The self-efficacy scale: Construction and validation. *Psychological Reports, 51*, 663-671.

Smith, N. (2002). New globalism, new urbanism: Gentrification as global urban strategy. *Antipode, 34*(3), 427-450.

Spielberger, C. D., Gorsuch, R. L., & Lushene, R. E. (1970). *Manual for state-trait anxiety inventory.* California: Consulting Psychologist Press.

Türker-Devecigil, P. (2005). Urban transformation projects as a model to transform gecekondu areas in Turkey: The example of Dikmen Valley–Ankara. *International Journal of Housing Policy, 5*(2), 211-229.

Uzun, C. N. (2005). Residential transformation of squatter settlements: Urban redevelopment projects in Ankara. *Journal of Housing and the Built Environment, 20,* 183–199.

vanEijk, G. (2010). Does living in a poor neighborhood result in network poverty? A study on local networks, locality-based relationships and neighborhood settings. *Journal of Housing and the Built Environment, 25,* 467-480.

Yıldırım, F., & Özgür İlhan, I. (2010). The validity and reliability of the general self-efficacy scale-Turkish form. *Turkish Journal of Psychiatry, 21*(4), 301-308.

7.
WOMEN'S MOVEMENT AND RESISTANCE

Different Women, Different Activisms

Ecehan Balta

The women's movement in Turkey, albeit under recognized, is one of the most active and vibrant contemporary women's movements at a historical moment in which the influence women have gained since 1970s is now being challenged throughout the West. The overall decline of women's movements is partly due to the sentiment that the achievements gained are sufficient and partly the result of economic and political crises.

In this chapter, I will examined the agenda, intellectual legacies and tensions that comprise the women's movement in 21st century Turkey. In the first section, I explain the milestones of the women's movement, going back to the beginning of the century. In the second section, I examine the position of women in political, social, and economic structures. In the third section, I explain the responses towards the women's movement from above; in other words, the state's attitude towards both the movement itself and the subject of gender equality. I will examine the responses from above within a path extending from state feminism to the familial context. In the final section, I outline the nature and composition of the contemporary women's movement, focusing on the attraction it has had for diverse groups, such as Islamists Kurds and what we might call the 'classical' feminists.

Background: Feminism and Women's Movement in the 19th and 20th Centuries in the Ottoman Empire and Republic of Turkey

Contrary to what was believed until the 1980s, women's movements in Turkey's territory had emerged as far back as the 1800s during the Ottoman times (Çakır, 2010). Similar to their contemporaries of the first wave women's movement, women during the Ottoman Empire demanded fundamental social rights, such as increased employment, education, and suffrage after the proclamation of the first constitution in 1876. The first women's newspaper was published in 1869 and by time of the Republic's foundation, in 1923, the number of such papers had reached 40 (Ergün, 2012). It is worth mentioning *Kadınlar Dünyası* (Women's World), which was occasionally published as a daily newspaper between 1913 and 1921. There were also about 30 women's associations during the same period (Ergün, 2012). The Ottoman women's movement was in interaction with the first-wave of its European counterparts and some of them identified themselves explicitly as 'feminists.' Along with women's associations that undertook the task of defense or organizing behind the frontline during the war, others were established for women's empowerment, giving vocational training or making efforts to provide employment.

As is typical during wartime (and economic crises), women replaced their fighting men in production processes during World War I and during the Turkish War of Independence (between 1919 and 1922). Nonetheless, it is worth noting that these two periods differ from each other: During WWI, the women working in textile and tobacco mills were non-Muslims (who composed 15 percent of the country's population at the time). Employment of Muslim women was culturally and socially disapproved of. However, immediately after WWI, a tremendous uprooting of a whole range of ethnic and religious communities in the Balkans and Asia Minor was witnessed. During the War of Independence, Muslim women started to work both behind the frontline and in production, especially agriculture.

An attempt at founding the first women's party was made after the proclamation of the Republic on October 29, 1923, and was to be led by Nezihe Muhiddin. The party's foundation, however, was not approved on the grounds that 'it would distract public attention' from the Republican People's Party (CHP)—the party that would end up ruling the country as the single governing power until 1946 (Ergün, 2012). For this reason, the Turkish Women's Union was founded in 1924 to fight for women's suffrage.

It is worth noting at this point that the platform of the women's movement had some similarities to Kemalism's 'modernization from above,' which played the role of constitutive will in Turkey. This fell short of providing equality between women and men but played a significant role in obtaining women's rights. From its very emergence, the women's movement existed as part of a broader modernization movement. That movement claimed that with the foundation of the nation-state, all social relationships, including the family, would change and equality and freedom for women would emerge. Therefore, the modernizing project overlapped with the demands of the women's movement. As the conservative-Islamist Empire was collapsing, Kemalism promoted concepts like 'Western,' 'modern' and 'secular.' The position of women played a very central role in this discursive struggle (Kandiyoti, 1997, p. 35). However, this parallel between Kemalism and the women's struggle should not lead one to claim that women's rights were handed down by the pro-Western elites, as the prevailing discourse in Turkey implies. Doing so ignores the women's struggle that has existed since the Ottoman times.

With the birth of the Republic, women's right to education was established through the 1924 'Law on the Unification of Education,' while women's right to divorce, inheritance, and custody were recognized in the Civil Code of 1926. Women were granted suffrage in local elections in 1930 and in general elections in 1934. However, shortly after these developments, in 1935, the CHP government closed the Turkish Women's Union.[47] This indicates that the parallel interests that had existed during the Republic's foundation split thereafter.

Between 1935 and 1970, there was no significant women's movement in Turkey, as well as many other European countries. The reason for this stagnation can be probably be found in the various pressures against women's mobilizations, the severe problems during both WWII and the post-war period, as well as the perception that women had already reached the limits of gender equality afforded by the law.

An awareness that law was an inadequate measure and tool for gender equality emerged within the libertarian atmosphere of 1970s Europe and in Turkey a few years later. With a short delay and small modifications, the repercussions of the European and American second-wave feminist movements began to be felt in Turkey. The raison d'être of 'the Progressive Women's Association,' which was

---

47 There are various speculations over why the Turkish Women's Union was closed. Some claim that since the Union voiced demands for peace against the upcoming war during the International Women's Conference hosted by Turkey, it was deemed a threat to Turkey's war efforts and thus closed (Ergün, 2012). It was officially closed on the grounds that it had 'completed its mission.' In my opinion, it was closed since it was decided that women would not be treated as interlocutors any more after the 'completion' of progress toward social gender equality was announced to the international public, which was the most crucial point for the CHP.

founded in 1975, was to organize working-class women for socialism, rather than abolishing social gender inequality. Nonetheless, a certain number of these women took their place in the movement as 'feminists' in the 1980s.

The second-wave feminist movement emerged in Turkey in the early 1980s. 'Consciousness raising' groups were composed of young women critical of leftist movements on the subject of gender equality, young women who returned to Turkey after studying abroad (particularly in the West), and female academics. The latter had resigned from the university in protest of the Board of Higher Education (YÖK), developing a brand-new analysis critical of the male-dominant Turkish society and state (Tekeli, 2004). As it was clearly stated in their 1989 'Feminist Manifest,' a total struggle had begun against men's domination over 'women's body, identity, and labor'—that is, the patriarchal order.

Since they had gained strength after the military coup of 1980, which had totally steamrolled the socialist movement, feminists were accused of splitting the workers' movement and putting identity politics ahead of class interests. In fact, this was not the case and socialist feminism left its mark on the first period of the second wave movement. However, it *is* the case that the socialist movement's decline after the coup generated an environment of self-reflection and self-criticism on the Left, which impacted the development of feminism in turn.

The post-1980s women's movement distinguished itself from Kemalism and modernization. Proclaiming this distinction became possible in 1990s; however, the movement had to deal with Kemalism as well, since it was launched with the stated intentions of equality, organization without hierarchy, horizontal relationships, considering and facing the social dynamics and discussing the problems of power. In this way, the movement had to reflect back on its history, and in doing so discovered the 19th century's Ottoman women's movement. While it was redefining itself as a political movement, the feminist movement settled accounts primarily with leftist movements and secondarily with Kemalism. The feminist movement attempted to identify itself as an independent political agent with a separate line. Interestingly, since 'consciousness-raising' involved small, face-to-face meetings, the feminist groups did not attract the attention of the military regime and they were not perceived as a threat. Consequently, they remained immune from the kinds of repression that other opposition groups experienced during the regime (Sancar, 2011, p. 70).

The Civil Code of Turkey, which had been adopted from the Swiss Civil Code (considered to be the most modern at the time), had not been changed since its creation in 1926. A married woman was dependent on her husband and had a restricted legal status. Thus, reforming the Civil Code was central to the movement's agenda from 1985 to the end of 1990s (Tekeli, 2004).

While the 1980s' movements were becoming institutionalized in the 1990s, the feminist movement introduced significant novelties to the substance and discourse of politics. It was, of course, the first movement to question the distinction between public and private spheres. Many issues that had long been deemed non-political became relevant to politics.

The struggle against control over women's bodies has been another primary feature of the women's movement since the 1980s and up to the present. It took very seriously the problems of virginity control, domestic violence, sexual harassment, rape, and honor killings. Partial success has been achieved in some areas: For those experiencing domestic violence, 'women's shelters' (such as *Mor Çatı*, the Purple Roof Women's Shelter Foundation) were created and municipalities were encouraged to establish these according to the movement's principals. With the adoption of the 1998 'Law on the Protection of Family,' the state recognized the necessity of protecting women subjected to domestic violence (Tekeli, 2004). The movement expanded the idea of economic equality to the cultural and political spheres with demands for consideration of domestic labor, the right to fertility, and the prevention of violence against women (Sancar, 2011, p. 56).

During this period, the movement found itself oscillating between the crisis of Kemalist modernization, on the one hand, and the rise of Islamism, on the other (Sancar, 2011, p. 72). It was acknowledged that Kemalist modernization fell short in terms of gender equality compared to European countries. But a specific ambivalence grew in the movement around the place of the headscarf; The headscarf was the embodiment of Islamism and thus the headscarf ban (from universities and public services) was a sign of the Kemalist victory over Islamist conservatives and defense of its modernizing project. The headscarf was thus at the center of a hegemonic struggle. Islamist conservatives—who gained strength in the early 1990s and have been in power with few interruptions—protested for the first time in demonstrations against the headscarf ban in 1994. The Islamist feminists who launched and maintained these demonstrations discussed the headscarf in terms of second-wave feminism and the demand for 'women's right to control their own body.'

The emergence of the Kurdish women's movement should be included into this picture. At the beginning, the movement was mainly centered on the politicization of motherhood. It was through this emphasis on motherhood that the women's movement (*Demokratik Özgür Kadın Hareketi*—Democratic Liberated Women's Movement) acquired legitimacy among Kurdish women. The feminist movement and the Kurdish women's movement had an impressive history of collaboration, albeit with tensions. These tensions usually reflected those between the socialist movement and the Kurdish independent movement.

The Current Situation of Women in Turkey: Employment, Education, and Political Participation

To examine the dynamics upon which the contemporary women's movement is premised, it is useful to outline the situation of women in Turkey today. To this end, I will examine indicators such as labor force participation, equality in education, participation in political life, and violence against women, comparing the situation in Turkey with international data.[48]

According to the Global Gender Gap report published by the World Economic Forum, Turkey was ranked 105th out of 115 countries in 2006 and 120th out of 136 countries in 2013 (Table 6.1). Although Turkey's overall score on inequality index increased, the report clearly shows that—as the 16th biggest economy in the world—the country has not made sufficient progress on gender equality.

Table 7.1. Turkey in Global Gender Gap Index

Year	Nr. of Countries	Score of Turkey	Rank of Turkey
2006	115	0.585	105
2009	134	0.5828	129
2012	135	0.6015	124
2013	136	0.6081	120

Source: World Economic Forum, 2006, 2009, 2012, 2013 Global Gender Gap Reports

Examining this table, it is clear that Turkey ranks rather low on employment and political participation and has made progress in education and health (albeit, not in proportion with its economic size). While the reasons for this situation are beyond the scope of this chapter, we should note that the statistics show that existence of women in public sphere is a yet to be socially or legally approved fact (Table 6.2).

According to the Social Gender Equity Index of Social Watch, Turkey was ranked 139th out of 157 countries in 2008, taking education, economic activities, and empowerment criteria into account. In addition, Turkey has been the second most regressing country between 2004 and 2007, showing a 12.7 percent decrease (Report of Sosyal-İş, 2009, p. 10)

---

48 While I was writing this chapter, I cited the thread of the Report on Women's Labor and Employment, published by Social Security, Education, Office, Commerce, Cooperative and Fine Arts Workers' Union (*Sosyal-İş*) by updating the data. I thank Onur Bakır who drafted the report.

Table 7.2. Turkey's Position According to Four Basic Criteria

Year 2013	Economic participation and opportunity	Educational Attainment	Health and Survival	Political Empowerment
Rank	124	104	59	132
Score	0.4269	0.9431	0.9755	0.0221

Source: World Economic Forum, 2013 Global Gender Gap Report

Furthermore, according to the Research on Structure of Family, published by the Turkish Statistical Institute (TÜİK) in 2006, 23 percent of men and 10 percent of women in Turkey believe that women should not work. The justifications are given below as to why women should not work.

Table 7.3. Justifications of Those who say 'Women Should not Work'

Why should women not work?	Women	Men
Housework is their main duty	64.7	60.7
It's against traditions	14.1	12
Workplaces are not safe	9.5	16.5
Children may suffer from it	7.8	7
Women may get exhausted	2.5	2
Other	1.4	1.8

Source: Research on Structure of Family, Turkish Statistical Institute, 2006

The biggest obstacles to women's employment have been the obligation, until 2001, for married women to obtain their husbands' permission to work and low rates of schooling that did not change until the 1980s. Research shows that women undertake more than 50 percent of housework, excluding payment of bills and small repair work. According to the same study, 92 percent of women take the responsibility for childcare. Firms that employ more than 100 women workers are obliged to have nursery rooms; nonetheless, large firms of this kind are primarily in the male-dominated industrial sector. Taken together, these factors have posed a significant obstacles to women's employment.

The sectorial distribution of businesses in which women are employed is as follows: One million women in Turkey are working in education and health care sectors, which are regarded as an extension of women's social role of providing care service. Out of 7.6 million employed women, 2.8 million are unpaid family workers in the agriculture sector, and only 25 percent of the employed women are working in jobs that correspond to their occupational qualifications (TÜİK, 2013).

While women in Turkey make up 9.9 percent of lawmakers and high-profile executives and managers in 2008, this percentage dropped to 3 percent in 2012, according to TÜİK data.

According to data compiled by TÜİK, women make up 14.4 percent of members of Parliament[49] and 4.2 percent of ministers in 2013. Women account for 0.9 percent of mayors, 4.2 percent of members of municipal councils, and 3.3 percent of provincial councils. These numbers demonstrate that women are underrepresented, both in Parliament and in local administrations.

Research on Domestic Violence against Women in Turkey, conducted in 2008 by the General Directorate on the Status of Women,[50] reveals that 41.9 percent of women in Turkey have been subjected to physical or sexual violence by their husbands or partners at least once in their life. 39.3 percent of women report having experienced physical violence and 15.3 percent report having been subjected to sexual violence. 12.7 percent of women in Turkey are subjected to both physical and sexual violence. 43.9 percent of women in Turkey have been subjected to emotional violence or abuse by their husbands or partners at least once in their lives. Despite steps taken to end violence against women, including legal regulations, women's vulnerability to abuse remains a problem and should be a top priority for public health authorities and human rights advocates.

Responses From Above: From State Feminism to Family Nexus

The state's attitude towards gender equality and the women's movement/ feminist movement can be summarily categorized by period: From the early 1990s until 2002, we can identify a form of 'state feminism'; from 2003 until today, we observe the framing of women in the 'family context,' where they are viewed not as individuals but in their role as mothers. It is important to note that I am not taking the concept of 'state feminism' to be unproblematic. Despite legal regulations in favor of women that were adopted under conservative-liberal-democrat party alliances in the 1990s and the forming of 'more' egalitarian measures, these changes were not entirely based on a feminist perspective. Furthermore, it should be highlighted that conservative parties within coalition governments

---

49　The majority of women lawmakers are members of the Peace and Democracy Party (BDP), which is the representative of Kurdish Freedom Movement in Parliament. The BDP applies a 50 percent women quota. The ruling Justice and Development Party does not apply any gender quota, while the main opposition social democratic Republican People's Party has been applying a 33 percent gender quota as of 2012.

50　'Kadına karşı şiddetle mücadele alanında çalışan personele yönelik el kitabı', http://kadininstatu-su.aile.gov.tr/data/542a8e0b369dc31550b3ac30/Kad%C4%B1na%20Y%C3%B6nelik%20Siddet-le%20Mucadele%20Kitap%201.pdf

approached and supported these measures with the intention of 'protecting' the family; thus, many feminists were extremely critical of the state's paternalistic attitude. Nevertheless, the enhanced legal protections for women should be seen both as a necessary precondition for Turkey's accession to the European Union and the result of pressures to absorb feminist discourses of gender equality.

In this context, it was not a coincidence that an institutional framework on gender equality emerged at a time when the feminist movement was beginning to gain strength. This institutionalization process began with the Advisory Board on Women Policies, which was founded within the State Planning Organization (DPT) in 1987 (Acuner, 2002, p. 126). The first official institution concerned with women was established as the General Directorate on the Status of Women in 1990. It should be noted here that Turkey was being governed by coalition governments formed by conservative and liberal parties, thus different wings of government had different interpretations of both the term 'woman' and what would count as a women's institution. However, when the structure of the General Directorate is examined—with its 20-personnel-staff, it's clear that this was primarily 'lip service' to the women's movement and an effort to appear pro-Western (Acuner, 2002, p. 131). In fact, the statutory decree on the establishment of the General Directorate states its duty as 'ensuring the orientation of voluntary women's institutions and associations that are members of international institutions within the direction of the national vision.'

The institution had been subordinated to the Ministry of State Responsible for 'Women' first and then with a change of name to 'Family.' It was then subordinated to the Ministry of Family and Social Policies, which was founded with a statutory decree instead of a law in 2011. The statutory decree clarifies the duty of the newly founded ministry as 'ensuring the hand[ing] down [of] the family structure and values to the next generations by protecting them against social and cultural erosion.' This statement probably reveals the true structure and purpose of the ministry. Along with women, the ministry is also responsible for disabled persons, children, elders, veterans, and people in need of protection.

Many legal regulations in favor of women and aiming to abolish inequalities[51] have been adopted since the foundation of the General Directorate of Status of Woman. However, these legal regulations did not have a decisive positive impact on either the public or private lives of women—a point I will discuss in the next section of this chapter.

---

51 That is if the removal of discriminations, such as a quarter abatement in the rape penalty against sex workers or the consideration of the honor motive as a mitigating circumstance in women killings, can be deemed progress!

Our discussion should be contextualized within the devastating impact of global capitalism after the 2001 economic crisis, which paved the way for the rise of Islam in the absence of other alternatives. Islam, which was relatively excluded from the political arena during the crisis, underwent an ideological transformation that enabled it to raise opposition in some places. We cannot disregard the fact that Islam gained legitimacy as a base for public opposition due to the Iranian Revolution and some recent national liberation movements. And yet, the rise of religious conservatism did not take shape due to the peculiarities of Islam. Neoliberalism's urgent need for conservatism led religion, which is one of the constituent elements of conservatism, to take place on the political stage. And, neoliberal governments, as the dauntless defenders of conservatism, favored the religion to strengthen their rule. The Justice and Development Party (AKP) is the consequential extension of this 'development.'

Under AKP rule since the early 2000s, we have witnessed severe attacks on women's rights that were obtained during the period of relative welfare. Though some of those assaults were repelled, depending upon the power of the specific women's movement, there have also been retreats in the legal sphere. For instance, the right to abortion has turned into a precarious entitlement that will be lost unless it is defended constantly.

Conservatism has been reviving since the 2000s, as a 'back to the past strategy' with an updated emphasis on the patriarchal family, heterosexuality, motherhood, as women's 'biological fate,' and women's role as domestic worker and primary caregiver. This can be understood as a 'new body regime.' Surely it is not surprising that conservatism advances through women's body. What lies beneath this is the belief that women's 'production functions,' along with their 'productive organs,' belong to nature. While head and arm are associated with men and labor, productive functions of women, the uterus for example, do not give the woman a 'status of wage slavery.' Therefore she is not free to sell her labor. Woman are deemed to be property.

In this way, population policies and biopolitics have always been one of the main regulatory instruments of capitalism. Focusing on family and women's biological role as mother not only enables to see the family and the woman as the main social security units, but also assumes the function of controlling the body and therefore fertility through biopolitics. Nevertheless, the characteristics of the specific state and the level of capitalist development also shape the direction of population policies.

Labor power in the neoliberal era emanates in the service sector in an unskilled form. Roughly, there is no need to qualify all of them. In the so-called 'growth without employment' model, the exclusion of the labor force from employment without reflecting it in statistics is a highly anticipated and desired phenomenon. Under conservative governments, those who are excluded are mostly women. The conservative government emphasizes the role of 'women' as 'mother.' This mother will raise children who will be the unskilled labor force. The tide of conservatism, which has risen as a result of this objective dynamic, also consolidates the conservative government.

We should underline the 'extra disciplining' function of conservatism as well. In the face of neoliberal attack, to discipline working class men, there cannot be a better reason than a wife and children at home to be taken care of. On the other hand, women's obligations as housewives are an obstacle to participation in paid labor. Within this context, the recently proposed law, 'Women Employment Package,' which claims to be in favor of women's participation, cannot be taken seriously. This proposal, which encourages women to find home-centered flexible work, seeks to decrease employment costs, on the one hand, and ensure childcare at no cost to the state, on the other. The proposal is one of the main topics on the agenda of feminist/women's movements that are against flexibilization/precarization and women's exclusion from public sphere.

Responses from Below: Feminism and Women's Movement

The Turkish women's movement is composed of independent individuals as well as more than 350 associations, foundations, initiatives, commissions, and university research centers that conduct in-depth discussions on every issue concerning women to find creative solutions. These organizations have been cooperating effectively in different platforms according to specific issues.

Nevertheless, the classical Western style feminist movement is not the sole form of the women's movement in Turkey. Rather, the women's movement since the 1990s had had three social bases: Islamist women, Kurdish women and 'classical' feminist women. The nomenclature of 'feminism' is nevertheless used by Islamist and Kurdish women's movement to some extent.

Islamist Feminism/Islamist Women's Movement

Islamist Feminism and the Islamist Women's Movement date back to the early 1990s. Working groups were formed to discuss gender equality through a contemporary interpretations of the Koran. Islamist Feminism, which was nurtured by the theoretical debates on Islam in Egypt, Iran, and Turkey during the 1990s, positions itself as modern but anti-orientalist and relies on the idea that a 'local' feminism is possible (Güç, 2008: 658). The reactions of radical Islamist circles against this movement had been cruel: Konca Kuriş, who became the flag bearer of Islamist feminism, was kidnapped and tortured to death by Turkish Hezbollah in 1998.[52]

The Islamist women's movement, which also includes Islamist feminists, became popular in the late 1990s with demonstrations protesting the headscarf ban. This was a time when Kemalism and 'statist secularism' were untouchables regardless of who was in power. During this period, women's demand for the right to appear with their headscarf in public offices—including universities—was interrupted by military memorandum of 1998.[53] However, after the AKP's coming to power in 2002, headscarved women started to take public offices, particularly in women's institutions and the ministry. Street protests came to an end after the issue was gradually resolved when the headscarf ban was abolished first at the universities and then in public offices. Islamist feminists continue to work within the Ministry of Family and Social Policies over violence against women.

The feminist movement has diverse approaches toward the Islamist feminist movement. Though they formed different alliances in various demonstrations, on the headscarf issue there is significant disagreement; in some circles the headscarf is described in terms of a 'woman's right to decide on her own body,' while others deem it 'woman's absolute abandoning of the right to decide on her own body.'

Although a number of Islamist feminists' utter criticisms that the AKP manipulated women's protests for freedom of headscarf during its struggle for power and exploited the protests for their own gain—that it did not use politics for women but through women—these issues are usually not publicly debated.

Kurdish Women's Movement

The Kurdish movement[54] gives a more active and constitutive role to women by relying on the 'image of women who will liberate the society together with

---

52 Turkish Hezbollah assumed the responsibility of killing of Konca Kuriş with this statement: 'Konca Kuriş, the enemy of Islam and a secular-feminist, has been kidnapped by Hezbollah fighters and interrogated in our bases for her actions and statements against Allah and Koran. Konca Kuriş, who acts in line with atheist-secular Republic of Turkey's rhetoric and instructions and who is also used by Zionists, has been punished as required by sharia rules for making attempts to disseminate suspicion among Muslims.

53 The Islamist conservative Welfare Party was the leading coalition partner in this period. In a memorandum that was handed down to the Prime Minister on February 28, 1997, the military stated that headscarf protests were provoked by the leading coalition partner and they were attempting to create chaos in the country. Violations by the Right against 'headscarved sisters' during the period between February 28 memorandum and the AKP's coming to power in 2003 became one of the main elements of the AKP's strategy as part of 'pro-oppressed politics.' In this regard, we can say that headscarf protests played a major role in the AKP's coming to power.

54 The last ethnic Kurdish rebellion in Anatolia has been continuing since 1983, resulting in major casualties throughout the 1990s. The movement founded political parties beginning in the early 1990s, which have been represented in Parliament. The Kurdish Freedom Movement had been 'separatist' at the beginning, but today they are advocating a kind of federalism under the name of democratic

herself' (Çağlayan, 2007, p. 87). Since they participate actively in legal political parties, as well as paramilitary forces, women have a strong place in the Kurdish movement that is not necessarily defined through their identity as women.

In the early 1980s, the issue of gender equality, examined through a classical Marxist approach, became a central point of discussion in the Kurdish movement (Çağlayan, 2007, p. 98). In the 1990s, the dominant ideology of the movement was 'women are slaves to be liberated.' Afterwards, women's active participation and change in the gender composition of the movement led to the rise of the idea, 'women will liberate themselves.' This change is closely related to the more active participation of Kurdish women in the movement since 1992. The Kurdish movement discussed the concepts of 'new woman' and 'new family' in its theoretical publications. Women are called to war through love with the motto of 'Who makes war becomes free, who is free becomes beautiful and who is beautiful is loved' (Çağlayan as cited in Öcalan, 1999). Abdullah Öcalan, the jailed leader of the armed wing of the movement—the Kurdistan Workers Party (PKK)—describes it as 'dialectics of love and victory.'

After ethnic identities became decisive in voters' preferences, beginning in the 1990s, a new Kurdish-oriented political party (People's Labor Party, HEP) was founded. New parties were founded consecutively under new names after the Constitutional Court closed down the HEP. Today, the Peace and Democracy Party (BDP), having been a key political actor for over 20 years, is represented with 27 deputies in Parliament.

In these new political parties, Kurdish women acquired new ground for collective discussion and feminist politics. After the foundation of the HEP, women unprecedentedly became active in Turkey's political life. The Kurdish political tradition implemented a 50 percent women quota and put the co-chairman system into practice. These circumstances paved the way for other leftist or social democrat parties to apply gender quotas.

As soon as the political party was founded, Kurdish women started to identify themselves as a 'women's movement,' and a women's commission was established for the first time within the People's Democracy Party (HADEP). Though the commission's objective was defined as 'unveiling the perspective on woman ideology and forming the collective administration,' this 'perspective on woman ideology' was not defined as 'feminist.' Without a doubt, there are many women within the Kurdish women's movement, particularly those living in the western regions, who identify themselves as 'feminist.' Yet, the 1990s debates about the local character of the movement and the extent to which its theoretical perspective is Western, are still under way. Moreover, there has been a move away

---

autonomy. They currently have political parties and armed units conducting guerrilla war.

from the term 'feminist' to 'jineoloji,'[55] which indicates a new synthesis of Eastern and Western approaches.

Unlike the feminist and Islamist feminist movements, the Kurdish Women's Movement had more success attracting working class women with little education by appealing to ethnic identity through the Democratic Free Women's Movement. Still, this mass movement has collaborated with the broader feminist movement in various platforms. The participation of many socialist movements rooted in Turkey's west and of socialist-feminist women from the newly founded Peoples' Democratic Party (HDP) made this relationship with the Kurdish feminist movement more organic.

Feminist Movement

The classical feminist movement, which is less homogeneous compared to its abovementioned counterparts, has also been influenced by socialist feminism. This is due to the fact that socialist feminists founded the movement after becoming critical of the sexist practice of 1970s' Left movements.

The feminist movement has been organized around diverse journals, political groups, associations, and platforms with separate emphases but shared practices of solidarity. The Association for the Support and Training of Women Candidates (KADER), the Library of Women's Works, Purple Roof Women's Shelter Foundation, and Women's Labor and Employment Initiative are among the organizations participating in this movement. Over the last decade in particular, these organizations have been working together on platforms founded under different themes, such as 'Abortion is a Right, Decision Belongs to Women,' 'We will Stop Women Murders,' 'Women's Platform against Sexual Violence' and 'Women's Platform for Constitution' (to name just a few). These platforms are founded with both long- and short-term programs and campaigns.

Beginning in the late 1990s, the feminist movement has made significant progress in purging sexism from Turkish law. This process continued with many legal acquisitions, such as the annulment of the Civil Code provision obliging married women to have their husbands' permission to work in the paid labor force and the adoption of the 'Law on Protection of Family,' which treats domestic violence as a crime.

The prolonged, low-intensity civil war in Turkey has also been a central topic on the feminist movement's agenda since the early 1990s, albeit losing momentum from time to time. The debate on the specific effects of war on women is one of the earliest contributions of the feminist movement in Turkey. Many

---

55 Jin means woman in Kurdish. Jineoloji can be translated as 'woman science.'

studies on women's exposure to war (as a specific group and as mothers and workers) have been conducted. Meanwhile, feminists staged the first 'anti-war' demonstrations in Turkey's Western regions.

On the other hand, beginning in the 1990s, and particularly after the AKP's coming to power in 2003, conservatism and its 'new body regime' have become major issues in the women's movement.

The 'new body regime' which calls women back to their fertility and motherhood functions and revives the 'holy family,' is an imminent and major threat against women in Turkey. Measures seeking the flexibilization of women's labor and a de facto ban on abortion, reproduce women's primary role as spouse and mother within the family context. These transformations are not peculiar to Turkey; forms of conservatism under the auspices of neoliberalism are emerging elsewhere to undermine women's control over their bodies and their lives. Under neoliberal capitalism, conservatism is on the rise, albeit within specific political, economic, and cultural structures. The distinction between advanced and backward societies that is made by the United Nations' various gender equity indexes makes no sense for women in Italy or Spain who are endeavoring to protect their right to abortion, or for women in the US who are fighting to keep their right to abortion.

Consequently, conservatism has been reviving under the auspices of neoliberalism as a 'back to the past strategy' emphasizing the patriarchal family, heterosexuality, motherhood ideology, the 'biological fate' of women, and her primary responsibilities in the home.

When it was announced that abortion may be banned, demonstrations in 2011 generated the largest participation by the feminist movement, apart from rallies on International Women's Day. Eventually, abortion was not officially banned; however, married women's abortions in state-run hospitals were banned in practice.

Violence against women is high on the agenda of the feminist movement in Turkey. Without a doubt, the state's use of violence power is in direct proportion to violence used in the private sphere. The spread of violence within society generally corresponds with an increase in violence against women. In fact, there has been a noticeable increase both in individual crime rates generally and in violence/offences against women in particular since 2005 (TÜİK, 2013).

It should be made clear that the state implements both direct and indirect violence against women. The direct violence can be openly seen and noticed in state politics, political strategies and legal regulations. The indirect violence, on the other hand, is the discourse and/or action against women (women's place is at home, women are not equal to men, women are mothers etc.). Therefore, although the 'modern state as the superior patriarch' has the monopoly of violence, it has handed down part of the violence to 'men as the individual patriarch' of the home

(Balta, 2013, p. 56). This 'handing down' of patriarchal control should be read as a regulatory measure rather than a 'total abandonment' of the state's role.

Two of the main functions of conservatism are to preserve the traditional family at the core of society and to discipline women through their biological and procreative roles. But explicit violence against women is also increasing in this conservative tide. According to the records of the Ministry of Justice, murders of women increased 400 percent between the period of 2003 and 2014 (Ministry of Justice, 2013). In the face of this terrifying number, stopping violence against women has to be one of the main priorities of the feminist movement.

Conclusion:

New Challenges, New Struggles

Violence against women is an outcome of sexist capitalism. The private sphere is the only space where the state gives up its monopoly on violence. When we examine the distinction between the private and the public through the lens of violence, we see that the monopoly of violence belongs to men in the private sphere and to the state in public sphere. This means that no matter how much the state becomes civilized, violence in the private sphere will not come to an end. This bears many connotations for the internal debate of the feminist movement: Obtaining equality before the law or increasing participation in the workforce will not be sufficient instruments for the prevention of violence against women. Even though Turkish women are living in a society where the law on the prevention of violence against women has been in place for 10 years, marital rape is counted as a crime and there is a 'relatively free' right to abortion, they are still witnessing an increase in violence against women (particularly in the form of murders). This contradiction challenges a so-called 'feminist myth', namely that women's equal social status would ensure equality. For this reason, the claim that the 'private is political' still stands as an important argument to be heard. Unless the distinction between private and public is abolished, women will be subjected to violence and exploitation as required by 'protection' of the private sphere. This should be the common agenda of not only women's and feminist movements but also all women living in an environment where sexism and homophobia prevails.

References

Acuner, S. (2002). 1990'lı Yıllar ve Resmi Düzeyde Kurumsallaşmanın Doğuş Aşamaları. In A. Bora & A. Günal (Eds.), *1990'larda Türkiye'de Feminizm* (pp. 125-159). İstanbul: İletişim.

Balta, E. (2013). Muhafazakarlaşmanın Gölgesinde: Kadınların İkincil Konumu Pekişirken. *Sosyalist Demokrasi için Yeniyol, 42*, 52-63.

Balta, E. (2012). The women's movement fights back. *International Viewpoint Online Magazine.* Retrieved from http://www.internationalviewpoint.org/spip.php?article2802

Bora, A., & Günal, A. (Eds.). (2002). *1990'larda Türkiye'de Feminizm.* İstanbul: İletişim.

Çağlayan, H. (2007). *Analar, Yoldaşlar, Tanrıçalar: Kürt Hareketinde Kadınlar ve Kadın Kimliğinin Oluşumu.* İstanbul: İletişim.

Çakır, S. (2010). *Osmanlı Kadın Hareketi.* İstanbul: Metis.

Ergün, Y. (2012). Osmanlı'dan Cumhuriyet'e Kısaca Türkiye Kadın Hareketi. *Cafrande.* Retrieved from http://www.cafrande.org/?p=37992

Güç, A. (2008). İslamcı Feminizm: Müslüman Kadınların Birey Olma Çabaları. *Uludağ Üniversitesi İlahiyat Fakültesi Dergisi, 17*(2), 649-673.

İlerici Kadınlar Derneği. (1996). *Ve Hep Birlikte Koştu.* İstanbul: Açı.

Kandiyoti, D. (1997). *Cariyeler, Bacılar, Yurttaşlar.* İstanbul: Metis.

Koray, M. (1999). Türkiye Kadın Hareketinin Soru ve Sorunları'. In Kolektif (Ed.), *75 Yılda Kadınlar ve Erkekler* (pp. 361-375). İstanbul: Tarih Vakfı Yayınları.

Moralıoğlu, A. (2012). 80'li Yıllarda Kadın Hareketi ve Kampanyalar. *TBB Dergisi,* 291-296.

Saktanber, A., & Çorbacıoğlu, G. (2008). Veiling and headscarf-scepticism in Turkey. *Social Politics, 15*(4), 514-8.

Sancar, S. (2011). *Türkiye'de Kadın Hareketinin Politiği: Tarihsel Bağlam, Politik Gündem ve Özgünlükler.* In S. Sancar (Ed.), *Birkaç Arpa Boyu: 21. Yüzyıla Girerken Türkiye'de Feminist Çalışmalar* (pp. 53-109).. İstanbul: Koç.

Tekeli, Ş. (2004). On Maddede Türkiye'de Kadın Hareketi. *Bianet.* Retrieved from www.bianet.org/bianet/kadin/43145-on-maddede-turkiyede-kadin-hareketi

Tekeli, Ş. (1990). (Ed.). *Kadın Bakış Açısından 1980'ler Türkiye'sinde Kadınlar.* İletişim: İstanbul.

Timisi, N., & Gevrek, M. A. (2002). 1980'ler Türkiye'sinde feminist Hareket: Ankara Çevresi. In A. Bora & A. Günal (Eds.), *1990'larda Türkiye'de Feminizm* (pp. 13-40). İstanbul: İletişim.

TÜİK. (2006). Aile Yapısı Araştırması. Retrieved from www.tuik.gov.tr/IcerikGetir.do?istab_id=16

TÜİK. (2013). Toplumsal Yapı ve Cinsiyet İstatistikleri. Retrieved from http://www.tuik.gov.tr/PreTablo.do?alt_id=1068

World Economic Forum. (2013). Global Gender Gap Reports. Retrieved from http://www3.weforum.org/docs/WEF_GenderGap_Report_2013.pdf

8.
PUBLIC EMPLOYEES AND PRACTICES OF RESISTANCE

The Ideology and politics of Education in Turkey

Orkun Saip Durmaz

What are the possibilities and loci of resistance against the education policies of the AKP regime? This question can be discussed in three separate but related contexts, each corresponding to a different level of abstraction: The labor process, unionization, and the political regime. The labor process refers to the organization and control of conduct in production and service work. It thus represents the micro scale of social relationships, where one is confronted with the smallest but most concrete manifestations of complex social and political relations. For example, this is the level at which tensions experienced between workers and employers in everyday working life are revealed. Yet, more macro-scale parameters must also be included to understand the extent to which tensions between workers and employers are class-based.

The unionization has a broader context in which meso-level dynamics are analyzed. In other words, the dynamics related to the collective struggles and labor organizations need to be analyzed through a larger context which cannot be provided by the term of labor process. It is approached at the meso-level, to examine both the more generalized social and political relations within the labor process and the greater dynamics of the political regime. The members of labor unions (and other organizations for economic struggle) are associated on the basis of their socio-economic interests; unionization replaces their direct work relations with processes of institutionalization and bureaucratization. Moreover, ideological and political developments across the country affect the organizational practices and political orientation of the labor unions.

The context of the political regime is the more abstract; its dynamics are the most macro-scaled and thus have strong effects on both the labor process and unionization. The basic characteristics of a political regime tell a story about the country's economic, ideological, and political developments. In this chapter, the three contexts will be examined to understand the ideology and politics of education and the practices of resistance of the public employees. Now, let us turn to the transformation in education in relation to the AKP regime.

The main orientation of Turkey's neoliberal economic policies—namely, liberalization, privatization, cuts in public spending, de-unionization, and deregulation—has not changed significantly since 1980.[56] That said, the neoliberal transformation of Turkey's economic and political structure took on a new institutionalized intensity with the election of the AKP in 2002. The notable cornerstones of the AKP agenda included: a total transformation of the labor regime, the formation of a new official ideology, the implementation of political Islam—which had a history of oscillating between state suppression and support—and the establishment of a new social policy regime. The coming to power of the AKP was the occasion for dramatic transformations in the political, ideological, and cultural spheres; consequently, it was also the catalyst for immense discontent and organized resistance.

A full analysis of both the neo-liberal transformation under AKP rule and the organized resistance is beyond the scope of this study. In this chapter, I will limit the discussion to the neoliberal transformations and practices of resistance within the field of education. The focus here is not on 'educational policies' per se, but on the education sphere as a field of labor, in which micro, meso, and macro dynamics are revealed. Specifically, I examine the labor process of teachers, collective organization practices, ideological and political dynamics influencing education policy, and economic forces regulating the field's labor market. I approach the AKP's transformation of the education sphere by examining the three

---

56 On January 24, 1980, an economic 'stabilization package' which is widely known as the 'January 24 decisions' was announced. The package constituted a turning point in Turkish economic history, signifying the end of planned development and the beginning of a market-oriented restructuring process.

contexts discussed above: First, the labor process of education services will be discussed, along with examples of resistance at this level; Second, unionization and other organizational practices in education will be discussed and interpreted within the context of the AKP's ideological-political character; Third the AKP regime will be analyzed in terms of ideology and politics, with an emphasis on its uniqueness in the history of the Republic.

A word about methodology: In my discussion of teachers' perceptions and experiences, I draw on in-depth interviews and focus-group discussions with 41 teachers from seven separate institutions in Ankara. This research was conducted as part of my Ph.D. dissertation, which was also published as *To be a teacher in Turkey: Labor process and re-proleterization.*

The Labor Process: The First Context for Understanding Transformation, and Resistance in Education

When analyzing the labor processes, the most direct relationships of exploitation are taken into consideration, along with the technical organization of the workplace and the power relations that emerge. At this level of analysis, the workplace is theorized as a social arena with specific economic, ideological, and political characteristics. Although school is made possible through the contributions of many different groups of workers (including janitors, technicians, and subcontracted workers), this chapter focuses on the group that constitutes the bulk of employment: teachers. At this point, it is necessary to state that teachers are examined and discussed not as *professionals* but as *individual workers* in the labor process. I am interested in the experiences created by social relationships between teachers that are realized as part of the labor process.

Ozga and Lawn (1981) analyze the problems of deskilling, the decreasing autonomy of teachers, and new administrative control mechanisms in education through the paradigm of the Taylorization of the labor process. Smyth (1991), focusing on collegial relationships among teachers and professionalism, claims that the perception of professionalization revealed among teachers does not always ensure autonomy; in fact, it may lead to reconstruct a new social and institutional agenda that aims to control the teachers in the labor process, by instructing them what they must do 'and how they must strive to meet national priorities and international competitiveness' (Smyth, 1991, pp. 324-325). Thomas (2005) and Robertson (2000) consider changes in the labor process of teachers as a necessary outcome of the commercializing tendencies in the sphere of education. They specifically highlight new administrative models that emphasize 'performance' over other priorities. While Robertson (2000) focused on macro-level political economic developments, Reid (2003) and Harvie (2006) combined debates on the teacher labor process with debates on surplus value and productive/non-productive labor, thus developing a more substantial approach. These studies shed only minimal light on the ideological-political aspects of education; in fact, ideology is either not mentioned at all or conceived as subordinate to political economy processes. For this reason, they are of limited value for analyzing the uniqueness of the AKP regime in Turkey.

Other studies focusing on labor processes have paid closer attention to the ideological, political, and cultural dimensions of teaching in a manner that does not subsume them to economic or technical factors (Grace, 1985; Sachs & Smith, 1988). Similarly, while Sachs and Smith (1988, p. 432) argue that the 'education system represents the social constitution it is involved in,' this can only be useful in developing a general view on the issue, but not in examining the specifics of Turkish context.

Özoğlu's (2012) study is the most applicable for our concern with labor processes of teachers in Turkey, although the transformation of the public personnel management under AKP rule is examined through the political-economic axis rather than the ideological-political axis. Other studies should also be noted: Adıgüzel (2013) examines the differences between marketization and commodification in the education context and the role of the education in a capitalist system, while Aksoy (2013) discusses the deskilling of teachers and the process of transforming the teacher into an unskilled worker. For their part, Ercan and Şimşek (2013) concentrate on the teachers' social role in Turkey, once again focusing on the political economy of neoliberal transformation rather than the political uniqueness of the AKP era.

To properly analyze the impact of the AKP regime on labor processes, the focus should be shifted from the political-economic axis to the ideological-political. The AKP has brought about much more than an intensification of neoliberal economic policies; religious fundamentalism has also become central to the political regime and to its education agenda in particular. This is evident not only in the regime's education policies per se, but also in the everyday experiences of teachers and students. In the context of the regime's education reforms and changes to course curriculums, the ideological and political functions of education are becoming the everyday subject of politics.

Teachers are forthcoming about how these changes have begun to effect their work life. One interviewee recalls a specific conflict that occurred at his school:

> When you try to do something, [the school administration] raises ludicrous difficulties and discourages you. For example, a teacher has been training

students semah [an Alevi ritual dance] at the school for as long as I've been here—that's seven years. Among the folk dances taught, there was a folk dance from the Black Sea region and a semah as well. Besides, this is a predominantly Alevi neighborhood. And here, Anatolia, is a mosaic of cultures. The mother of my student who performs semah best is headscarved [Sunni]. Although semah is part of Alevi culture, we are living together here, and children don't refrain from performing it. They are eager for it. But our school's principal said that we cannot perform semah. Obviously, he did not want to be at odds with the District Education Directorate. Maybe he did not want to go against the government. Semah or Mevlevi dances [whirling dervish dance] are being performed everywhere, normally there's no problem with them. But he started to stir up concern with them. Moreover, semah usually receives the most enthusiastic applause. He said 'I don't allow it on May 19 [Youth and Sports Day].' 'Why?' 'It has political content. [Caliph] Ali is mentioned,' he said. When we said 'It is the same performance as previous years,' he said, 'No, you changed it.' May God give us patience! (Interviewee 1)

These remarks make it clear that interactions in the school and curriculum debates, including those pertaining to extracurricular activities, have political, ideological, and cultural dimensions. When school administrators maintain prohibitive and punishing attitudes toward these activities, they may become politicized. The issue of whether a folk dance will be performed in the school cannot simply remain a problem between the administrator and the teacher who organizes the show. In the teacher's own words, the fact that 'the school principal is leery of the District Education Directorate or government...' coincides with the ideological-political divisions across the country (Durmaz, 2014. p.200). While other cases of the influence of religious thought over school activities emerged during the research, this example will suffice for now to show the everyday impacts of the AKP's ideological-political agenda on education.

What kind of resistance practices can occur within the labor processes of the school? How can the individual teacher resist the AKP's pressures to reorganize educational practices? On this matter, one's level of employment security becomes significant. The response of a full-time, permanent teacher to the question of 'What is the most fundamental problem of the teaching occupation' is a useful point of departure for our discussion:

It's very difficult to teach in crowded classes. We don't teach in ideal classrooms of 18 to 20 students ... For example, if the curriculum was less intensive, we could have the opportunity to take better care of students. Then we could find a chance to pay attention not only to teaching but also to the education of the students. (Interviewee 2)

These remarks suggest that the problems for teachers with job security are primarily occupational. However, the response to the same question from teachers with precarious employment, who are called as *contracted teachers* and *temporal instructors* in Turkey, is quite different because, contrary to permanent teachers, they have uncertain and unwarranted future. One interviewee notes:

We have many problems from every angle. We don't have any problem-free area. I don't think we have enough [employee] rights. We have a very heavy workload. But despite that, we aren't rewarded economically or socially for our efforts. It's not financially satisfying either. (Interviewee 3)

Here, the interviewee refers to his basic socio-economic needs, rather than the specific challenges of teaching. This suggests that different degrees of employment security create different points of emphasis in the identification of occupational problems. Yet, interviews also show that teachers holding positions with the same level of job security may also express different solutions for the same problem. In other words, the fact that individual teachers are subject to similar labor processes does not necessarily mean that they will participate in identical practices of resistance. One can identify, however, that a shared ideological-political tendency among interviewees in response to the question, 'Who can solve the problems of teachers ' may also be different:

Government should do something on this matter ... The first thing the government should do is maybe to shut down 70 or 80 of the 90 faculties [of education]. As the number of faculties of education and their graduates increased, the occupation of teaching has been discredited. Changing the system and so on is the policy makers' job. (Interviewee 4)

If there's a problem of unassigned teachers, this shows that there's a problem in the education system. What is the problem of the education system? A fundamental reform in the education system should be made. People like us will make that reform. Those people will change this system. There's no other alternative, I think. (Interviewee 5)

Two teachers who have similar jobs and are subjected to the similar labor process may have different approaches in dealing with any problem. At this point, the ideological-political context comes into play. In other words, the responses to the question of 'why some consent to the regime while others revolt against it?' are related with the ideological and political context of the labor process.

Unionization: The Second Context for Understanding Transformation and Resistance in Education

At the meso-level, we are interested in examining legislation on collective labor law during the AKP reign, the importance of collective labor contracts for teachers, and the relationship between unionization and job security. An examination of resistance at this level would focus on the actions of teachers' labor unions and collective organizations.

Studies on teachers' unions in the international literature tend to focus on country-specific unionization processes and thus cannot be applied to the particular Turkish union movement during the AKP rule. Stevenson's (2007) comprehensive study on labor unions and education reforms in England has become a key text in the field. In the Turkish context, Aksoy (1974) examined in detail the period of 1965 to 1971, during which union struggles and political struggles became intertwined with judicial developments. Durmuş (2006), Güvenç (2008) and Koç (2013), on the other hand, investigated teachers' unions in Turkey's recent history, reviewing the important developments of the period chronologically. Yet, it should be noted that teacher unions cannot be said to be influential in social struggles compared to the pre-1980 era. The impacts of the teachers' unions were minimal throughout the post-1980 period, except for those struggles that peaked in the early 1990s and led to the establishment of the Education and Science Workers *Union (Eğitim-Sen) and Confederation of Public Sector Labor Unions* (KESK) (Koç, 2013, p. 15). I will return to this point; however, now, let me discuss, not contradictory, but cooperative relations between the AKP and some syndical organizations. In the following discussion, I focus on the Education Personnel labor union (Eğitim-Bir Sen).

The extraordinary increase in the number of members of this specific labor union confederation between 2002 and 2013 (the period of the AKP rule) should be emphasized. The number of members of the Confederation of the Public Servants' Labor Union (Memur-Sen) increased from 41,871 in 2002 to 707,652 in 2013. The largest labor union within the confederation, *The Education Personnel labor union (Eğitim-Bir Sen), accounts for* most of this expansion. Eğitim-Bir Sen is the biggest labor union in the education service sector, with 251,111 members as of 2013.[57] Most importantly, this expansion should be interpreted not as the result of

---

57 See *Statistics of Public Servants Labor Unions*, released by the Public Employers Union of Turkish

a sudden revival of solidarity between teachers but rather an indicator of stronger relations between labor unions and political parties and elites. When Eğitim-Bir Sen's orientations are inspected closely, cooperation with political powers is far more pronounced than any struggle on behalf of working teachers. Union discourse expresses this ethic of cooperation by redefining labor unions as civil society organizations aiming to influence government rather than oppositional organizations in conflict with the regime. Eğitim-Bir Sen clearly distinguishes its perspective from what it terms 'ideological unionism,' a kind of 'quarrelsome unionism' that refuses to cooperate with the state, seeks to disrupt the labor peace, and ultimately fails to protect workers' rights (Göktürk et al., 2012, p. 116).

In 2012, Eğitim-Bir Sen declared support to Law No. 6287 58 (popularly known as the '4+4+4 bill') that would divide 12 years of mandatory schooling into three levels. He described it as 'breaking the shackles of February 28.'[58] Eğitim Bir-Sen's other attitudes and stances in line with the AKP's ideological and political orientations can be exemplified as well.[59] The most striking among them is the Labor and Social Security Minister Faruk Çelik's participation in the May Day celebrations jointly organized by Memur-Sen and Confederation of Righteous Trade Unions (Hak-İş) in 2012.[60] This collaboration reveals a union perspective that promotes harmony between labor and government.

Under the AKP rule, four resistance practices led by unions come to the foree: The first is KESK (henceforth Eğitim-Sen) and the second is the Platform for Teachers who are not Appointed (AYÖP), which was established to act on behalf of teachers who are not appointed. A mass protest (of which KESK was an important constituent) was launched in Ankara on April 1, 2008, against the Social Security and General Health Insurance Bill.[61] It was one of the most significant protests in recent history. Ankara's symbolic Kızılay Square, which had been closed to mass protests for a long time, was de facto opened to workers for this protest.[62] Another

Heavy Industry and Services Sector (2013) for the chart containing detailed information about the members of the trade union confederations between 2002-2013, http://www.tuhis.org.tr/resim/files/tum_kitap_2013_N.pdf

58 'February 28' refers to bloodless 'post-modern' coup which is known to have led to the fall of the country's first Islamist head of government, the now-defunct Welfare Party's (RP) Necmettin Erbakan. This occurred after a parade of tanks passed outside Ankara and an ultimatum was put to Erbakan to resign, following a National Security Council (MGK) meeting on February 28, 1997.

59 'Kesintili eğitim ile geçmişin prangalarından kurtulacağız', http://www.egitimbirsen.org.tr/manset-haberleri/kesintili-egitimle-gecmisin-prangalarindan-kurtulacagiz/1349

60 'Memur ve işçilerin 1 Mayıs coşkusu Tandoğan'a sığmadı', http://birlikhabersen.org.tr/memur-ve-iscilerin-1-mayis-coskusu-tandogana-sigmadi/2133

61 The Social Security and General Health Insurance Bill corresponds to a very important legislative regulation to realize the neo-liberal transformation of the social security system in Turkey. Therefore, it must be accepted as one of the most significant protests against neo-liberal transformation in the recent history.

62 'Ankara'da SSGSS karşıtları Kızılay'da', http://arsiv.kizilbayrak.net/index.php?id=249&tx_ttnews%5Btt_news%5D=24776&cHash=9e72d268ce60a9678c5c92c40c40ae3f

striking rally during the AKP era was the protest staged by Eğitim-Sen against the '4+4+4 bill' in Ankara on March 28 and 29, 2012. The protest was one of the few labor union protests to directly dissent against the ideological-political orientation of the AKP regime. Public workers across Turkey participated in work stoppages and parents were encouraged not to send their children to school.[63] Lastly, let me discuss a *boycott campaign,* introduced by several Alevi associations, Eğitim Sen, and the United June Movement (a political platform, composed of political parties and individuals participating in Gezi protests, and aiming to struggle against the AKP's reactionary and authoritarian policies) claiming *scientific and secular education.* Parents, once again, were advised not to send their children to school across the nation on February 13, 2015. It was an effective campaign. The government realized the campaign as a serious threat to its religion-oriented educational policies, and so, some of the members of United June Movement were arrested.[64]

For its part, the AYÖP has drawn attention as a platform struggling against the unemployment of teachers, which has become an important problem under the AKP regime. Though weakly institutionalized, it made the voice of those teachers who are not appointed heard through many protests. The AYÖP is an important organization, as it brought together those teachers who are not represented by unions either due to legal obstacles or because they lie outside of union priorities. Members of the AYÖP staged effective protests despite their limited means and institutionalization challenges. The protests of the AYÖP, such as a press statement on August 15, 2010 and a two-day-long sit-in staged in Ankara, were rather successful. Prime Minister Recep Tayyip Erdoğan's agenda should be remembered in light of his words: 'What in the world is the Union of those who cannot Become Teachers? What's that? ... Some things in Turkey are really becoming ridiculous.'[65]

Political Regime: The Third Context for Understanding Transformation and Resistance in Education

For an analysis of the ideological-political role of education, one has to examine the general ideological-political agenda of the AKP, rather than the regime's political economy ambitions. From this perspective, the education is approached as a field through which the regime extends its reach into social life.

To this end, I examine the relations between education policies and the ideological-political aspects of the regime. I want to highlight here, within a brief

---

63 'Eğitim-sen greve gidiyor', http://www.dunya.com/egitim-sen-greve-gidiyor-149554h.htm
64 '4 günde 4 genç tutuklandı', http://www.dha.com.tr/4-gunde-4-genc-tutuklandi_874581.html
65 'Erdoğan'dan emekçilere: Direnmeyin, birbirinize düşmanlık edin!', http://haber.sol.org.tr/devlet-ve-siyaset/erdogandan-emekcilere-direnmeyin-birbirinize-dusmanlik-edin-haberi-55264

overview of the continuities and breaks in Turkey's political history, how the education reforms of the AKP era are unique.

Bourdieu and Passseron (1977) and Illich (1971) regard education as the field in which the dominant ideology is reproduced, focusing on the impact of education on people at the macro level. Apple (2004) and Greaves et al. (2007) similarly take education as a field of reproduction, situating their analyses within neoliberalism and the transformation of the state. Literature on critical pedagogy in Turkey should be interpreted within this context (İnal, 2004; Ünal, 2005). According to Hill (2003, pp. 4, 19), teachers are guardians of labor power; playing a crucial role in the social reproduction of labor power by transferring skills, qualities, and capacities to future workers, teachers can nevertheless serve a counter-hegemonic function by equipping students with the critical capacities needed for resistance and struggles for economic or social justice. Indeed, teachers stood at the forefront of social opposition in Turkey in the 1960s and 1970s (Durmaz, 2014, p. 130). One of the most significant characteristics of that era was the intensification of social struggles and the gains won in favor of labor classes. Teachers participated in the social struggles of the time as educational workers formed democratic institutional mechanisms like the Teachers' Labor Union of Turkey (TÖS), the Primary School Teachers' Labor Union of Turkey (İLK-SEN), and the Association for Union and Solidarity of Teachers of Turkey (TÖB-DER). In the capacity of these organizations, teachers were struggling against unjust working conditions and for greater employee rights; at the same time, they participated in broader political struggles, endeavoring to build anti-imperialist and anti-fascist lines of resistance.

Highlighting the peculiarities of AKP's conservative and Islamist agenda, Okçabol (2005) examined the Turkish education system through an historical periodization. Okçabol's study is significant for its comprehensive empirical data as well as its grounding of education policies within an ideological-political analysis. While Okçabol does not discuss labor processes or unionization, his study is valuable for our discussion of changes in the ideological-political content of education. Yücesan-Özdemir and Özdemir (2012), on the other hand, discuss neoliberal transformation in education within its political economy dimensions, regarding the reforms as a result of transformation in labor-capital relations.

While a comprehensive analysis of education must take into consideration labor-capital relations, this approach is not sufficient in the case of Turkey. Neoliberal educational reforms cannot be properly scrutinized by concentrating only on the labor process or unionization practices apart from its ideological-political context. In contemporary Turkey, we do find a kind of crystallization of the capitalist and modernizing processes that have been at work since the birth of the Republic. On the one hand, teachers have become members of a profession that 'the bourgeoisie has stripped of its halo' (Marx & Engels 2002, p. 119); on the other hand, teachers, who were playing significant roles in building a modern and secular nation-state, have become instruments in raising a pious generation. Said otherwise, while the transformation of education serves as a unique example of the neoliberal re-proletarianization of white-collar workers, it also reveals a network of social relationships marked by ideological-political polarizations and conflicts. Moreover, one should bear in mind that acquisitions in favor of the working classes in Turkey between 1960 and 1980 were achieved as a result of resistance practices that had, at their core, a pro-Enlightenment, secular, and anti-imperialist focus, rather than a narrowly defined class-based perspective.

In Marxist literature, education is defined as an ideological and political institution working in the service of social (class) reproduction and determined by relations of production. From this perspective, education protects the power of dominant classes, legitimizing relations of exploitation in the eyes of the exploited classes and oppressed social groups. Education has a similar function in contemporary Turkey. The dominant class/classes in Turkey made efforts to constitute an ideological-political formation, expressed in education policies that protect their interests and legitimize that formation in the eyes of the masses. The ideological-political mission attributed to teachers in the early years of Republic was to ensure the future of the young Republic and nation-state, which was built step by step. Mustafa Kemal Atatürk's speech in his address to the Teachers Union of Turkey in 1924 explicitly demonstrates this:[66]

Devoted teachers and educators of the Republic ... the new generation will be the product of your work. The value of your work will be proportionate to the extent of your proficiency and devotion. The republic needs mentally, scientifically, technically, and physically strong guards of upright character.

This speech shows how modern education was an element of the Kemalist regime; it was used as an instrument of nation-state building, with nationalist and pro-independence content. Under the Kemalist rule, certain education policies were implemented to secularize the state apparatus and to break the influence of religion over society. About 80 years after Mustafa Kemal Atatürk's speech, Prime Minister Recep Tayyip Erdoğan indirectly addresses teachers as follows:[67]

What I said was ... raising pious generations ... I'm still at the same point. Do you expect from us to raise an atheist youth as a party, which has a conserva-

---

66 For Mustafa Kemal Atatürk's address on the occasion of Congress of Teachers' Union of Turkey on August 25, 1924, see Bilir (2011).

67 See 'Dindar gençlik yetiştireceğiz' (We will raise pious generations), February 18, 2007, Retrieved from http://www.hurriyet.com.tr/gundem/19825231.asp

tive-democratic identity? We will raise conservative, democratic generations that protect their principles inherited from history. We are here for it.

The statements of Mustafa Kemal Atatürk and Recep Tayyip Erdoğan show that educational activities are shaped within a certain ideological-political axis and these axes shift according to governments' political projects. Of course, it is worth noting that the ideological-political axes of the statements are quite different from each other. Above all, the promise of 'raising pious generations' by the most authoritative persona reveals the ideological-political character of the new political regime. Moreover, that discourse has had many practical equivalents. As a result of amendments in the curricula, the books in the list of '100 Fundamental Literary Works' recommended to students by the Education Ministry were re-translated into Turkish with an Islamic interpretation. One pillar for the project of raising pious generations was thus built. Eğitim-Sen, drawing upon a book on Islamic interpretations, revealed that the original texts of the literary classics were altered to have an Islamic twist. Characters in Oscar Wilde's *Happy Prince* wish each other a 'blessed morning,' while Pinocchio asks for food in 'Allah's name,' and even a fox in a La Fontaine tale tells a fisherman, 'May Allah keep your path free.'

One of the most remarkable examples of the AKP's religious influence is the opportunities offered to graduates of Imam Hatip schools. Rather than being raised as religious functionaries, graduates of Imam Hatip schools were designated by the new regime as a future pool of personnel for various occupations after receiving religious education. The crucial question about Imam Hatip schools is this: Are those schools designated as vocational schools for raising religious functionaries? Or is the main aim that of state-oriented religious education for future civil servants and employees? (Coşkun and Şentürk, 2012, p. 168). Evidence suggests that Imam Hatip schools are now oriented to the religionization of the whole society through education. For example, since women cannot become imams or muezzins according to Islam, the only option for female graduates of Imam Hatip schools is to become teachers of religion courses in schools. However, the number of female students in Imam Hatip schools dramatically exceeds the number of vacant positions for religion teachers (Coşkun & Şentürk, 2012, pp. 168-169). Hereby, it can be realized as an example of the religion-oriented educational polices of AKP government.

A survey disclosed that not only female students but also male students of the Imam Hatip schools intend to work as neither religious functionaries nor religious educators. 62 percent of the students in Imam Hatip schools do not want to be an imam or muezzin; they are instead aiming to become doctors, teachers, or lawyers (Coşkun & Şentürk, 2012, p. 169). This shows that Imam Hatip schools are no longer considered vocational schools by the public because the conservative parents whose children are learning at Imam Hatips have never recognized them as disadvantaged educational institutions preventing their children, for example, from being a doctor, a teacher, or a lawyer since the AKP came to power. Besides, it is important to state that the social perception mentioned above did not spontaneously emerge, but it was created by the AKP itself.

It is worth commenting briefly on the ideological-political character of the bill popularly known as '4+4+4' (Law No. 6287). This law amends the Primary School and Education Law (and some other laws), by dividing mandatory schooling into three tiers, increasing it from 8 to 12 years, and reinforces religious education. By reintroducing junior high school branches of Imam Hatip schools, enrolment in these schools from the fifth grade onwards was enabled. In addition, courses such as 'The Quran' and 'The Life of our Prophet [Mohammed]' entered secondary school curriculum as elective classes (Okçabol, 2013, p. 42). As a result, religious teaching in accord with Sunni Islam was unprecedentedly reinforced.

At this point, important questions should be raised: Why are branch teachers for classes such as mathematics or Turkish in primary schools deemed unnecessary? Are mathematics or Turkish lessons easier to teach compared to religion lessons? Answering these questions by taking the basic requirements of teaching activity into account would be inadequate. In other words, it is impossible to answer these questions without taking into account the conservative worldview of the AKP. This situation is just one of the reflections of the political cleavages in Turkey over the education system.

When religious thought becomes an organic element of the political regime, it paves the way for transformations not only in state institutions and official ideology, but also in the individuals' daily lives. The examples mentioned above confirm this situation. Moreover, religious thought in general—and the ideological-political orientations of the AKP in particular—also affect intermediary organizational forms between state administration and individuals. In other words, organizations/institutions in the social/political structure are more or less affected by this transformation.

Conclusion

In this study, the transformations within the Turkish education system have been examined in terms of the ideological-political dimensions of AKP. In lieu of a comprehensive analysis of AKP reforms in relation to the continuities and breaks in educational policies throughout the history of the Republic of Turkey— indeed a necessary future project—I have offered an introduction for a tentative study focusing both on the general ideological-political character of education reforms that refers to the reproduction of relations of exploitation and power, and the ideological-political orientations of the AKP sustaining anti-secular polices to raise pious generations who are realized as loyal subjects to the new political regime. The hegemony of political Islam over education and Turkish society is not insignificant, nor is it a 'Kemalist illusion' as liberal arguments claim. In Turkey, it is clearly known that liberal intellectuals are very critical of Kemalist secularism referring to a radical modernization project against traditional structures and political Islam. Furthermore, liberals usually argue that there is no real danger threatening secularism, and most of the claims drawing attention to conservative/Islamic project of AKP are just arguments of 'Kemalist elites' who have been losing their privileged situation under AKP rule. However, liberal arguments mentioned above cannot be realized as true. As shown in this study, the AKP has an aim to create a new society by raising pious generations as Erdoğan declared before.

Therefore, any viable opposition to educational reforms should not limit itself to economic struggles within the context of labor unions; instead, it should build a clear and compelling ideological-political line against the dominant discourse of the AKP regime. Having examined education reform and resistance at three levels of analysis—through labor processes, unionization, and the political regime—we can summarize the potential for effective resistance as follows: If the encroachment of the political regime into schooling (and social life in general) is to be contested, then the locus of resistance is neither the individual teacher (worker) nor labor unions; rather, it is the highly politicized social movements to struggle against the AKP regime. To this end, the ideological-political dynamics that characterized the Gezi Resistance of 2013 should be examined. This should be the endeavor of the intelligentsia; the rest, as they say, will be left to revolutionary politics.

References

Adıgüzel, E. (2013). Eğitim Metalaştırılırken Okullar Ne Yapar? *Sendika*. Retrieved from http://www.sendika.org/2013/04/egitim-metalastirilirken-okullar-ne-yapar-er-gul-adiguzel/

Aksoy, H. H. (2013). Eğitimde Teknoloji Kullanımına İlişkin Eleştirel Bir Değerlendirme. In N. Kurul & T. Öztürk (Eds.), *Kamusal Eğitim Eleştirel Yazılar* (pp. 107-129). Ankara: Siyasal.

Aksoy, M. (1974). *Devrimci Öğretmenin Kıyımı ve Mücadelesi*. Ankara: Gündoğan.

Apple, M. W. (2004). Creating difference: Neo-liberalism, neo-conservatism and the politics of educational reform. *Educational Policy, 18*(1), 12-44.

Bilir, A. (2011). Türkiye'de Öğretmen Yetiştirmenin Tarihsel Evrimi ve İstihdam Politikaları. *Ankara Üniversitesi Eğitim Bilimleri Fakültesi Dergisi, 44*(2), 223-246.

Bourdieu, P., & Passeron, J. C. (1977). *Reproduction in Education, Society and Culture*. London:Sage.

Coşkun, M. K., & Şentürk, B. (2012). The growth of Islamic education in Turkey: The AKP's policies toward Imam-Hatip schools. In K. İnal & G. Akkaymak (Eds.), *Neoliberal transformation of education in Turkey: Political and ideological analysis of educational reforms in the age of the AKP* (pp. 165-178). New York: Palgrave Macmillan.

Durmaz, O. S. (2014). *Türkiye'de Öğretmen Olmak: Emek Süreci ve Yeniden Proleterleşme, Ankara:* Notabene Yayınları.

Durmuş N. (2006). Bir Eylemi Örgütleme: 1969 Genel Öğretmen Boykotu. *Eğitim Bilim Toplum, 4*(15), 142-160.

Eğitim ve Bilim Emekçileri Sendikası. (2012). *Eğitimde AKP'nin 10 Yılı*. Ankara: Eğitim-Sen Yayınları.

Ercan, F., & Şimşek, G. (2013). Öğretmenlik Mesleğinin Dönüşümü/Dönüştürülme Çabaları: Ulus-devletin Muhafızlarını Yetiştirmeden Sermaye İçin Emek Gücü Yetiştirmeye. Sendika. Retrieved from http://www.sendika.org/2013/01/turkiyede-ogretmenlik-mesleginin-donusumudonusturulme-cabalari-ulus-devletin-muhafizlarini-yetistirmekten-sermaye-icin-emek-gucu-yetistirmeye-giz-em-simsek-fuat-ercan

Grace, G. (1985). Judging teachers: The social and political context of teacher evaluation. *British Journal of Sociology of Education, 6*(1), 3-16.

Greaves, N. M. (2007). Embourgeoisment, immiseration, commodification-Marxism revisited: A critique of education in capitalist systems. *Journal for Critical Education Policy Studies, 5*(1).

Güvenç S. (2008). Türkiye'de Öğretmen Sendikacılığı ve İLK-SEN. *Eğitim Bilim Toplum, 6*(22), 164-187.

Harvie, D. (2006). Value production and struggle in the classroom: Teachers within, against and beyond capital. *Capital and Class, 30*(1), 1-32.

Hill, D. (2003). Global neo-liberalism, the deformation of education and resistance. *Journal for Critical Education Policy Studies, 1*(1), 1-50.

Illich, I. (1971). *Deschooling society*. New York: Harper and Row.

İnal, K. (2004). *Eğitim ve İktidar: Türkiye'de Ders Kitaplarında Demokratik ve Milliyetçi Öğeler*. Ankara: Ütopya Yayınları.

Koç, Y. (2013). Öğretmenlerin Sendikalaşmasında Yaşanan Sorunlar. Öğretmen Dünyası, *400*, 15-19.

Marx, K., & Engels, F. (2002). *The Communist Manifesto*. Penguin Classics.

Okçabol, R. (2005). *Türk Eğitim Sistemi*. Ankara: Ütopya.

Okçabol, R. (2013). Son Otuz Yılda Eğitim Alanındaki Dönüşümler. In N. Kurul & T. Öztürk, T. (Eds.), *Kamusal Eğitim Eleştirel Yazılar* (pp. 33-46). Ankara: Siyasal.

Ozga, J., & Lawn, M. (1981). Schoolwork: Interpreting the labor process of teaching. *British Journal of Sociology of Education, 9*(3), 323-336.

Özoğlu, B. (2012). *New ways of organizing work in the public sector: The Turkish public education case*. Ankara Üniversitesi: Tartışma Metinleri.

Reid, A. (2003). Understanding the teachers' work: Is there still a place for labor process theory. *British Journal of Sociology of Education, 24*(5), 559-573.

Robertson, S. L. (2000). *A class act: Changing teachers' work, the state and globalization*. New York: Falmer.

Sachs, J., & Smith, R. (1988). Teacher Culture. *British Journal of Sociology of Education, 9*(4), 423-436.

Smyth, J. (1991). International perspectives on teacher sollegiality: A labor process discussion based on the concept of teachers' work. *British Journal of Sociology in Education, 3*, 323-346.

Stevenson, H. (2007). Restructuring teacher's work and trade union responses in England: Bargaining for change. *American Educational Research Journal, 44*(2), 224-251.

Thomas, D. (2005). Restructuring the teachers' labor process: The case of Greece. *Mediterranean Journal of Education Studies, 10*(2), 1-17.

Ünal, I. (2005). 'İktisat İdeolojisi'nin Yeniden Üretim Süreci Olarak Eğitim. *Ekonomik Yaklaşım, 16*(57), 35-50.

Yeom, M-H. (2005). *Professionalization and the reform of teaching, teachers and teacher education in the United States and the Republic of Korea: A critical discourse analysis* (unpublished doctoral dissertation). University of Pittsburgh.

Yücesan-Özdemir, G., & Özdemir, A. M. (2012). The political economy of education in Turkey: State, labor, and capital under AKP Rule. In K. İnal & G. Akkaymak (Eds.), *Neoliberal transformation of education in Turkey: Political and ideological analysis of educational reforms in the age of the AKP* (pp. 3-16). New York: Palgrave Macmillan.

PART II
STRUGGLING FOR COUNTER-PUBLICS IN 21st CENTURY TURKEY

9.
COUNTER-PUBLICS AND ORGANIZED LABOR

Beyond the Limits of Bourgeois Democracy

Ali Murat Özdemir

We are now faced with a deep helplessness in Turkey. It is very deep in two respects: First, either people cannot find a job or the jobs they have yield less but demand more. Second, people are subjected to the negative impacts of commodification and primitive accumulation processes: Pasture areas of villages are converted into private property, coasts are transformed into hotel resorts, forests are set on fire and then sold to the private sector under the name of 'degraded forest lands,' and brooks are taken over by owners of hydroelectric power plants. In short, privatization dispossesses women and men living in Turkey of earth, air, and water.

One can argue that these processes already existed before the Justice and Development Party (AKP) rule was established. But they were not in place extensively. Substantial changes have taken place in regulations on tenders, municipalities, privatization, tobacco, energy, land property, husbandry, and other areas. More than 10 million people have been displaced by these processes (Boratav, 2012). The structure of agriculture, which was dependent upon small producers, has been dissolving at a greater pace than ever before (Aydın, 2005). Our strained dependency on the little income we earn in cities is higher than ever. Turkey has become well acquainted with urban poverty under the AKP rule. Social security systems are placed on the market and new accumulation units for the private sector are formed. The pension rights of working people are at risk because of the insufficient pension payments. Healthcare service is about to be taken out of social security coverage. The costs of health services are increasing constantly. Indeed, the public sector has almost relieved itself of the burden of social reproduction in the transportation, education, and health sectors. There is widespread social and economic inequality in Turkey and poverty is sure to increase (Yücesan-Özdemir & Özdemir, 2008).

The future is rather ambiguous. Even that sense of familiarity we once felt in the repetitive workings of our social institutions has eroded, leaving us isolated and disconnected. New crises lead to further dislocation; people are scattered and unable to collectively organize against their structurally imposed helplessness.

In this chapter, the labor struggle over current legislation will be examined, along with an assessment of how things should change. The first section provides an overview of the (real) subordination of labor. The second section focuses on contemporary organizational conditions for resistance against destructive processes of commodification. Taken together, these sections contribute to a better understanding of the organized 'helplessness' in Turkey today.

Demands Within the Limits of Bourgeois Democracy: Matters that Should be Changed in Current Legislation

In this section, the current legislation in Turkey will be discussed under several subheadings. Both individual and collective elements of the labor legislation will be discussed throughout. Suggestions for change within the current system are also made, although one should bear in mind that these are dependent upon the actions of organized labor; their success will be proportionate to the scale of organized resistance.

Working Hours

The labor force in Turkey today accepts lengthy work hours in dangerous environments. Average weekly working hours in all sectors of industry increased between 2002 and 2012. Turkey is globally competitive when it comes to wages, work safety, and working hours, but it has not developed national policies over energy, transportation, and goods for competitive costs for laborers. Even the provisions of Labor Law No. 4857, designed to bring some protection to the unemployed or those working within informal work structures (50 percent), are not widely applied. This situation is related not only to the structure of bourgeois power and that of its international allies, but also to the global conjuncture. Policies under current conditions are deeply punitive against labor.

According to Labor Law No. 4857, the maximum working time is 45 hours per week. Nevertheless, articles 41 and 64 of the Labor Law increased the daily working hours up to a level that prevents laborers from fulfilling even their biological needs. For instance, article 63 paved the way for overtime work without overtime payment: 'Providing that the parties have so agreed, working time may be divided by the days of the week worked in different forms on condition that the daily working time must not exceed 11 hours.' In other words, daily working time had been increased to 11 hours in practice.

I recommend that references to Article 63 that pave the way for excessive working time should be removed. If this suggestion receives intensive objections, then 11 hours of working time should be decreased to 9 hours. Moreover, the sanctions in Article 104, titled 'Violation of the provisions on organization of work' should be strictly implemented given the prevalence of repeated violations. Fines should be increased in cases of repetition and other sanctions should be imposed. The structure of committees given the task of determining both the regulations and the violations should be revisited within this framework.

Precarious Work

Informal labor markets occupy a significant place on the agenda, since a substantial part of the labor force in Turkey is excluded from full-time and secure employment. Subcontract work, home-oriented work, on-call work, temporary contract work, part-time work, and other precarious contract work have become the most common employment forms.

Dismissal (the termination of labor contract) has been facilitated through Labor Law No. 4857. Indefinite duration labor contracts that require severance payment in case of dismissal have been replaced by definite duration labor contracts that do not require severance payment at the end of the contract. Seeking judicial remedy has been abolished because of a provision in Article 11 of the Labor Law, namely, 'an employment contract for a definite period must not be concluded more than once, except when there is an essential reason which may necessitate repeated (chain) contracts.' Yet, the protective provisions of International Labor Organization (ILO) conventions and of the European Union consider indefinite duration labor contracts as the basic form of wage relation and general protective provisions are predicated on this legal form. In addition, subcontracting practices that found a broad range of field of application in the public sector provided employers the opportunity to hand over the responsibility to the subcontractor.

Different forms of work should be subjected to the same sanctions, and the indefinite duration labor contract should be the principal form of work. When it comes to subcontracting, the tendency to distribute work to subcontractors that was previously performed by a business firm in the total production process of a particular commodity should be prevented.

Last but not least, regulations on dismissal, which have been facilitated in the Labor Law, should be re-regulated in favor of laborers and severance payments should be implemented for definite duration labor contracts. Procedures in accord with workplace democracy for dismissals should be developed.

Minimum Wage, Unemployment Insurance, and Employment Agencies

The monthly minimum wage in Turkey is rather low (less than one fourth of the amount sufficient for a family of four). The so-called unemployment insurance is not applicable for employees working informally (accounting for approximately 50 percent of the working population). There are also very strict conditions that one must satisfy to benefit from this insurance, even for the formally employed population. Employment agencies, for their part, have lost their public mandate, becoming profit-seeking mediators in the business of marketing workers. The right to establish labor unions should be provided for students as well as the unemployed for them to protect their interests. The means of organization and operation of these labor unions, like all other unions, should be improved.

The monthly minimum wage should be increased to a level that is sufficient for subsistence, and the entitlement conditions to receive unemployment benefits should be re-regulated in favor of labor; the scope of unemployment insurance should be extended to the informal sector. Employment agencies should also be reorganized on the mandate of providing a public service.

Social Security and Healthcare

In the previous section, we have offered suggestions for improving the working conditions for labor. In this section, we will discuss social provisions of health care, education, and retirement public services that are, of course, predominantly produced by the state, non-profit seeking, and aimed at securing the common interest of the public.

There is an increasing orientation away from public provisioning towards the marketization of social security and health. The state is withdrawing from its social reproduction responsibilities. This is clearly seen in the transformation of the pension system. The law on Private Pension System was drafted in 1999 and adopted in October 2001 and the legal and institutional framework was completed in 2002. The law (No. 4447) was drawn up in accordance with the advice of the World Bank and with backing from the Association of Turkish Industrialists and Businessmen (TÜSİAD). When the dramatic decrease in public pension payments is taken into account, the significance of the private pension system can be comprehended. While the former is a collective right originating from service to the public, the latter corresponds to an individual right established through a contract and based on the weakening of social policies.

Another significant example of the orientation away from society toward the individual is Law No. 5510 on Social Security and Universal Health Insurance, which was introduced after the restructuring of social security institutions. The law is part of the 'Program for Transformation of Healthcare,' which was presented to the public in June 2003, and is comprised of regulations in accordance with the programs and principles of the World Bank and the International Monetary Fund (IMF).

To provide health and a secure future for everyone, it is important to grant citizens social rights guaranteed in the Constitution, such as healthcare and social security, and it is important to render the state responsible for this guarantee. In addition, above-mentioned services should be produced as a public service without profit-seeking. In short, the social state should be brought back into the agenda again, even though the political and ideological conditions that created it are no longer in place. This suggestion, which appears to some to be impossible, is based to a certain extent on the idea that the current crisis cannot be overcome by pursuing current (neoliberal) policies.

The freedom of organization and the freedom of expression should be protected and citizens should be permitted to exercise their rights within new organizational forms. Labor organizations should be supported to better incorporate the demands of the working class for social rights and a social state. These suggestions, like those outlined above, are contingent on the existence of struggle, both inside and outside the labor union.

Organized Labor

We can summarize the overall picture as follows: The number of unionized workers is decreasing dramatically. Less than six percent of private sector workers are members of a labor union. The objective bases for labor unions are eroding in the deregulated and flexible labor market, where the share of formal workers is shrinking day by day. While employment of definite-duration contracted personnel prevails over secured employment (civil servants) in public offices, temporary, contracted, and/or subcontracted employment in private sector obstructs union-ization.

Solidarity networks are also being established as aid organizations that operate under the patronage of the government and Gulf capital, instead of workers' own organizations or traditional institutions. In recent years, the activities of aid organizations against the government, even those driven by religious ideology, are being blocked. The involvement of labor unions in social solidarity networks has been hampered by current legislation: Since labor unions cannot establish membership relationships with anyone but active workers, and the scope of their activities are limited to defending economic rights of workers against the employer, their activity outside the factory has become almost impossible. They can neither act like an association, nor have characteristics of a cooperative, nor manage properties like foundations.

The situation gets even direr when labor unions are examined in the field of industrial relations to which they are confined: Today, labor unions in Turkey are encountering very crucial legal restrictions that include elements of both collective labor law and individual labor law. Collective labor law is based upon two codes (Law No. 2821 on Labor Unions and Law No. 2822 on Collective Labor Agreement, Strike and Lockout) that remained valid until very recently. These provisions have also remained valid up until today, almost without any amendments. Even though Law No. 6356 (on Labor Unions and Collective Bargaining Agreements) replaced Law No. 2821 and 2822 in 2012, the situation is no different.

Articles 51 to 54 of the Constitution, which was drafted after the 1980 military coup, were formulated to regulate industrial relations in favor of capital. Since the decision in 1999 on Turkey's candidacy for European Union membership, Turkey has adopted numerous important Constitutional and legal reforms intended to strengthen democracy, the rule of law and the protection of human rights. However, these efforts did not include any positive development in the Constitutional articles regulating collective labor law in Turkey. The main body of the Constitutional text on the collective rights of the labor front still holds the institutional design of the 1980 military takeover, which primarily targeted the working class and its allies. Today, the Constitutional articles regulating the collective rights of workers have massive discrepancies when compared with the Constitutional systems of Western European States.

Articles 51 through 54 of the 1982 Constitution pertain to the collective rights of labor. The right to organize labor unions is described in Article 51, which limits the right to establish labor unions in various ways. It is important to note that the definition of 'worker' is not included in the article. This is a source of subsequent violations of the right to organize. Governments can interfere with the right to organize, without infringing on the Constitution, by way of employing restrictive definitions of the term in the relevant parliamentary laws. Currently, what the labor front in Turkey needs is a broad definition for organizing, for instance, the retired and the unemployed, into labor unions. In addition, Article 90 of the Turkish Constitution states that Turkey is bound to let international agreements in the realm of human rights prevail over its own parliamentary laws.[68] The ratified UN Declaration and 1966 twin agreements on human rights and the European Declaration on Human Rights state that everybody has the right to form trade unions to protect his or her collective and personal interests. Currently, despite court rulings stating otherwise,[69] there is no clear and satisfying reason why a retired worker and/or unemployed person should not have the right to establish and/or be a member of a trade union.

Furthermore, the first paragraph of Article 51 states that the activities of labor unions should be limited solely to the economic and social interests of their members. This is extremely problematic since political rights cannot be separated from workers' economic and social rights or interests. Moreover, the ILO Convention 87 on freedom of association is ratified by Turkey. Article 3 of Convention 87 states that 'workers' and employers' organizations shall have the right to draw up their constitutions and rules' and that 'the public authorities shall refrain from any interference which would restrict this right or impede the lawful exercise thereof.'[70] Last but not least, labor unions cannot be forced to represent their individual members who, under the current situation, are actively working under a labor contract. Labor unions represent, to a certain extent, the working class as a collective entity composed of retired, unemployed, and actively working people under various statutes.

The right to collective bargaining is regulated in Article 53. The first paragraph of the Article states that collective bargaining agreements regulate reciprocally

---

68 The revised European Social Charter was signed by the AKP government in October 2004. The AKP government expressed reservations and the Turkish parliament refused to ratify the articles of the revised Charter regulating the rights of workers.

69 On October 9, 2007, Ankara's 17th Civil Court of General Jurisdiction, following the Court of Appeals order, ruled to close Emekli-Sen (a trade union that was established for protecting the benefits of retired people in Turkey) on the basis of Article 51 of the Constitution. However this groundless verdict did not, in any sense, undermine Turkey's position in the accession negotiations with the EU, nor did it echo in European labor circles. The same attitude applied to the trade unions of students and of unemployed. Umut Sen, a trade union established for the purpose of organizing the insecure workers and unemployed, is under pressure to be closed. In the same vein Genç-Sen (a trade union of students) was closed in 2011.

70 This matter brings back memories of the case of the teachers' union, Eğitim-Sen The union has always been under severe pressure for its proposals on the necessity of education in one's own mother tongue. The authorities tried over and over again to close down the union on the basis of an annulled clause stressing the necessity of mother tongue in education, notwithstanding the fact that this demand and its formulation in the text was perfectly in line with international legislation in the realm of human rights.

economic and social positions and conditions of work. The third paragraph acknowledges the right of public servants and public employees' right to collective bargaining. The problem rests in the following paragraphs. Paragraph four clearly announces that in case a conflict arises during the negotiations, public officials and other public servants will not be entitled to strike. The only remedy for the holders of these positions is an arbitration tribunal established solely for dealing with conflicts between government and public servants. Additionally, paragraph four affirms the arbitration tribunal should be established by the government by way of a parliamentary law. Before the 2010 amendments, public servants and public employees had the right to conduct meetings with the relevant administrative body. In case of disagreement, all the trade unions composed of public servants and public employees could do was to compose a text, which would be submitted to the Council of Ministers regardless of the nature of the disagreement. The novelty of the 2010 amendment to article 53 rests here. Public servants are now entitled to apply to an arbitration tribunal whose members shall be elected by the government and who has the power to issue absolute decrees.

The last paragraph of article 53 furnishes for the government a vast space to decide on the content and scope of the collective bargaining agreements. Furthermore, the paragraph states that the exceptions, beneficiaries, and procedures of the collective bargaining agreement shall be decided by law.

Constitutional Article 54 regulates the right to strike. The first paragraph of Article 54 clearly states that workers have no right to strike if the dispute in question does not arise from the collective bargaining process. This clearly means that if the employer decides to waive his obligations arising from the collective agreement, workers will not be entitled to strike on the basis of this violation. The Constitution clearly states that the conclusion of a collective bargaining agreement is distinct from its application. Put differently, Turkish workers can only call for a strike in the event that the dispute arises during the collective bargaining negotiations. Workers cannot go on strike to force employers to keep their word, for political reasons or for solidarity (they cannot support other workers by way of strikes). This article clearly repudiates the right to strike rather than regulating the right to strike.

Currently the law regulating strikes requires the trade union in question to prove it had the necessary majority to start a strike. In case of an objection, the conflict has to be settled in court. As a rule of thumb, it takes more than one year to decide the case. In addition, it is relatively easy in the Turkish legal system to fire a worker. Furthermore, the unregistered employment is the main legal instrument to weaken unionization and is used liberally (in more than 50 percent of contracts). In sum, the employer has the power to fire the unionized workers and to subordinate working people in its plant. Assuming that a group of workers manages to start a strike under these conditions, they must be extremely careful. They cannot, according to the second paragraph of the article, use their right 'in a manner contrary to the principle of goodwill, to the detriment of society *or* in a manner damaging national wealth.' If they are still determined to strike, then our constitution reminds workers on strike to research whether their strike plans fall within the scope of the law regulating 'the circumstances and places in which strikes and lockouts may be prohibited or intervened.' Because if not, 'the dispute shall be settled by the Supreme Arbitration Board at the end of the intervention period.' And don't forget that 'the decisions of the Supreme Arbitration Board shall be final and have the force of a collective bargaining agreement.' Under these conditions, politically motivated strikes and lockouts, solidarity strikes and lockouts, occupation of work premises, labor slow-downs, and other forms of obstruction become illegal.

Despite all assertions of reform, Law No. 6356 on Labor Unions and Collective Bargaining Agreements (dating back to 2012) adopted the same restrictions of its predecessors, with a few exceptions. Article 25 of Law No. 6356, which replaced Law No. 2821 on Labor Unions and Law No. 2822 on Collective Labor Agreement, Strike and Lockout, is in line with these restrictions. Article 25 of Law No. 6356 limits union security to workers who are working in a workplace employing at least 30 workers with indefinite duration labor contracts. Besides numerous legal restrictions, there is an endeavor to produce the prototype of 'yellow' unions and unionists. Unionists who do not fit this type are being dragged out of the system.

A certain part of the problems originates from the persistence on a single form of unionization. Industrial unionism and workplace unionism are in fact two interconnected organizational levels that complement each other. An attempt to abolish the former and to promote the latter paralyzes the structure of unionism. Allowing only workplace labor unions leads to the disorganization and disintegration of the labor union movement, yet allowing only industrial unions produces oligarchical union structures. When workers cannot create their own organizations on the basis of their own experiences, forming union structures that emanate on the workplace level and evolve into regional federations, then confederations and branch-of-activity-level labor unions are possible while they are becoming centralized without sacrificing democratization. Unionization practices in Turkey between 1946 and 1980 demonstrated this truth (Özveri, 2014).

It is particularly regrettable that, despite the very limited progress in EU negotiations, Turkey has achieved no significant progress in the field of collective labor rights. Moreover, case law has become more hostile to collective rights of labor than it was before the 2001 crisis. The AKP's 2003 'flexible' Labor Law (No. 4857) eroded the rights of labor in the realm of the technical division of labor. It is very clear that the Turkish labor legislation is not in line with the already weak international standards.

To resolve the current problems of the recent period, unions' field of activity should be enlarged to an extent exceeding the classical union law. The unemployed, the retired, and students should simultaneously have the right to establish associations, foundations, cooperatives, and independent legal entities that possess the qualification of being a labor union. Suggestions for organized labor will be examined in detail in the second section.

Demands Beyond the Limits of Bourgeois Democracy: New Organizational Forms and Opinions on Resistance

These assertions have focused on the scope and principles of labor organizations, the need for a new organizational form, potential demands of this organizational form, and the similarities and differences between new organizational forms and existing social organizational forms. Most of the assertions are not groundbreaking; they are drawn from the past and owe much to the old terrain of Marxism.

Scope of the Organization

The labor movement should have influence both *in* the extended reproduction process and *against* commodification and primitive accumulation processes. In other words, the workers' organizational activity should be involved at all levels on which the dictatorship of the bourgeoisie is established. Every opportunity of resistance missed is a moment of reestablished bourgeois power. Hence, a working class politics solely focused on extended reproduction processes. If labor persists on strictly adhering to the classical organization schemes even though power scales now correspond to infranational and supranational dimensions, labor movements will not succeed (see Balibar, 2003).

The scope of labor organization should reach to an extent that it can conduct struggles on many levels and in cooperation with other organizations. First, it should be strong enough to struggle against the 'new working relations,' which aim to peak the surplus value and to suppress the resistance. Second, it should reach to an extent that it struggles in all levels against the general economic structure itself.

Third, labor organization should extend into alliances with environmentalist, feminist, and peasant groups, to the extent that the latter share an awareness of processes of primitive accumulation. Participants struggling in the name of 'reforming the system' can fight along side those who are 'against the system.'

Principle of Organizing

Organizing is the activity of forming, reregulating, and stabilizing relationships. People in relationships are unique but the relations that they form are not. In fact, these relations correspond to certain abstract and general forms, and they impose themselves within a scope of identifiable spaces and processes (see Althusser, 2011). On the other hand, the thing that is being organized is not a factory or shipyard, it is people. From this perspective, organization can be moved from one production space to another. It can encompass the space of production, the level of contracts between 'equals,' and political formations at the same time. Organizations cannot be reduced exclusively to private or public spaces.

Organizational activity develops on the basis of the participants' common interests. In other words, we cannot imagine 'an organization dependent upon a particular interest externalized its participants.' Labor organizations are founded with the intention of representing—and working on behalf of—a group of people. They establish or protect a collective interest beyond those that can be converted into market terms.

We said that the common interests pursued by labor organizations and the collective rights that are demanded and advocated for correspond to an aggregate of class-based rights. Yet, the opposite is also possible. Ethnic or religious collectivities may have demands of rights and these rights can be properly placed under the index of collective rights as well. Advocacy of these rights may exclude the class axis. This is the tendency we have seen in recent years. The organization that emerges in this case—though its may be against primitive accumulation in some cases—does not take a stand against private property established upon the means of production, the subordination of labor to the process of valorization, and the commodification processes and primitive accumulation system that are regenerated constantly.

Out-of-class demands of collective rights attribute their legitimacy to the 'natural rights' of the collectivity for which they demand rights. In this case, demands are not made for those who are outside of this collectivity or those who cannot join this collectivity because of its historical and psychological characteristics. The 'other' of 'out-of-class collectivities' and the 'other' of the 'class collectivity' is fundamentally different. The former is based on the belief that the self can exist outside of commodification, proletarianization, and globalization processes. It would have nothing to say about class contradictions. There is no other term that can access helplessness that directly. There may be many reasons why your admittance to hospital is refused; yet, none of them would be as decisive as your class. Acts of solidarity can encompass everybody only on the basis of this term. Having emphasized that, let us turn back to the assertions over class-based organizing.

It is possible to organize wherever people engage in productive activity or affect productive activity due to their presence. The labor organization should remain mobile, with relationships comprising its basis, and it should defend its right of existence along with the collective interest that it protects or produces.

What has been said up to now can be summarized as follows:

1) An organization of laborers prioritizes collective rights discourse over individual rights rhetoric. The collective rights in question correspond to an aggregate of class-based rights.

2) Labor organization is an indispensable social space for transcending the imagination of the liberal individual and market individualism. This space needs anti-capitalist principles, Marxist theoretical positions and practices, and it must transcend ethnic and/or religious collectivities in order not to be paralyzed with communitarianism. These are reasonable elements of any effort of socialist/ Marxist organizing. In the absence of these elements, the organization will not succeed.

Demands

Acting in the opposite direction encourages a socialist social policy horizon. However, in the event of converting fields of healthcare, education, housing, pension, environment, and natural resources into the common property of society and linking up the common property with collective labor of society, a socialist/ Marxist intervention into the related field would be possible.

Those who provide the collective labor potentials of society (workers, the unemployed, those who perform unpaid domestic labor, producers of goods produced as part of non-value form) have the right to demand the common property of society by the very reason that they are part of this collectivity.

Therefore demands of labor organizations should encompass all façades of politics. We should bear in mind that collective labor does not drop out of the sky all of a sudden—it is the product of current production relations.

Organizational Capacity

With which capacities should our new social organization form/forms be equipped so that it can deal with the aforementioned issues and transform those into a common language and practices? If our question is correct, then our effort will not be wasted.

We have examined two aspects of helplessness common to capitalism. We have stated that socialist activity (resistance) should be organized despite all the helplessness. There is a need for a new social organization form (or forms), which can perform in both fields or provide coordination between social organization forms that have special features peculiar to these fields. For instance, the need for a new union form stands in the first field of the helplessness (against the private ownership of the means of production). Union forms that only think of economic struggle, that only organize the employed workers, and that only consider factories as worplaces cannot accomplish any goal.

Thus, we can argue that the new union form(s) should encompass the unemployed, pensioners, students, domestic labor, and street vendors. Questions of 'Why will you organize those people ... in order to increase their non-existing wages?' and 'How will such an organizing cover its own expenses?' will be brought forward. Appealing to those questions requires acknowledging the fact that the struggle is not restricted to the wage relationship; rather, it includes everything required for the moral and material reproduction of those who have labor power.

Organization capacity should include many demands: building day nurseries for childcare and schools in neighborhoods, demanding day nurseries and schools from locally or nationally organized power networks, lending a hand for potable water, and taking healthcare service. Therefore, wherever people carry out social production there is a kind of factory–the factory is everywhere. However, this factory is not the one where the capitalist imposes workplace rules. The motto of 'production is realized in private space of the owner of means of production' loses its meaning here. I am talking about an organizational capacity that would insist on these responsibilities. In other words, I am talking about an organizing that would push for the representation and demands of those who were alienated from the so-called state field. I am not talking about voluntary work or charity. I am talking about collective rights and public services.

Therefore, the new form of union is something more than a hybridization of current social organization forms (foundation, labor union, association, cooperation, party etc.).

Within this social imagination, the process of negotiations is conducted by participatory democracy (see Zizek, 2005). While the bourgeois content of the term of reconciliation' settles on actions of exclusion and postponement, the performance of new forms of Marxist social organization progresses through the discourse of inclusion. While formal (neo-liberal) democracy is seeking its nation, the latter is forming its class. While the former is closed, the later is open to newcomers, new thoughts, new freedoms, and new forms of activity on the axis of class solidarity. While the former is covered with a conservative/pious or modern/progressive nationalism, the latter enjoys the opportunities of being able to be internationalist.

A second space of the resistance (socialist activity) has to be built up against commodification and the primitive accumulation system. New form of organization should demand the collective properties of the society.

New forms of organization should direct their actions to both the national and supranational level. They should aim to be both one and many. Organizations should be a part of internal and external communication networks.

These organizations may make efforts to play their roles within legally separated but sociologically united units. Their roles include the regulation of reproduction in neighborhoods, conducting wage unionism, organizing new forms of working and/or resistance in the face of new labor processes, designing instruments of international solidarity building, and generating legitimate demands against political power holders.

While actors are exercising their right to 'free' movement, they may have to cope with the illegality originated from 'collective and organized action.' Yet, let us not forget that if something started to create obstacles, it means that it started to move forward.

Conclusion

This chapter has emphasized six points:

First, the current labor legislation in Turkey is more backwards than it is in states linked to the international capitalist system.

Second, the current system can be partially ameliorated through struggles. The act of pushing the limits is the precondition of capacity building.

Third, the current organizing methods and fields of activity of labor organizations should be questioned and changed. Labor organizations possess the right to deal not only with extended reproduction (of both capital and labor), but also commodification and primitive accumulation processes.

Fourth, there is a need for a new union-form. This new form cannot be established or realized simply by bringing the current ones together. The new form should be debated. Thus, any ideas about what should change should be discussed and developed through debates. Penning down this list is important even if it will transform through practices. What new organizational forms will be capable of beyond anti-capitalism is a question not only for practice but also for theory.

Fifth—although it seems contradictory—producing socialist social policy demands in a capitalist society is possible, albeit difficult. A number of collective rights should be advocated on the basis of being owners of common property.

The owners of this common property are those who constitute social labor power. The collective owner of labor potential is the constituent element of society, and this element must have the unlimited right to organize. Your rights—in our theoretical construction—derive out of your contribution to the production (and re-production) of life. This contribution is never reduced to the production of tangible commodities; rather, it encompasses the production of affection and love and the protection of hope. We cannot imagine collectivism without laborers nor a socialist republic without laborers' unlimited right to organize.

Sixth, organized resistance on both the micro and macro levels is essential.

References

Althusser, L. (2011). *Sur la Reproduction.* Presses Universitaires de France.

Aydın, Z. (2005). *The Political Economy of Turkey.* London: Pluto Press.

Balibar, E. (2003). *We, the People of Europe? Reflections on Transnational Citizenship* (J. Swenson, Trans.). Princeton University Press.

Boratav K. (2012). *Türkiye İktisat Tarihi (1908—2009).* Ankara: İmge Kitabevi.

Özveri, M. (2014). İşçi Hakları ve Hukuk. In A. M. Özdemir & M. Ketizmen, M. (Eds.), *Türkiye'nin Hukuk Sisteminde Yapısal Dönüşüm* (pp. 173-216). Ankara: İmge.

Yücesan-Özdemir, G. & Özdemir, A. M. (2008). *Sermayenin Adaleti: Türkiye'de Emek ve Sosyal Politika.* Ankara: Dipnot.

Zizek, S. (2005, July-August). Against Human Rights. *New Left Review, 34,* 115-131.

10.
COUNTER-PUBLICS AND LOCAL PRACTICES

The Struggle for Revolutionary-Popular Government

Ahmet Kerim Gültekin

*When it comes to local government,
the lack of a common, institutionalized perception
that is based on practical knowledge prevents us from
progressing in a systematic and scientific manner. Those of
us with the intention of building a socialist future must draw
lessons from the struggles being waged in the field of local
government and bring these lessons together.*

Tekin Türkel (Mayor of Mazgirt)

We have a saying in Turkey: 'There is still hope until the final breath is drawn.' No matter how grim the situation is, hope will endure until things reach a definite conclusion. Hope endures and the struggle continues. For the past couple of years, this phrase has been an adequate expression of the general state of mind prevalent among workers, peasants, students, and representatives of various groups who have been struggling for their economic, social, and political rights against the neo-liberal depredation and destruction that was intensified under the AKP's 12-year rule. For years, the anti-capitalist political and economic struggles had a very limited base of mass support. However, the Gezi Uprising lit a beacon of hope in the darkest of times and carried these struggles onto a qualitatively new stage. These protests intensified various struggles that had faced the most brutal political repression for many years. The Gezi events gave these struggles new voice and legitimacy. Moreover, the struggle in the field of revolutionary-popular local governments, despite facing constant political attacks and economic reprisals by the AKP government, has also garnered strength due to the new voice and legitimacy of the Gezi events. It is these movements that are the focus of this chapter.

The struggle in the field of revolutionary-popular local government is an important historical focal point for the recent mass uprising—the long-term effects of which are yet to unravel. It is also an area that has been mostly overlooked in analyses of the people's struggle for democracy. In providing a tentative overview and evaluation of this field of struggle, I note at the onset that while there are many alternative forms of local government describing themselves as 'popular,' 'progressive,' or 'neo-progressive,' I focus on those attempts at 'revolutionary-popular' local government, distinguished for their socialist perspective. Aggressive neoliberalism in Turkey and elsewhere over the past decade has led to the various kinds of dissent that have aided the development of alternative local governments that do not necessarily have at their core a socialist vision. An example would be the emergence of ethnicity as an important determinant in alternative political and economic movements. In this chapter, I will focus on struggles for the formation of local representation with the following characteristics: they uphold anti-capitalist economic, social, and cultural programs for local government; they organize through the initiative of the people and are based on the people's own mass organizations; and they determine and supervise their candidates and mechanisms of administration through popular organizations.

With the exception of literature dealing with the Fatsa events of 1979 and 1980,[71] scholarly work on struggles for revolutionary-popular local governments (characterized by independent socialist candidates) is nonexistent. Unfortunately, the information we have on the subject is quite fragmented and meagre. New paths for research, however, have been opened up by the The Symposium of Revolution-

---

71 For recent studies evaluating the experience in Fatsa, see Türkmen (2006) and Morgül (2007).

ary-Popular Local Governments,[72] which was held in 2011 and is the basis for the arguments made in this chapter.

The Symposium brought together scholars, municipalities aiming for administering along revolutionary and popular principles, as well as dissident professional chambers. Propositions presented towards the end of this chapter are based on the very important theoretical and practical lessons to be drawn from the experiences of the participants, namely the Diyarbakır Metropolitan Municipality, the Hatay-Samandağ Municipality, the Hatay-Aknehir Municipality, the Dersim (Tunceli)[73]-Pertek Municipality, the Dersim-Hozat Municipality and the Dersim-Mazgirt Municipality. In this context, I shall attempt to examine the example presented by the Municipality of Mazgirt, which, since the municipal elections of 2009, is being governed by an independent socialist candidate who was elected on account of his alternative economic, social, and cultural program.[74]

This chapter has been written from an anthropological perspective and its principal goal is to evaluate the experiences of the Municipality of Mazgirt to contribute theoretical and practical knowledge of anti-capitalist, egalitarian and participative local governments that seek to defy the ravages of neoliberalism. It also aims to offer a humble contribution for future forms of struggle.

---

72 The Symposium of Revolutionary-Popular Local Governments, in whose organizational processes I actively participated, took place in Ankara on December 3 and 4, 2011 with an unexpectedly large turnout. It can be said that the discussions held were critical and quite productive. In the months following the event, the symposium and the various panels, meetings, and trips organized in Dersim as a part of it, as well as the Revolutionary-Popular Local Governments Workshop (16. 06. 2012) were targeted by 'counter-terrorism operations' and were subjected to an investigation by the state. More than 80 people were detained and 32 people—including the author of this article—were arrested. The total number of years people are being tried for exceeds one hundred and the judicial process is still on going. The speeches of the participating mayors and some of the presentations in the symposium were published by the Patika Kitap publishing collective. For this book, whose foreword I have written during my period of incarceration, see Gültekin and Gündoğdu, (2013). Also, to view the presentations during the symposium see: http://www.youtube.com/playlist?list=PL90F5D4D0EC748823

73 Both 'Dersim' and 'being from Dersim [*Dersimli*]' are ethno-cultural and socio-political indicators of identity. When we take a brief glance at the history of the region, it can be seen that during the *Tanzimat* [reorganization] period of the Ottoman State, there existed a large Dersim province encompassing the area of today's Tunceli, Elazığ, Erzincan, and Bingöl provinces. But with the coming of the Republic, it was divided and turned into modern day Tunceli. Recently, the ethno-cultural and socio-political differences of the region, characterized by the rebellions and uprisings of its Alevi and Kurdish communities as well as the state's campaigns of 'suppression,' have once again brought to the forefront in the age of neo-liberalism and identity politics. In this sense Dersim and *Dersimli* both sociologically and spatially characterize the Alevi-Kurds of Tunceli as well as the *Kurmanci* and *Kırmancki* speaking Alevi-Kurdish communities inhabiting a vast area covering Erzincan, Muş, Bingöl, Malatya, Maraş, and Sivas. This is because these communities are historically tied to this identity and in this sense the *Dersimli* identity indicates a common origin. Because of this, the terms Dersim and *Dersimli* have been used in this article to describe the Kurmanci and Kırmancki speaking Alevi-Kurdish communities, as it is their preferred spatial and ethno-cultural identity.

74 The independent socialist candidate Tekin Türkel was re-elected as the mayor of Mazgirt in the 2014 Municipal Elections. The Municipality of Mazgirt continues its activities through the people's councils formed during his previous term.

Local Government: The Evaluation of the Concept in the Context of Globalization and New Public Policy

With the process of globalization, discussions regarding locality have gained prominence. The debate over local government constitutes one aspect of such discussions, and when we take a look at various evaluations of local government, we clearly see that there are two main trends in this field. The first envisions a form of local government that will serve as an agent of the free market in this age of neo-liberalism to convert the social and biological existence of human beings, as well as all natural elements, into commodities. Such policies are often put into practice by governments and aim to restructure local governments as active intermediaries of the neo-liberal economic system in local markets (which have been dissociated from one another and have been socio-economically or culturally re-identified by international capital). The fact that terms such as 'autonomy,' 'local initiative,' 'liberal democracy,' and 'freedoms' are essential to this discourse can probably be considered one of the paradoxes of our age. On the other hand, a second trend also exists, which bases itself on a criticism of the dominant political structure and the free market economy. While there are many examples historically that fall into this category, we focus here on alternative forms of local government that rely heavily on contemporary socialist views.

A concept that has gained importance in the context of globalizing processes is the active role of localities (in Turkey, this refers to rural areas) in the process of neo-liberal capitalist industrialization and the new paradigms of modernization that this leads to. The process through which localities 'rediscover' their pre-modern identities relies, both politically and economically, on capitalism's strategy of renewing itself. The general tendency of modern capital accumulation was to become even more homogenous; in the post-modern era, however, capital spreads/expands through differentiation based on dissimilarities and thereby directly organizes and revives itself in localities. Hence, all administrative systems are being re-identified and re-structured. Forms of thought that present themselves as an alternative to the current system are actually reproduced within the confines of this system.

The present day policies of local government are better understood in light of the general trend displayed by neo-liberalism when it comes to local administration. According to this new understanding of public administration, the Weberian model of bureaucracy—dominant during the Keynesian times—had contributed to the progress of democracy and prosperity for a while (at least in the West). However, this model has now turned into the main cause of unwieldiness and ineffectiveness. Therefore, the organizational structure of the state needs to become more flexible; it has to be downsized and a broad system of local administration must be formed. In this context, public services are separated from the state and handed over to private enterprises. Public authority is relegated to the status of a mediator and public institutions are re-structured and operated as though they were private businesses. This itself leads to an important point of discussion, namely, the attempted removal of the distinction between those who make decisions for a more efficient free market system (i.e. the politicians) and those who execute these decisions (i.e. the bureaucrats). To put it in other words, the balance between criteria set forth by the state in the name of the public good (such as efficiency and productivity) and the policies of those holding political power is being reshaped to favor those in power (or more precisely, big business). In the process, civil servants are expected to take 'customer (citizen) satisfaction' into account and to carry out the state's tasks for the realization of this goal (Eryılmaz, 2002). Naturally, this is all done to attain a higher level of cooperation with the private sector and the objective is the transformation of public institutions in accordance with the administrative and operational principles of the private sector. Therefore, as with all other spheres of life, the discourse on local governments is being infiltrated by concepts such as 'productivity,' 'quality,' 'entrepreneurship,' 'supervisor,' 'set,' 'vision,' 'mission,' 'customer,' and 'market' (Günal, 2010, pp. 39-49).

In sum, the shrinking of the public sector, the expansion of the private sector, and the transformation of localities into enterprises are among the results of the new accumulation strategy adopted by the capitalist system. The restructuring of public institutions, goods, and services to match the functioning of the free market and the transfer of these elements into the hands of private sector have led to massive inequality. The determining principles of public service, such as 'fairness,' 'objectivity,' and 'public responsibility' have disappeared due to the market and management-based understanding that dominates the private sector. In this renewed model of public administration, the state, though in the position of a 'mediator,' operates in the interests of 'politicians' and continues to play an important role in a system that victimizes the vast majority.

Continuity and Renewal in Struggle: From Fatsa to the Symposium of Revolutionary-Popular Local Governments

The restructuring in the field of local governments caused by globalization, in carrying neoliberal market relations to the locality, has had identifiable negative effects. Also, in the context of administrative reforms that keep the system together, this transformation has opened up political spheres in favor of local government. In this sense, policies of localization produced by globalization have created certain unique dynamics of dissent or resistance. After all, local governments—even though they are under the political and economic control of the state—continue to hold an image as institutions that enable the people, in one way or another, to make and implement decisions concerning their everyday lives. It can also be stated that this general perception held by the people has led dissenting socialist movements to perceive local governments as an important stepping-stone to the people's struggle for self-government. The discussion concerning revolutionary-popular local governments, as well as struggle in this field, gained prominence in the early 2000s. One reason for this was the implementation of certain administrative reforms that strengthened this perception among the people. Many dissident political institutions attempted to take advantage of these partial opportunities.

Certain aspects of the current system—such as the present electoral thresholds, the fact that the professionalized understanding of politics in accordance with neo-liberalism is determined by the centers of capital and the obstruction of the people's participation in parties governed by certain elite circles—hamper the people's representation and constitute significant problems of the current 'democratic order.' Unique economic, political, and cultural demands posed by the localities have no representation in the aforementioned mechanisms and are simply ignored by the central administration. In spite of this, local governments, part of the very same governmental system, are still viewed as a particular political arena that facilitates the people's participation in local politics. While the 'democratic' system in this field bears similar faults to the 'democratic' system at the central level, it also has certain more favorable aspects in terms of regulating day-to-day life and monitoring decision-making. This situation becomes much more apparent in the context of districts and counties in the rural areas where the population is low and the economic and social differentiation is insignificant (Yıldırım, 2006, pp. 67-70).

In this sense, the understanding of revolutionary-popular local governments in Turkey is not one that aims to abolish the neo-liberal capitalist system on a local level. Futhermore, the main emphasis is on the democratization of the processes of decision-making concerning economic, social, and cultural issues. In this context, the term 'participation,'[75] used to express the inclusion of the people in

---

75 As representative crises become ever more perpetual in contemporary democracies, the term 'representation,'—with all its economic and political aspects—is gradually becoming a reference to a widely discussed model of alternative democracy. In this context, the crises of the traditional electoral, representative system and demands for direct democracy are emphasized. The current administrative model, where representatives come to office through legally sanctioned and regularly held elections and then elect representatives amongst one another (even though, on paper, these people are supposed to be accountable to the people) is seen as the fundamental problem. Because this system, in form, appears to be based on the will of the majority, in essence it leads to a structure of repression on the will of the minority. In addition, in this system the will of groups that are victimized or discriminated against—such as women, immigrants, workers, and ethnic minorities—is disregarded entirely. Representative institutions favor capital and are closely tied to lobbies and relations of privilege and patronage. These factors have generated intense discussion concerning processes of transition from representative democracy to direct democracy. A look at discussions regarding a

the process of decision-making, has gained importance on many levels over the past years. This is only natural, since the primary aspect of revolutionary-popular local government is the participation of the people—either directly or through an elected and monitored representative—in the process of making decisions. Another highly important issue worth noting is that practices of revolutionary-popular local government in Turkey have, in the past as in the present, taken place in small rural settlements. At first glance, this situation seems connected to the geographic, spatial, and cultural context shaping the relations between the rulers and the ruled. In addition, in settlements with a small population, it is easier to enable direct participation in processes such as decision-making and supervision.[76]

Before the 1980s, local administrations in Turkey had little significance in processes of democratization. Despite the limited nature of opportunities, the first fifty years of the Republic witnessed important experiences in this field.[77] The most important historical reference point for present-day discussions and practices concerning revolutionary-popular local governments is, without doubt, the 'socialist' oriented experience in Fatsa.[78]

If we attempt to compare the important practices of the Fatsa experience to contemporary examples of revolutionary-popular local government, we can

---

new model of governance shows that topics such as the raising of social consciousness, the sharing of responsibilities, emphasis on cultural rights, and the assurance of minority rights are stressed quite frequently. In accordance with this, the understanding of self-governance, where participants are active in all processes of administration, implementation, and supervision is seen as one of the fundamental principles of the participatory model. Thus, in this system, representation is based on a number of different social movements and, with the sharing of institutional power, all groups are able to participate in processes of decision-making. This is widely regarded as the theoretical basis of a new understanding of democracy—one which is characterized by the concept of participation (Kurtuluş, 2005).

76 For narratives and discussion on the subject (on the basis of district governance) see Gültekin and Gündoğdu (2012, pp. 199-240), Yıldırım (2006, pp. 75-84) and more specifically, for the experience in Fatsa see Morgül (2007) and Türkmen (2006).

77 For an important study concerning the history of relations between the central authorities and local governments, as well as the period of neo-liberal transformation, see Günal (2010).

78 If we wish to further our understanding of contemporary revolutionary-popular local governments, then we need to fully understand the specific historical and social conditions that have given rise to this particular experience. The second half of the 1970s was one of the most tumultuous periods in the history of Turkey. On the one hand, aggression against the popular opposition—both by official institutions and civilian paramilitaries—was widespread. Yet on the other hand, the scope of the struggle for a revolutionary democracy had expanded to its full limit (or at least as far as the particular conditions of that era allowed it to). It was under such conditions that the popular opposition won the right to local governance, through elections, in the district of Fatsa. Bordering the Black Sea, Fatsa had a population of 19,000, mostly comprised of people engaged in agricultural production. During that period there existed a contradiction between the hazelnut producing peasantry and the moneylenders and merchants. The revolutionaries interfered and tipped the scale of balance in economic life to favor the interests of the people, thus gaining popular support. When the previous mayor lost his life in 1979, elections were held and the independent candidate Fikri Sönmez, with the support of people affiliated with the publication *Revolutionary Path* (Devrimci Yol), was elected into office. This signaled the beginning of the first experience of revolutionary-popular local government in Turkey, which lasted 270 days (Morgül, 2007, pp. 132-180). Also see Türkmen (2006, pp. 54-89).

clearly see that the first alternative policy to stand out is the reform concerning the people's participation in—and supervision of—local administration. In addition, there were efforts to devise new social policies, reform the town's infrastructure, embrace local culture and, to an extent, regulate economic life.[79] For example, a new administrative structure was formed to pave the way for the participation of the people in municipal activities. Moreover, a public relations unit was formed. Its purpose was to work alongside the people, keep track of the people's municipal activities, and supervise and evaluate the activities of the local government. In places where the intended regulation could not be put to practice, creative solutions to enable the people's supervision and evaluation of municipal policies were implemented. For instance, in some cases, the meetings of the municipal council were broadcasted live from the speakers of the municipality for all the people to listen. This way, even if all of the people were unable to participate in meetings, they were able to hear what was being said in them. It also needs to be stated that during the Fatsa experience, the municipality did not officially hire any staff other than the aforementioned unit. The initiative required for participatory government was provided by 'municipal representatives' elected by the people's committees of every neighborhood. In the second half of the 1970s, Fatsa had 7 quarters. These were divided into 11 'People's Committee' zones. Councils formed by these committees enabled the collective designation, supervision, and implementation of municipal activities. Through the 'Executive Committee,' the various issues resolved in committee meetings (which were open to the participation of all) were conveyed to the municipal council (itself an entity recognized by the law). The goal of the people's committees was to replace the representative system with one that permitted people direct participation in decision-making (Türkmen, 2006,

---

79 In a compilation on the Fatsa experience, some examples of the abovementioned economic, social, political and cultural practices have been described: 'People's Committees were formed right after the elections. People affiliated with other political parties—except fascists and moneylenders—also took part in the activities of these committees. The first major municipal policy implemented in Fatsa was the 'Away With Filth' campaign. Many thought that the completion of such a task would take years, but it was over in a mere matter of months. Fatsa was all cleaned up. After this, the People's Cultural Festival of Fatsa was held. The cultural and artistic activities took place with the direct participation of the people. In addition to folk dances, musical and theatrical performances by the Fatsa Community Centre were positively received by an audience comprised of people from all over the country. After Fatsa, important gains were made against the fascists in the surrounding districts as well. In Fatsa, important struggles were waged against alcohol abuse, gambling, and domestic violence. Loan bills in possession of moneylenders were annulled. Through the direct participation of the people, important steps were taken to resolve problems concerning the road, water, and sewer systems. Demonstrations on the hazelnut issue were held and the vast majority of the peasants participated in these as well. In time, the people started bringing all kinds of problems (land conflicts, blood feuds, public and domestic disturbances etc.) to the attention of the revolutionaries and the revolutionaries strived to solve these problems with the people's participation.' See 'Fatsa'da devrimci halkçı belediyecilik deneyimi', http://www.atilimhaber.org/2012/10/19/fatsada-devrimci-halkci-belediyecilik-deneyimi/. For further articles, see Morgül (2007), Türkmen (2006), and Yıldırım (2006).

pp. 95-105; Morgül, 2007, pp. 157-180). Such policies are important milestones in the process of creating a collective will, which is an important objective of revolutionary democratic practice. In sum, the example of Fatsa, for the first time in the history of people's struggles in Turkey, quite concretely demonstrated that it is possible to replace representative democracy with direct democracy through the struggle of revolutionary-popular local government. The economic, social, and cultural achievements of the Fatsa experience have proven that this model is quite attainable in the historical epoch following it. The popular support for these policies by people both on the left and right ends of the ideological spectrum should be regarded as one of its most important achievements. The overcoming of the unequal division between the administrators and the administered, the improvement of accountability, and the practice of a revolutionary democratic understanding are extremely significant gains, and the lessons to be drawn from these experiences remain relevant.

Held in Ankara nearly half a century later (on December 3 and 4, 2011, at the Cultural and Educational Centre of the Ankara Law Association) the Symposium of Revolutionary-Popular Local Government brought together alternative revolutionary and democratic perspectives, and it represents an important historical turning point. At this congregation, historical and contemporary experiences of local government—both on a national and an international level—and their various economic, social, political, and cultural dimensions were discussed at length. What made this meeting unique was that, for the first time in history, municipal authorities that had been elected due to their promises of waging a struggle of revolutionary-popular local government (and discerned by their independently running socialist candidates) came together to share their experiences with each other and the public. Another distinctive feature of the symposium was that the remaining participants were individuals from either the academia or dissident political groups and possessed a high level of knowledge in the discussion regarding revolutionary-popular local governments.[80] Some points about the background of the symposium should be mentioned: In spring 2011, through the initiative of the municipalities of Dersim-Hozat and Dersim-Mazgirt (where 'independent socialist candidates' were elected into office in the Municipal Elections of 2009), several meetings were held in both Ankara and Istanbul with the participation of academics and union representatives. Following these, a large group

---

80 The symposium received a significant amount of attention, both in the socialist press and the national press. In the mainstream media, an article, titled *Terzi Fikri Kardeşliği* (The Terzi Fikri Brotherhood), was published about the 'socialist mayors.' For this, see http://www.sabah.com.tr/Yasam/2010/11/22/terzi_fikri_kardesligi. For an article from a popular internet web portal (which can be considered among the mainstream press) see http://t24.com.tr/yazi/dersimden-sosyalizm-manzaralari/2639. For an example from the socialist press see http://www.mazgirt.bel.tr/basinda-belediyemiz/sosyalist-belediyecilik-dersim-de-de-yasiyor.html.

comprised of academics, trade union activists, and students travelled to Dersim on the invitation of the municipalities of Hozat and Mazgirt. They were met with the hospitality of the Hozat and Mazgirt municipalities, represented respectively by their mayors Cevdet Konak and Tekin Türkel. For 5 days they had the opportunity to attend debates, meetings, and panels and to travel through the region; thus, they experienced and evaluated the activities of revolutionary-popular local governments first-hand.[81] After a concrete experience as useful and stimulating as this, the participants conveyed their observations and thoughts to a wider audience in the academia and unions. These activities were determining factors in the emergence of the Symposium. For the first time since Fatsa, current practices in the field were discussed and compared to examples in other countries, with the objective of creating a roadmap for revolutionary-popular local government.

The local administrations that participated in the symposium (Aknehir, Akpazar, Pertek, Hozat, and Mazgirt) must be evaluated in light of fields of struggle that emerged within political-administrative and socio-economic conditions following the 1980s. This is highly important because the issue of 'cultural identity' and 'ethnicity,' which had been regarded as an extension of class struggle prior to 1980, presently plays an important role in discussions within the ranks of the people's opposition. For example, if we were to place those localities participating in the symposium on a map of the country, we would find ourselves looking at a map of Turkey's impoverished and ethnically oppressed areas. It is no secret that today that certain ethnic groups face working conditions much harsher than others. Kurds, Zazas, Arabs, and Alevis residing in Eastern and South-eastern Anatolia (where the Hatay, Dersim and various BDP (The Peace and Democracy Party) municipalities are found) are among those groups whose members find themselves working under extremely hazardous conditions, usually without job security or insurance. This can be seen as the ethnicization of poverty. The same evaluation applies to space as well. Dersim, Hatay, and the BDP municipalities, representing most of the Kurdish areas, are important points on this map of poverty. In sum, it is evident that poverty and ethnicity, or in other words, class and identity (or political economy and culture), as intertwined dynamics, determined the policies of the people's opposition in important ways. In addition, those participating localities have utilized cultural policies as an important tool of politicization— both in the programs announced prior the elections and in their activities after.[82] Thus, the junction points of these two determining dynamics (labor and identity) are constantly becoming more important as they are the important determinants

---

81 For an example of the kind of panels attended by academics during these trips, see http://piyaportal. de/index.php/forum/5-piya-forum/22-qdersimde-kimlik-tartmalarq-paneli-gercekleti

82 To further develop this point, see the suggestions for alternative cultural policies in regards to revolutionary-popular government (Özbudun, 2012).

of revolutionary-popular local governments and facilitate the spread of radical, pro-labor, pro-liberty, and solidaristic ideas aiming at direct democracy.

The Municipality of Mazgirt in Dersim: A Contemporary Example of Revolutionary Popular Local Government[83]

Prior to the previous municipal elections (in 2009), the platform known as The Democratic People's Solidarity of Dersim (DDHD) comprised of various mass organizations, nominated certain independent socialist candidates in the districts and town center of Dersim. These candidates won the elections for the second time in Hozat and the first time in Mazgirt. The candidate for the town center lost the elections only by a bare margin but two representatives were elected to the city council.

A distinguishing aspect of the DDHD experience was that—as stated in its program for local administration[84]—these candidates were determined by the people's direct participation in people's councils (and their women's, youth, worker's, peasant's etc. sub-committees) formed in the neighborhoods. Other local administrations participating in the symposium, such as Aknehir, had similar practices. Before the elections, the program for local administration and the policies specific to the conditions of Mazgirt were also formed through the participation of the people. The mayoral candidates were also discussed and determined at these meetings. This is a discerning quality of the DDHD's work as—in accordance with a participatory understanding of administration—the future administrative representatives were determined through processes of mass meetings and mass discussion. The fact that the individuals intended to represent the will of the people's councils were determined prior to the elections can be seen as proof that the principles of people's supervision of—and participation in—government were embraced as an integral part of the organization's institutional functioning. In Mazgirt, these goals have been mostly achieved.

---

83 Mazgirt is one of the 8 districts of the province of Dersim (Tunceli). It lies in the southeastern part of the province. As of 2009, the district center has a population of approximately 1700. Along with the surrounding villages and hamlets, the district has a total population reaching 8000. The history of the settlements in the region can be traced back to ancient Anatolian civilizations. It is known that throughout history, the area has been home to the settlements of important cultures. Today, it is home to (mostly Kurmanci speaking) Alevi and Sunni Kurdish communities, as well as Sunni Turkish communities. The Mazgirt district center, in terms of its cultural identity, reflects the Alevi-Kurdish atmosphere dominant in Dersim. However, some towns, villages and hamlets are entirely Sunni. For first hand economic, social and political data on the district of Mazgirt, see http://www.mazgirt.bel.tr/

84 The Initiative for Democratic Local Government, 2009.

At this point it is worth noting that 'mayoral elections,' at least in rural communities with low populations, have everything to do with the specific individual running for office. In the rural areas of Turkey, where traditional perceptions and attitudes are still prevalent, the individual candidate is a determining factor in the outcome of the election. The standing of such individuals in the eyes of the public is shaped by the social acceptance of the political movement this candidate represents as well as his or her social status. The candidates suggested and determined at the people's meetings (held on the initiative of the DDHD) were generally no exception. Some of the most important factors in determining an appropriate candidate were ethnic identity (namely that the person was a Kırmancki speaking Alevi, but also the religious and social status of his/her clan), political views, and socially accepted individual traits (such as honesty, diligence and modesty etc.). The experience of revolutionary-popular local government in the eastern Black Sea district of Hopa, during the 2004 municipal elections, witnessed a similar process whereby the candidate's identity played an important role alongside his political acceptability. In an evaluation of the Hopa experience, Yıldırım (2006, pp 91-95) states that, in addition to the 'people's councils,' which facilitated the people's participation in local administration, the 'Hemşinli' cultural identity of the candidate played a determining part in his electoral victory.

Today, despite all kinds of repression and economic difficulties, the Municipality of Mazgirt continues the struggle for revolutionary-popular local governance. Along with the Municipality of Hozat, it spearheaded the Symposium of Revolutionary-Popular Local Governments, thereby enabling a systematic and complete evaluation of alternative forms of struggle in Turkey. This event opened up new channels of discussion for those who have been victimized by the neo-liberal depredation and social-political policies of the various governments up to this point. Indeed, we can compare the humble practices of the experience in Mazgirt to those of Samandağ, Aknehir, Pertek, and Hozat and to the historical examples of Fatsa to identify certain discerning aspects of the revolutionary-popular approach to local government.

In this context, it might be helpful to take a brief look at the practical policies implemented in Mazgirt for the past three years:

In the Elihatun Quarter of our district, an area of approximately 2.5 decares was converted into a public park for the people to use. Again in Elihatun, asphalt was lain on the path from Kale İbo Street to the Özgürlük ve Demokrasi Park. As the women from the villagers coming to visit our district had no warm place to stay, a women's guesthouse was built. 300 suits, 50 coats, trousers, and shirts were distributed to those with a limited income. In the district center, stationery was distributed to all elementary schools and high schools for the students to use. A public library was set up on the first floor of our public services building and books relevant to the curriculum were purchased for the students to benefit. For the unemployed youth in our district, three month programs were formed through cooperation with the Turkish Employment Association and 35 people found employment this way. In the Karapınar locality, where there was need of a sewer system, 600 meters of sewer pipeline were lain. In Mengüçlü street (behind the health center), in Yeni Mahalle, 150 meters of sewer pipeline was lain and the area's sewage problem was completely solved. In various parts (Kale Arkası, Zahpan, Aktoprak) old fountains were repaired for the people's use. The necessary preparations were made for the Nature & Culture Festival, in 2009, so it could be celebrated with mass attendance and support. Trips were organized to the Kırklar Baba Mountain, which had not been visited for many years. As the road leading to the Kale Arkası hamlet had been dusty and dirty, renovation activities were started so as to mend the path. The sewers leading to the cesspits at the entrance of the district center were expanded approximately 150 meters and the revealed parts were covered to make it aesthetically more pleasing. People's meetings were organized where the people's problems were discussed and solutions were put forth. Our municipal staff has also held monthly meetings to discuss how to serve the people more productively and give and receive feedback on how to solve various issues (Güntekin and Gündoğdu, 2013, p. 36).

When we look at practices reflecting some of the policies implemented in the economic, social, cultural, and various other spheres, we see that local government, utilized as a tool of social transformation, can be useful in many areas of life—from infrastructure repair to the creation of alternative economic resources. In the example of Mazgirt, the most important point worth stating is that the general idea—consistent with the political perspective in action—is that local governments can be utilized as a tool through which the people can experience direct democracy, and that in this manner, the level of democratic consciousness can be developed. Once the revolutionary-popular government gains the right to govern, its principle task is not to create an 'island of democracy' in a sea of reactionary exploitation, but to create examples of the most advanced forms of direct democracy, with the utmost level of people's participation and supervision. The principal goal here is to help the democratic consciousness develop and become institutionalized. In such a process, the main actor is neither the local government, nor the political organization implementing these practical policies. While these are quite determining and important factors, according to the general perspective, the principal actor is none other than the people. The advancement and consolidation of experiences of direct democracy—both in Mazgirt and in other revolutionary-popular local governments — is only possible if the people uphold their own forms of self-governance. Moreover, the problems faced by the people of various localities on a national level can only be fully solved if the people obtain political power. If this is not done, then local governments will eventually find themselves encroaching upon the limits set by the dominant system and face repression. The example of BDP municipalities and the experience of the DDHD (and the case of Fatsa) are proof of this, for in the last three years alone, many 'counter-terrorism' operations have been conducted against local governments and hundreds of people (dozens of them mayors and their assistants) have been arrested and their municipal activities obstructed.

Practical policies emanating from the understanding outlined above serve the goal of utilizing local governments for social transformation. This approach, while within the bounds of the legal procedure set for local governments, is based on the practice of using resources—through the collective participation of the people—to serve the interests of the people themselves. However, the long term aim of this perspective is not merely limited to using existing opportunities to benefit the people, but to politicize the masses by enabling people's participation in the processes of decision-making. With recent examples of local government like Hopa, as well as with radical revolutionary movements around the world, such as the Zapatistas, the goal has been to contribute to the development of a revolutionary consciousness of political power shaped by the direct participation of the people in local government through organs of direct democracy such as people's committees or people's councils. For example, in his work on the Zapatistas, Özünlü (2006) gives an example from the leader of the movement Subcomandante Marcos, who constantly stresses that the alliance with the indigenous people and the construction of local autonomous organs actually serve the goal of creating a form of power directly representing the people's will.

Solving poverty and difficulties faced by women, youth, and minorities by using the resources of the local governments and through mobilizing alongside the masses are the main goals of such practices. For these practices to advance towards this goal—enabling the people's participation in self-governance within a framework of direct democracy—there exist certain spatial organizations (on the level of district quarters) such as 'people's committees' and 'people's councils.' These organizations place emphasis on the interest of the community, foster relations of solidarity and mutual cooperation, and support the development of a democratic consciousness defending the people's interests. Most of the practices described above in the activity report of the Municipality of Mazgirt have been consistently undertaken through the mobilization of the collective labor of the people. Facilitating the people's direct participation in the struggle for local government by developing new social policies, as is seen in Mazgirt, is in fact a characteristic of almost all such experiences throughout the world. For example, in India, where in addition to economic problems, feudal dynamics (examples of which also exist in Turkey) intensify the oppression of the people, there are similar experiences spearheaded by socialist parties in Kerala. In this example, there are important achievements in the participatory determination of the public spending budget and the collective evaluation and supervision of economic and social policies. Fundamentally, the practices in Kerala are also being conducted with the goal of a revolutionary transformation of society (Fund and Wright, 2001, pp. 15-16).

Last Words

Today, as in the past, local governments in Turkey are under the control of the state. They are under the supervision of powerful groups that shape the government both politically and economically. Therefore, the resources available to localities and the scope of their political activities are confined to certain limits. However, as local government is a field where the administrators and the administered are intermeshed and the people have easier access to these administrators, there exist certain possibilities for implementing democratic and autonomous practices. The neo-liberal project asserted that such characteristics of local government would be constitutionally guaranteed and even, in certain cases, transformed into autonomous institutions. Without a doubt, the goal here was to regulate the new actors and markets of the free market system, which had spread into the localities. With such motives, certain partial amendments were made to local government legislations, both in the West and in dependent countries such as Turkey. Yet in practice, the rapid privatization of the public services meant that the resources were, in fact, transferred to the hands of those holding economic and political power in the localities. With this process, new areas of unearned income appeared and free market relations became ever more widespread. Instigated by various international financial organizations such as the World Bank and the IMF, these policies triggered the beginning of a process where the centralized administrative structures of the state were gradually dissolved through local governments. While this was all done in the interests of capital, certain concepts used traditionally by the people in processes of struggle, such as 'autonomy,' 'democratization,' and 'emancipation,' were emptied of meaning and adopted by the official discourse. Local governments, already deprived of adequate resources, infrastructure investment, and support due to the power relations imposed by the central authority, were forcibly pressed further into capital's rapacious cogwheels of exploitation.

However, this same process also witnessed the emergence of new alternative policies, embraced by localities with a history of democratic struggle. In the first decade of the 21st century, apart from the expansion of the BDP's influence in various municipalities, there are certain examples worthy of notice where politics in the field of local government were undertaken with a socialist perspective, either through independently running socialist candidates or through candidates who were determined through the alliance of various socialist organizations and were elected on a socialist party's list. The municipalities of Artvin-Hopa, Yozgat-Bahadın, Hatay-Samandağ, Hatay-Aknehir, Dersim-Hozat, Dersim-Pertek, and Dersim-Mazgirt were exemplary cases in the 2000s and were widely reported on by the national press. In spite of all limitations, the abovementioned district and county municipalities have proven that the project of designing local governments as economic, political, and social agents of the dominant system can be upturned through struggle. As well, local administrations, by integrating with the people's own self-organizations, can be converted into tools that transform the local relations of resource distribution in favor of the people.

A look at historical and present-day examples of struggle for revolutionary-popular local governments in the world, and in Turkey in particular, shows that the actual goal of such struggles is the seizure of state power by the people. The determining aspect is the implementation of alternative economic, social, political, and cultural policies with the aim of creating 'sustainable cities/habitats.' The access of individuals on the basis of their victimized identities (women, children, minority ethnicity, the impoverished etc.) to positions in local government, their participation in processes of decision-making, implementation and supervision, and the determining of the local budget within this framework are among the common traits of all revolutionary-popular local governments worldwide. In this context, it can also be said that experiences of revolutionary-popular local government (unless physically obstructed in one way or another) develop and even consolidate the participatory consciousness of the people. This, in turn, demonstrates that through the humble but instructive examples presented by local governments, political-administrative mechanisms paving the way towards 'a different, better world' can gain widespread recognition and lead to more radical and fundamental results.

References

Adda, J. (2006). *La Mondialisation de l'Economie*. Paris: La Decouverte.

Aladağ, A. (2013). *Hegemonya Yeniden Kurulurken: Sol Liberalizm ve Taraf*. İstanbul: Patika.

Aydemir, C., & Kaya M. (2007). Küreselleşme Kavramı ve Ekonomik Yönü. *Elektronik Sosyal Bilimler Dergisi, 6*(20) 260-282.

Bingöl, Ö. (2003). *Küreselleşme Sürecinde Devletin Yeni İşlevi* (unpublished master's thesis). İstanbul Üniversitesi.

Ellywood, W. (2010). *No-Nonsense guide to globalisation*. Between the Lines.

Ercan, F. (2006). Küreselleşme Sürecindeki Yerellikler: Homojenleşme ve Farklılaşma/ Güç ve Eşitsizlik İlişkileri Üzerine." In D. Yılmaz (Ed.), *Kapitalizm, Küreselleşme, Azgelişmişlik* (pp. 19-83). Ankara: Dipnot.

Eryılmaz, B. (2002). Belediyelerde Demokrasi Geleneği ve Değişim İhtiyacı. Çağdaş Yerel Yönetimler Dergisi, *11*(3) 58-60.

Fung, A. & Wright, E. O. (2001). Deepening Democracy: Innovations in Emprowed Participatory Governance. *Politics and Society, 29* (1), 224-239.

Giddens, A. (1998). *The third way: The renewal of social democracy*. Polity Press.

Günal, V. A. (2010). Türkiye'de Merkezi Yönetim – Belediye İlişkileri: 1999-2006 Arası Siyasal, Yönetsel, Ekonomik İlişkiler. Akdeniz Üniversitesi, Sosyal Bilimler Enstitüsü, Kamu Yönetimi Anabilim Dalı. Antalya.

Gültekin, A. K., & Özbudun, S. (2012). Kültür-kimlik politikaları atölyesi. In Kolektif (Ed.) *Devrimci Halkçı Yerel Yönetimler Atölye Sonuç Metinleri*. Ankara, 94-108.

Gültekin, A. K., & Gündoğdu, İ. (Eds.). (2013). *Devrimci Halkçı Yerel Yönetimler: Umut ve Mücadele Mekanlarından Deneyimler*. İstanbul: Patika.

Köse, H. Ö. (2003). Küreselleşme Sürecinde Devletin Yapısal ve İşlevsel Dönüşümü. *Sayıştay Dergisi, 49*, 1-49.

Kurtuluş, H. (2005) (ed.) *İstanbul'da Kentsel Ayrışma: Mekânsal Dönüşümde Farklı Boyutlar*, İstanbul: Bağlam

Morgül, K. (2007). *A history of the social struggles in Fatsa 1960-1980* (unpublished master's thesis). Boğaziçi Üniversitesi.

Pehlivan, V. (2008). *Küreselleşme, Yoksulluk ve Türkiye* (unpublished master's thesis). İstanbul Üniversitesi.

Türkmen, H. (2006). *Radicalisation of politics at the local level: The case of Fatsa during the late 1970s* (unpublished master's thesis). Middle Technical University.

Yeldan, E. (2006). *Küreselleşme Sürecinde Türkiye Ekonomisi*. İstanbul: İletişim.

Yıldırım, Y. (2006). *Radikal Demokrasi Teorisi ve Uygulanabilirliği: Farklı Yerel Yönetim Deneyimleri* (unpublished masters' thesis), Hacettepe University.

11.
COUNTER-PUBLICS AND SOCIAL MEDIA

Different Channels for Self-Organization and RedHackers

Şafak Etike

Social media has recently become a main target of the AKP's assault on free speech. While this article was being written, YouTube was blocked and Twitter was blocked, unblocked, and then blocked and unblocked again. The AKP's ferocious campaign against social media triggered intense resistance in this medium; indeed, it is in social media that the resistance was first organized and then grew. Directly after Twitter was blocked, within a few hours, a record number of tweets were posted by Turkish users who had discovered new techniques for bypassing the ban. Within one hour, over 137,000 tweets were posted under the single hashtag: #twitterisblockedinturkey.[85]

Thanks to social media, publics around the world have been informed of unveiled corruption, unlawfulness, secret bargaining, government's crimes against humanity, and war crimes. Publics rely on social media and new communication technologies to keep informed, communicate, organize, and resist. On the other hand, there is organized and networked capitalism, which means that conflicting

---

85 'Kökü kazınıyor', http://www.hurriyet.com.tr/ekonomi/26086389.asp

powers are benefiting from and competing over technological communication instruments to strengthen their struggle (Castells, 2006). This new era compels us to reconsider the opportunities and restrictions that the Internet offers for class struggle.

Government attacks on social networking and video-sharing platforms are nothing new in Turkey. There are two turning points, however, in the AKP's campaign against social media. The latest was the recent local elections of March, 2014, in which public anger surfaced. Right before the elections, AKP's dirty secrets were revealed, including millions of dollars lost in corruption, shady relations with media moguls, manipulation, and plans to hurl missiles over Turkey as a pretext to declaring war on Syria. Although leaked phone recordings and secret documents about corruption were not published by mainstream media, this information was shared and discussed through social media. Prime Minister Recep Tayyip Erdoğan, speaking at a rally in the western city of Bursa on March 20 (10 days before the local elections), vowed to eradicate Twitter, claiming that national security is under threat and there was an international conspiracy against Turkey.[86] That very night, access to Twitter was blocked.[87] Erdoğan, speaking at a live televised interview on March 6, alleged that social media platforms were promoting all kinds of espionage and immorality, and said that this cannot be considered as an expression of freedom. Erdoğan also stated that his government would take all necessary precautions, including the closure of sites, saying: 'We will not leave this nation at the mercy of YouTube and Facebook.'[88] Access to YouTube was also blocked.[89]

The second turning point of the AKP's approach to social media occurred during the Gezi resistance. Erdoğan described Twitter as 'trouble,' and social media as a 'troublemaker.'[90] Turkish media sunk into an inconceivable silence within the first four days of Gezi resistance and then went through its darkest and

---

86 ' Turkey blocks Twitter, after Erdoğan vowed eradication'http://www.hurriyetdailynews.com/turkey-blocks-twitter-after-erdogan-vowed-eradication.aspx?PageID=238&NID=63884&-NewsCatID=338

87 'Ankara Cumhuriyet Başsavcılığı'na', http://www.barobirlik.org.tr/dosyalar/duyurular/TiB.pdf

88
'Turkey calls Syria security leak villainous blocks youtube', http://www.reuters.com/article/2014/03/27/us-syria-crisis-turkey-idUSBREA2Q17420140327

89 Some people were still able to access Twitter and YouTube after these blockings. However, the government cracked down on users' methods of circumventing the blocking and tweets posted from Turkey gradually decreased by half in the following days. Blocking YouTube, which become an object of derision in Turkish public opinion after a court ordered unblocking one night and another court ruled for blocking on the following day. This process was still continuing when this essay was being written. 'Youtube to remain blocked in turkey despite court order:BTK', http://www.hurriyetdailynews.com/youtube-to-remain-blocked-in-turkey-despite-court-order-btk.aspx-?pageID=238&nID=64850&NewsCatID=339

90 'Twitter is a troublemaker: Turkish PM', http://www.hurriyetdailynews.com/twitter-is-a-troublemaker-turkish-pm—-.aspx?pageID=238&nID=48084&NewsCatID=338

most shameful days. Turkish televisions that had broadcasted live for hours from Tahrir Square when uprisings began in Egypt turned a blind eye to the demonstrations of millions taking place in the very streets where their headquarters are located and so close that their employees were able to watch what was going on from their windows. At the moment when protests peaked and police staged their heaviest crackdown, CNN Türk broadcasted a documentary on penguins. Nature documentaries, sports programs, and beauty contests were widely broadcasted as Turkish citizens met the batons of police.

In the first four days of the Gezi resistance most Turkish television channels neither ran a single news story about the incidents nor conducted even a short live broadcast. That was unbelievable! Intense conflicts were taking place in city centers, with people wounded and even killed, but the Turkish media chose to be blind and silent.[91] This infuriated the protesters even more and they began to demonstrate outside of media buildings.[92] Demonstrators waved money in front of the TV channels' buildings, revealing the public's awareness of the capitalist structure of media ownership (Bulut, 2013). After media criticism turned into full-scale protests, some mainstream media outlets started to cover demonstrations; however, there was no indication that the 'partisan media'[93] of the AKP would broadcast a single news story. We have witnessed a situation unforeseen by communication theorists of the Propaganda Model or of Culture Imperialism. Simply put, getting informed by conventional media during the social uprising was impossible.

Yet the uprising snowballed. Korkut Boratav (2013), describes the Gezi resistance as the reaction of those who object to political powers' pillaging of common assets that have been inherited from previous generations. He identifies the resistance as 'a mature class-based uprising against capitalism.' This class-based uprising makes use of new instruments of communication, especially social media. Sharing photos, videos, and information about police violence and those wounded or killed explicitly exposed the brutality of the government and carved a place in the collective consciousness for unforgettable moments of resistance. Social media was so prominent in the struggle that a simple # (Twitter's 'hashtag' sign) became a symbol of the resistance.[94]

---

91 For a comprehensive analysis on the AKP's building of its own media groups, dissident elements' movement away from mainstream media, the suppression of critical media outlets, and media editorial policy during periods of resistance, see Bulut (2013a).

92 'Turkey's media under fire:protests at NTV', http://www.euronews.com/2013/06/03/turkey-s-media-under-fire-protests-at-ntv/

93 'Partisan media' is a widely accepted term referring to media organizations that are close to the AKP government and publish and broadcast solely in line with government's interests (Bulut, 2013a).

94 This symbol frightened the government. An administrative investigation of Professor Timuçin Köprülü (Uludağ University) was launched after he attended the university's graduation ceremony wearing a t-shirt that read '#diren' (which means resist in Turkish). Although it received a series

This chapter is composed of two sections. In the first, I will discuss the opportunities offered by the Internet for class-based political struggle, new organizational forms peculiar to the online world, and the limits of new struggle practices of this kind. I address the criticism that the concept of 'class struggle' has been at the margins of political economy studies of communication. Making 'class struggle' a central concept in the theorization of 'media and struggle' is among the most important tasks for political economists of media (Wittel, 2012). In our era, the struggle of the 'multitude' or 'alternative' struggles are highlighted and class becomes invisible; yet to explain the developments in the field of communication, class struggle must be placed at the center of our analyses.

In the second section of the article, I examine the class struggle in Turkish social media through an analysis of the group 'Red Hackers Association,' which disclosed its class-based identity and declared itself as part of the class struggle in the digital field. RedHack conveyed inside information about the Gezi Resistance to the public in the least structured form. RedHack's posts were valuable for conveying information to protestors about one another and about the developments across Turkey. RedHack became an information leader that was formed independently of the existing social opposition and received wide support despite the political heterogeneity of the resistance (Bulut, 2013b). Within this context, RedHack can be examined as an alternative communication experience.

And yet, 'resistance' in the online world of communication goes far beyond alternative modes of information sharing. Cyber attacks against the ruling party and elite institutions and establishments—such as hacking and revealing secrets to the public—are also significant forms of resistance in the field of communication. In this way, RedHack serves as a good case for thinking through other forms of online resistance.

Capitalism Without 'Capital' or Class Struggle that Becomes Invisible in Networks?

The claim that digital networks are democratizing the world and undermining capitalism is a modern myth. This myth tells us that classes, and therefore class struggle, are becoming irrelevant due to the developments related to new communication technologies. According to the proponents of this myth, we are now living in a new era (Bell, 1973; Toffler, 1984; Masuda, 2009); capitalism has either been dissolved or radically transformed. A 'new capitalism' (which we are

response from the government, this little sign also united protestors wherever it was seen (Bulut, 2013a, p. 91). Police raids were conducted in numerous cities of Turkey for social media posts. People were taken into custody because of their social media posts, and some of them were arrested and imprisoned. Retrieved from http://www.news.az/articles/turkey/80268

told does not resemble capitalism at all) or a 'computopia,' composed of entirely new communication instruments, will dissolve class-based relations.

According to information society theory, the production and reproduction of information transforms all other sectors. Hence, the collectivization of info-property provides the opportunity to share the wealth of the society. In this perspective, the labor theory of value is replaced by the information theory of value. The idea is that new forms of information sharing will transform the whole society; all political, cultural, and economic structures will be reshaped. Information is seen as immune from property regimes and, thus, from authority and power. We can look forward then, to a dissolution in power relations and a wave of democratization, so the theory goes. McLuhan and Powers (2001) argue that the global village, which was supposed to be established by television, will be founded certainly by new communication instruments.

As the myth goes, political mechanisms will function more democratically, there will be total access to information and thus political participation will increase dramatically. This is the modern version of Habermas' public sphere, in which each one of us can communicate and participate in social activity whenever we like. Applications such as e-government will make administrations transparent and technology will promote enhanced education for all. Masuda (2009), in his *Computopia,* further echoes that class relationships would be eliminated in the information society and adds that a classless society would be established evolutionarily. Machines become the real creators of social change. In this way, the tough rival of socialism is now the computer (Dyer-Witheford, 1999).

Claims of this kind have been widely received both in academic circles and online publications. They were even placed on top of the agendas of international organizations, presuming that new information and communication technologies had made this rosy picture realizable through immediate access to knowledge and interaction. Underlying these claims is a pro-enlightenment perspective that takes knowledge as the key to social development and transformation. Closely aligned to development theories, proponents argue that a country's development depends on the extent to which it is integrated into the global information society.

We should ask how these theorists might respond to basic questions, such as 'If there is now an e-government, why are we still starving?', 'If there is e-democracy, why am I not still represented?' or 'Is information extraneous to capitalism?' These theories neglect the fact that information is itself a commodity. Developments in the new communication technologies go back to military and industrial structures of the United States, and the field of communication production remains one of power and force (Yücesan-Özdemir, 2009b, p. 30). While the average citizen may make creative use of these technologies, he or she has no say over the production of the technologies themselves. The elite engaged in technology production remain global corporations, the US Army, and the capitalist state. Thus, one should not be surprised that new technological advances are devoted to strengthening capitalism and providing security by military control (Hirschkop, 1998). One should also bear in mind the ideological function of these technologies in determining political and social choices. In sum: Technology is not impartial (Levidov, 2003).

Dan Schiller (1999) emphasized that the driving forces in information and communication technologies are enhanced control over labor, increased productivity, accumulation of capital, and domination of world markets. New communication technologies are thus the outcome of class struggle (Levidov, 2003); indeed, they enhance, rather than eliminate, class struggle. As Beniger (1986) says, they provide opportunities for overcoming the production, distribution, and consumption crises of capitalism. There emanates not only flow of information, but also the new infrastructure of a new economical order. Therefore digital capitalism is not a simple outcome of technology; it emanates in line with the needs of capitalism and pioneers capitalism's new accumulation processes (Dawson & Foster, 1998). What is digitized is nothing but structures belonging to capitalism (Menzies, 1998). This digitization comes forth as a historical necessity for capitalism. In the 1970s, inflation, unemployment, and escalation in class struggle brought the movement of capital to a crisis point. Capitalism overcame this crisis by internationalizing capital and removing the obstacles to its further global expansion. Precisely at this point, it used the opportunities provided by information and communication technologies to secure its continued existence. The capitalist character of information activity makes all the arguments of information theorists questionable.

According to Holloway (2006), the more successful the capitalist class is, the more invisible class struggle becomes. In this internationalized phase of capitalism, the capitalist class and its ideologues have been quite successful. The class struggle has not dissolved; rather, it has become concealed. Moreover, the domination over labor has been increased and exploitation of surplus value has been intensified. Holloway (2006) also says that wherever the capitalist class exists, class struggle exists as well. If the existential condition of the capitalist class is exploitation of surplus value, then this necessarily implies the existence of a working class that would produce surplus value. Because the latter is the basis of antagonism, it would also produce class struggle (Holloway, 2003). As Daniel Bensaïd (2009) rightfully highlights, everybody asks whether class is fading away, yet nobody seems to ask whether the bourgeoisie still exists. Class struggle, although invisible, is continuing fiercely.

Autonomist Marxists, who separated themselves from the information revolution theorists by theorizing the current digital era as a phase of capitalism, nonetheless agree that the struggle is not class-based any more. In this way, the Autonomists—often faced with the counter argument that a thing that is everywhere cannot be completely captured anywhere—do not regard class as a central concept. They lay emphasis on the concept of the 'multitude,' which, according to their claim, expands the proletariat. This is the most important point of commonality between the Autonomists and the Information Theorists (ITs) I have discussed above; social struggle is no longer seen as class-based. Even Castells (2006, 2012)—who argues that old relations of domination are continuing within new forms—omits class from his analysis of social struggle (2012) and thus echoes the Autonomists and ITs in this regard. In Castells' view, struggle is organized through networks, creating flexible oppositional forms that are centerless, horizontal, non-hierarchical, leaderless, individual, and thus no longer 'organized' (in the traditional sense) nor conducted by a collective community.

Hardt and Negri also canonize these forms of struggle in *Empire* (2001), *Multitude* (2005) and *Declaration* (2012). However, when class is excluded from this field of struggle, the target of the struggle becomes ambiguous. That capitalism aims to intensify the exploitation of surplus value falls completely out of the analytical frame and class relations are totally obscured in the process. Nevertheless, Hardt and Negri provide a valuable effort to annihilate the pessimistic view of technology and to understand the role of new communication technologies in social relations. Highlighting the 'rhizomatic formation of networks,' they attempt to outline the potential for resistance that is inherent within them. And yet, surveillance, control, censorship, and bans should be kept in mind when thinking about the democratic possibilities inherent in new forms of communication.

Inspired by Marx, many theorists, such as Innis (2007) and Enzensberger (1970) and Özdemir (2009b) have outlined the paradox of modern technology; while the production of technology is under the control of the capitalist class, technology can never be fully controlled and thus opportunities emerge for all classes. This should be acknowledged as an outcome of a dialectical relation; class struggle will determine the direction of the struggle over technology.

In short, new communication technologies did not evaporate the class struggle but they made it invisible. Capitalism is more active and dominant but more invisible in networks (Menzies, 1998). Institutions that are presumed to belong to network society are actually institutions of capitalist society (Törenli, 2011). Consequently, a new battlefield of capitalism has been opened up, rather than a democratic e-republic era in which capitalism is overcome. The struggle continues through and on networks.

Calling Class into the Digital Field

It is true that the Internet, as a new communication instrument, provides opportunities to the working class to organize a collective resistance. These opportunities can be summarized as follows: fast and frequently updated communication; immediate interaction; flexible political organization; participatory-collective decision making; political transparency and accountability; building associations for distant groups across space; rapid spread of tensions and frustration; organization of solidarity; anonymity, invisibility and reproducibility (Yücesan-Özdemir, 2009a; Wittel, 2012). The restrictions on these opportunities are as follows: common conceptualizations and goals are limited; accessibility of communication and discussion channels is limited; impact is relative; prohibition-censorship-control-intimidation mechanisms are easily put to work; collective action is weakened by abolishing social and class-based ties; reduction of class belonging; interactions rarely develop into solidarity; classlessness ideology of globalization is disseminated; physical gatherings are reduced and individuals are isolated from social relations; and monopolization and commercialization lead to a widening of social stratification, the knowledge gap, and culture imperialism (Yücesan-Özdemir, 2009b; Hirschkop, 1998; Törenli, 2011). The struggle for expanding opportunities against these restrictions is continuing fiercely. In the process, both sides (power versus the oppressed) are transforming themselves to respond to or nullify the strategies of the enemy (Dyer-Witheford, 1999). Dawson and Foster (1998) emphasize that this struggle should extend across the battle for controlling the technology; it should be extended into social relations in general.

In this case, both self-organizations and political organizations of the working class should be called into the digital field. But how? Digital and distributed media unveiled new opportunities for an alternative to capitalisml; however, neither of these chances can be realized unless fundamental changes take place through the struggle of the oppressed (Wittel, 2012). Castells (2012), who is criticized for falling into technological determinism due to the importance he attributed to the role of Internet and wireless communication in today's network-forming social movements, says that 'Neither Internet nor any other technology alone can be a source of causality. Social movements emanate from contradictions and conflicts in specific societies and represent people's revolts and projects originating from their multi-dimensional experiences' (2012, p. 34). Therefore, technology will not overcome the logic and the power of capitalism; rather, it is the level of organization and strength of the people's collective forces that will determine it (Dawson & Foster, 1998). As, Yücesan-Özdemir (2009, p. 152) notes, 'What really matters is not how technology fought its struggle [but] what kind of technology the struggle made use of.' In this way, the Internet can take its place among instruments of class struggle but it cannot replace the struggle itself.

What, then, could be the goals of struggles conducted in networks? Capitalism organizes the order of accumulation and reproduces itself again and again in networks. However, making these interests visible is a fundamental part of the class struggle. One should take courage from turning uncertainties into certainties. This was precisely the strategy of RedHack. Making the invisible visible and breaking knowledge monopolies, it showed that those deemed untouchable were anything but. RedHack creatively responded to networked capitalism in its own language.

RedHack as a Class-based Resistance Organization

While it has been argued that hacking is not a site of political struggle (Demirkıran, 2013), there are valid grounds for rejecting this claim: First, hackers place themselves at the center of the informational economy as subjects who resist against the commercialization of networks and control over the knowledge. As Wark (2006) notes:

The hacker may be the symptom of a broader class struggle over information, which pits those who produce it – hackers in the very broadest sense – against   those who own the means of realizing its value – the corporations whose value   is increasingly defined not by tangible assets, but by portfolios of patents,   copyrights and brands. Thus, the hacker may turn out to be a very important   social category for understanding labor, the commodity and private property in   the information age. (p. 321)

For us, RedHack became an interesting case study not only because it was a hacker group but because it explicitly identified itself in class terms. Linus Torvalds, the founder of Linux and a world-renowned hacker, categorized hacking motivations in terms of 'survival,' 'social life,' and 'entertainment.' The fundamental element that distinguishes RedHack from other hacker groups is its motivation: it does not hack for entertainment or social life, but as an act of survival against capitalism. Hacking, for RedHack, is thus one instrument among others.

Founded in 1997, the Red Hackers Association (later 'RedHack') defined itself as 'the force of the proletariat of Turkey and the World in the field of technology for attack, defense and development.'[95] Article 1 of the Charter of Red Hackers Association, which was drafted in 2006, states:[96]

---

95 'RedHack (Kızıl Hackerlar)', http://www.sosyalistforum.net/archive/index.php/t-57383.html
96 'RedHack (Kızıl Hackerlar)', http://www.sosyalistforum.net/archive/index.php/t-57383.html

R.H.A. is the attack, defense, and development force of proletariat of Turkey and the World from different nationalities and of the oppressed people in the field of technology. R.H.A. consists of workers and experts working in information and communication sector. R.H.A.'s principles are based on the RedHack philosophy that takes shape with the common ideology of the oppressed classes and peoples. This is nothing but the interpretation of the Marxist dialectics in this field.

RedHack was the first hacker group in the world accused of being a terrorist organization.[97] Operations were staged against them with this charge, and the people who were taken into custody and detained on the grounds that they are associated with RedHack were sentenced to dozens of years in prison.[98] Our analysis approaches RedHack as an organized form of digital resistance that conducted the first class-based political cyber-fight and challenged digital capitalism in its own language.

In article two of their charter, RedHack members describe their mandate to develop 'and use war between the oppressors and the oppressed in favor of the oppressed in the technological field.' They used slogans such as, 'Hack for people!' and 'Anybody who is unfair will be hacked!' Under the same article, they define their duty as supporting Turkey's revolutionary movement in the information and communication field. Article four of the charter explains RedHack's relationship with technology:[99]

R.H.A. regards technology as revolutionary because of its progressive essence, although it is under the control of imperialism and is being manipulated in line with the interests of the dominant powers. R.H.A. is not against technology; it is against imperialism that uses technology as an instrument of repression against oppressed people and as an instrument of profit by substituting it within its own subjective conditions. R.H.A. condemns monopolist capitalist bandits who claim technology and its branches through their power for their dirty goals. R.H.A. acts in line with the consciousness that technology will be used in its

---

97 'Prosecutor demands RedHack be declared terrorist organization', http://www.hurriyetdailynews. com/prosecutor-demands-RedHack-be-declared-terrorist-organization.aspx?pageID=238&- nID=24891&NewsCatID=341

98 Youngsters detained on charges of 'being members of RedHack' were accused of 'being members of terrorist organization' and the prosecutor sought prison sentences of up to 24 years. Nonetheless, a number of campaigns launched in support of these youngsters and RedHack repeatedly stressed that people on trial have no links with them other than sympathizing with their previous actions in social media and having dissident identities. Following these developments, imprisoned defendants were released. In fact, attempts at labeling RedHack as an 'armed terrorist organization' had no legal basis' (Uçkan, 2013, p. 70).

99 'RedHack (Kızıl Hackerlar)', http://www.sosyalistforum.net/archive/index.php/t-57383.html

own essence, in favor and for the service of people collectively and freely, once the revolutionary movement wins its fight for socialism and glorious communism.

In his article, written on the 160th anniversary of the publication of the *Communist Manifesto*, Harvey (2010, p. 257), says that there are millions of communists among us, ready to creatively pursue the political imperatives that the Manifesto defines and working incessantly to produce a different future to that which capitalism portends. RedHack is perhaps one of the leading communists organizations that shapes those 'creative forms.' It is doing what was never tried before in the digital field and staging one of the most important instances of class based struggle:[100]

We overcame the bourgeois censorship by making direct propaganda for communism. Our actions were launched and developed with the Marxist principle of 'concrete analysis of concrete conditions,' instead of 'prescriptions' or written formulas. When we first started this act in 1997, we were the first communists in this field, we can say. We have shaped this experience not with our own way but through the 'scientific guidance' of Marxism.

In their charter, RedHack state that they were organized in a Leninist manner and have a democratic centralist structure. Their goal and organizational style definitely distinguishes RedHack from other hacker organizations. The goal of all hackers is to attract attention to a certain social problem and to create change in the real world (Demirkıran, 2013, p. 28). Yet, the main goal of RedHack is to abolish capitalism, and it is organized for this very goal. This is its main difference from Anonymous, which can be defined as a 'formation' or 'randomly formed dynamisms' rather than a group or organization (Yaman, 2013, p. 49). Moreover, RedHack is not an artificial organization of the working class; on the contrary, it is an organic structure associated with this class. They often repeat the class positions of their founders and members in their charter and in interviews: 'We are all workers.'

Examining the structure more closely, we see that there is a 12-person central cadre and around this cadre there are enlarging circles of friends, sympathizers, and supporters named the 'Redhack Family.' The group has a charter, as we have discussed, which declares its 'democratic centralist' structure. Before it was withheld by Twitter administration, @TheRedHack main account had about 766,000

---

100 'Red!' is a documentary about RedHack. Director: Mustafa Kenan Aybastı, Independent Cinema Center, 2013.

followers and 23,730 tweets were posted from this account.[101] The English-language account @RedHack_En was about to reach to 95,000 followers before it was suspended.[102] It has become a substantially influential organization in social media platforms with blogs and accounts opened by those who are not in the core cadre.

What are the elements that made RedHack so influential and enabled it to move into a leadership role in digital mobilizations? The absence of a political will to direct the social struggle against the Turkish government has been discussed as a major problem (Yücesan-Özdemir, 2014). How, then, did RedHack manage to suddenly occupy the center of digital resistance? The attention that RedHack attracts cannot be considered apart from its social and political context, and specifically the repressive governing mentality of the AKP that culminated in the 2010 Constitutional changes. As the government became more repressive, support for RedHack increased even more. Before the Gezi Resistance broke out, some of the most important actions that brought relief to the people were actually staged by RedHack. At a time when the state had taken on a holy role, mystified with religious connotations, both Erdoğan and the AKP became 'untouchable.' But RedHack struck the myth of holiness head on, revealing the dirty secrets and scandals of the government precisely when fields of struggle were shrinking and technical dominance seemed to be invincible. While broad segments of society were feeling weak and helpless in the face of the expanding powers of political elites, RedHack broke the façade of both the people's impotency and the immunity of government. It gave the people confidence. And despite the fact that the government attempted to crack down on RedHack, it did not succeed. If the political power had the tools and the brute power, then the resistance had the intellect. The revenge of those who felt oppressed finally took place, leaving people with a sense that they had increased their numbers, strength, and self-respect. Moreover, the actions of Redhack, along with the documents that they shared with the public, tore down the reputation of those in power. In this sense, RedHack deployed an agenda of destruction in the fight for survival, while raising the hopes of the people.

RedHack succeeded to steer social mobilizations in the digital field, calling for accountability and change. Examining how RedHack constructed a collective political will is crucial for developing effective digital resistance move-

---

101 The Twitter account of RedHack was suspended many times for hacking the Turkish Foreign Ministry's website in July 2012 and participated in joint hacking activities with Anonymous against Israel in April 2013. The account was again withheld in Turkey as a result of AKP government's pressures over Twitter administration. 'Twitter suspends RedHack suggests another Turkish user delets political tweet', http://www.hurriyetdailynews.com/twitter-suspends-RedHack-suggests-another-turkish-user-deletes-political-tweet.aspx?pageID=238&nID=69184&NewsCatID=339

102 After the main account was suspended in June 2014, RedHack officially started to use this account. Therefore, the number of followers and tweets posted from this account rapidly increased.

ments; specifically we can consider RedHack's political form and activities and its language through the categories offered by Yücesan-Özdemir (2014) regarding how political protest should be organized for a socialist future.[103]

'Hack for People'

RedHack is estimated to be composed of employees and high-profile executives of the information sector and academics. Nonetheless, RedHack members perceive themselves as members of the working class. This perception corresponds to a position against attitudes that divide and fragment the working class. RedHack members define everybody who has to make a living by selling their labor power as a worker. They approach intra-class stratification with an embracing and inclusive attitude.

Their attitude toward political differences within the working class is also quite inclusive. They do not divide the working class by positioning themselves in a broad political spectrum as leftists or rightists. They do not exclude supporters of the AKP or supporters of fascistic formations. They proclaim themselves as the supporters of those who are under the domination of the bourgeois class in their struggle against this domination. They are speaking on behalf of the 'people' to emphasize this collectivism. They hack for people. When needed, for example in a child abduction incident, they do not refrain from helping the police. The needs of the class during the struggle determine their core principles. They also receive support from broad segments of people as a result of this inclusive approach. In fact, among RedHack supporters, thousands of people position themselves on the right or extreme right on the political spectrum.

Sharing a Sense of Justice

RedHack is revealing what is hidden from people and what is done against them. Unveiling the members of foreign intelligence services working in Turkey,[104] Higher Education Board (YÖK) documents,[105] intelligence documents about bloody bomb attacks in Reyhanlı[106] are among RedHack's acts of exposure.

---

103 While I was generating data about these three categories, interviews with my fellow academics have been very useful and decisive. I thank them all.

104 After attacking the website of Turkish Foreign Ministry, images of the hundreds of identity cards the Ministry had issued for foreign diplomats working in Turkey were disclosed via a Dropbox file-sharing address.

105 RedHack hacked the website of the Higher Education Board (YÖK) on New Year's Eve of 2013. The group hacked the website of the YÖK for the second time on January 8, 2013, and revealed documents proving corruption

106 On May 11th, 2013, two car bombs exploded five minutes apart in the southern province, Hatay's Reyhanlı district on Syrian border, leaving 52 dead. The government and mainstream media accused

These documents provided evidence of corruption, injustice, fraud, and murders that everybody knew but could not prove. RedHack thus comes to the fore as the one who uncovers the deception of the Turkish people. It creates a feeling of moral rightfulness that transcends all political levels.

This sense of rightfulness that brings RedHack together with the masses is provided by their openness in determining their targets. What lies beneath their success is the centralist structure and organizational form that they adopt and translate into the digital field. Thus they can manifest quick reflexes in the face of new developments and stage intervening actions that yield results. The Gezi resistance demonstrated that their organized and on-time interventions enable them to take the lead during a mass mobilization. Besides providing communication and coordination, the cyber-attacks that they staged in protest of police violence and political developments enabled RedHack to gain a respected reputation and the support of the people. Their activities, which were not limited to the Gezi resistance, took place on three fronts: First, in moments of crisis and protest, they provided coordination between protesters; Second, they staged cyber attacks[107] to lend support to mass protests against unjust political practices; Third, they attacked centers of misinformation and manipulation and ideological apparatuses that enabled power to produce and maintain itself. They hacked the police department's websites and revealed documents in support of academics and journalists who were threatened due to their support of RedHack and they encouraged people who got into trouble because of tweets or e-mails to defend themselves by saying 'We were hacked by RedHack.' These approaches consolidated a sense of trust in RedHack.

Bashar al-Assad's Syrian regime of being behind this attack and used it as a pretext for warmongering rhetoric against Syria. In response, many demonstrations were held in several cities to protest the Turkish government's alleged responsibility for the attack. While the government's propaganda and dissidents' protests were continuing, RedHack leaked an intelligence report over the attack drafted by the Turkish Gendarmerie. It was not the Syrian administration but a Syrian opposition group supported by Turkish government (Al Nusra Front) that was planning attacks with car bombs, according to the report (Etike, 2013).

107 Dissident activities include: Erasing of all traffic fines of İstanbul in 2005, hacking the websites of the Police Department in protest of police violence in 2013, hacking the website of Fethullah Gülen, Turkish Islamic cleric who lives in self-imposed exile in the US, in protest of his followers' infiltrating into the judiciary in 2012 and issuing a statement titled 'Damn the Imam and his abettors! Long live revolution,' hacking the website of Turkish Airlines in support of ongoing strike staged by Turkish Airlines employees in May 2012, hacking the website of the Ministry of Environment and Urban Planning in support of demonstrations against Hydroelectric Power Plants in 2012, hacking the website of the Ministry of Family and Social Policies on Mother's Day of 2012 and devoting their activity to oppressed mothers and mothers who lost their children as victims of 'unsolved' murders and war (Gökdemir, 2013).

About the Limits of Putting a Spanner in the Works

The bold, self-confident, and aggressive language of RedHack succeeded to influence broad segments of society. RedHack was outraged but humorous at the same time. Humor directed at power provided a psychological relief from oppression and exploitation. It also revealed that the political regime is the weaker opponent against the intelligence of the people. By ridiculing representatives of power who are purportedly untouchable, RedHack broke the perception of their immunity. RedHack successfully combined the conventional left discourse with the humorous language and culture of the Internet, which tends to say everything in 140 characters or fewer.

RedHack also deployed a new practice in which the leftist symbols of hammer and sickle were combined with contemporary technological methods. They produced a rhetoric and content that gained recognition within Internet culture; they also discussed labor, called people to the revolution and received support from hundreds of thousands of people who did not typically adopt socialist values. Within a couple of seconds, they did what political parties could not achieve despite years of trying.

One of the greatest impacts of RedHack's language was that it fostered a sense of belonging among its followers. Having close ties with a group of tech-savvy people who have significant talents in this information age impressed people. This was cultivated through RedHack's references to 'our children,' 'we are a family,' and 'us.' People started to feel that they belonged to this family, especially when they received support from RedHack in their own activities or when RedHack staged an action at a moment when they were subjected to unjust treatment. This built up self-confidence and courage in the face of injustice.

Conclusion

RedHack attracts a great deal of attention. The interviews that group members gave to dissident organizations were widely received and a documentary titled 'RED!' was shot. In addition, academic studies are now underway about the success of RedHack. The dissident activities of RedHack have a significant peculiarity in terms of public approval and support. This is perhaps even more important than the technical success it had in penetrating digital networks or even the information that it shared (Yaman, 2013, pp. 50-51). However, revolution will not be realized in the digital field. Technology cannot be the driving force behind social development and struggle. It can, however, be a key instrument. Using technology in favor of the working class and oppressed segments of society is a matter of power. In capitalist society, any adjustment within the structure of the means of mass communication is bound to remain a relative reform. The means of communication can change only if the capitalist system that determines it is also fundamentally transformed. While the Internet is used by capitalism to control the working class and advance its ends, it also offers opportunities for the resistance. This is a great struggle. Who will win this struggle and what capitalism (and thus the Internet) will evolve into remains an open question. What is certain is that the real flow of history is not a technical matter; it is determined within class struggle (Bensaid, 2009; Ollman, 1991).

Opportunities that digital media offers to both classes have expanded when compared with the previous period. However, social media remains an instrument; it cannot be a substitute for the struggle itself. The case of RedHack is proof of this. The digital activism that escalated in parallel with social mobilization calmed down together with the decline of social activism. For this very reason, the number of followers of the @RedHack_En, which began to be used after the Twitter administration suspended the main account of RedHack, stayed consistent (around 104,000). RedHack has declined along with the decline in social mobilization. A new social explosion—both online and on the streets—could indeed be on the horizon. To intervene in the flow of history or to turn the tide of history, a political will extending to all arenas of social life is necessary.

References

Bell, D. (1973) *The Coming of Post Industrial Society.* New York: Basic Books.

Beniger, J. R. (1986). *The Control Revolution.* Cambridge: Harvard University Press.

Bensaid, D. (2009). *Marx, Mode D'Emploi.* La Decouverte Poche.

Boratav, K. (2013, June 22). Olgunlaşmış bir Sınıfsal Başkaldırı. *Sendika.* Retrieved from http://www.sendika.org/

Bulut, G. (2013a). Direniş ve Medya: Gözümüzün İçine Baka Baka. *Praksis*, Ağustos, 79-93.

Bulut, G. (2013b). Gelin Şu İşin İsmini Bi Koyalım. *Sendika.* Retrieved from http://www.sendika.org/2013/07/gelin-su-isin-ismini-bi-koyalim-gokhan-bulut/

Callinicos, A. (1998). *The revolutionary ideas of Karl Marx.* London: Bookmarks.

Castells, M. (2012). *Networks of outrage and hope: Social movements in the Internet Age.* Chichester, UK: Wiley.

Castells, M. (2007). Communication, power and counter-power in the network society. *International Journal of Communication, 1*, 238-266.

Castells, M. (2004). *The power of identity: The information age: Economy, society and culture,* Vol. II. Oxford: Blackwell.

Demirkıran, P. (2013). Hacktivizm. In A. R. Keleş (Ed.), *Hack Kültürü ve Hacktivizm: Yeni Bir Siyaset Biçimi* (pp. 27-33). İstanbul: alternatif bilişim.

Dyer-Witheford, N. (1999). *Cyber-Marx: Cycles and circuits of struggle in high technology capitalism.* University of Illinois Press.

Dawson, M., & Foster, J. B. (1998). Virtual capitalism. In R. McChesney, E. M. Wood, & J. B. Foster (Eds.), *Capitalism and the information age* (pp. 42-54). New York: Monthly Review Press.

Etike, Ş. (2013). Türk Basınında Suriye Haberleri: Eleştirel Bir Çözümleme Denemesi', 1. In B. Arık, A. Ayhan, & O. Öksüz (Eds.), *Uluslararası Medya Çalışmaları Sempozyumu Bildiriler Kitabı* (pp. 539-552). Antalya: Akdeniz Üniversitesi Yayınları.

Enzensberger, H. M. (1970). Constituents of a theory of the media. *New Left Review, 64*, 13-36.

Geray, H. (2002). İletişim Teknolojileri ve Toplum. Ankara: Ütopya.

Gökdemir, O. (2013). *Redhack: Sanal Alemin Klavyeli Asileri*. İstanbul: Destek Yay.

Hamelink, C.J. (1986). Is there life after the Information Age?. In M. Traber (Ed.), *The myth of the information society* (pp. 46-63). London: Sage.

Hardt, M., & Negri, A. (2012). *Declaration*. Argo-Navis.

Hardt, M., & Negri, A. (2001). *Empire*. Harvard University Press.

Hardt, M., & Negri, A. (2005). *Multitude: War and democracy in the age of empire*. Penguin Books.

Harvey, D. (2010). 160 Yıl Sonra Komünist Manifesto. In *Komünist Manifesto ve Hakkında Yazılar* (Ş. Alpagut, Trans., pp. 239-257). Ankara: Yordam.

Himanen, P. (2001). *The hacker ethic? A radical approach to the philosophy of business*. Random House Trade Paperbacks.

Hirschkop, K. (1998). Democracy and the new technologies. In R. McChesney, E. M. Wood, and J. B. Foster (Eds.), *Capitalism and the information age*. New York: Monthly Review Press.

Holloway, J. (2003). Where is class struggle? In A. Saad-Filho (Ed.), *Anti-Capitalism: A arxist Introduction* (pp. 224-235). London: Pluto Press.

Innis, H. (2007). *Empire and communications*. Rowman and Littlefield.

Levidov, L. (2003). Technological change as class struggle. In A. Saad-Filho (Ed.), *Anti-Capitalism: A Marxist introduction* (pp. 94-106). London: Pluto Press.

Marx, K., & Engels, F. (2002). *The communist manifesto*. Penguin Classics.

Masuda, Y. (2009). Computopia: Rebirth of theological synergism. In M. Castells & R. Mansell, R. (Eds.). *The information society: Critical concepts in sociology, Vol. 1* (pp. 128-138). London & New York: Routledge.

McLuhan, M., & Powers, B. R. (1993). *Global Village: Transformations in world life and media in the 21st Century*. Oxford University Press.

Menzies, H. (1998). Challenging capitalism in Cyberspace: The information highway, the postindustrial economy and people. In R. McChesney, E. M. Wood, & J. B. Foster (Eds.), *Capitalism and Information Age* (pp. 322-338). New York: Monthly Review Press.

Ollman, B. (1991). *Marxism: An uncommon introduction*. New Delhi: Stirling Pub.

Schiller, D. (1999). *Digital capitalism: Networking the global market system*. Cambridge: MIT Press.

Schröter, J. (2012). Internet and 'Frictionless Capitalism.' *Triple C, Journal for a Global Sustainable Information Society, 10*(2), 303-312.

Taş, O. (2007). Şebeke Toplumunda Direniş: Hacker Kültürü ve Teknoloji Etiği. In M. Binark, (Ed.), *Yeni Medya Çalışmaları* (pp. 309-344). Ankara: Dipnot.

Toffler, A. (1984). *Third Wave*. Bantam.

Torvalds, L. (2001). Prologue: What makes hackers tick? In P. Himanen, P. (Ed.), *The hacker ethic? A radical approach to the philosophy of business* (pp. xiii-xvii). Random House Trade Paperbacks.

Törenli, N. (2011). *Küreselleşmenin Yol Haritaları Tekno-Siyasal Paradigmalar.* Ankara: Ütopya.

Uçkan, Ö. (2013). Dijital aktivizmin Sınır Boyunda hacktivizm: Anonymous ve Redhack Örnekleri. In A. R. Keleş (Ed.), *Hack Kültürü ve Hacktivizm: Yeni Bir Siyaset Biçimi* (pp. 53-79). İstanbul: alternatif bilişim.

Wittel, A. (2012). Digital Marx: Towards a political economy of distributed media. *Triple C, Journal for a Global Sustainable Information Society, 10*(2) 313-333.

Yaman, U. (2013). Hack'ikatin Red'di in A. R. Keleş (Ed.), *Hack Kültürü ve Hacktivizm: Yeni Bir Siyaset Biçimi* (pp. 48-52). İstanbul: alternatif bilişim.

Yücesan-Özdemir, G. (2014). Sınıf İradesi ve Dayanışma Hareketi. *Birgün,* 25 Mayıs.

Yücesan-Özdemir, G. (2009a). *Emek ve Teknoloji.* Ankara: Tan.

Yücesan-Özdemir, G. (2009b). Küresel İletişim Çağı: Egemen Yaklaşım Versus Ekonomi Politik Yaklaşım. In S. Bulut (Ed.), *Sermayenin Medyası Medyanın Sermayesi* (pp. 15-46). Ankara: Ütopya.

12.
COUNTER-PUBLICS AND FREEDOM OF EXPRESSION

New Forms of Journalism in the Digital Environment

Emek Çaylı Rahte

Freedom of the press [...] has its beauty [...] Which one must have loved to be able to defend it. If I truly love something, I feel that its existence is essential, that it is something which I need, without which my nature can have no full, satisfied, complete existence. The [...]defenders of freedom of the press seem to enjoy a complete existence even in the absence of any freedom of the press

(Marx, 1842)

When the AKP won the 2011 elections with 49.9 percent of the votes, a new period had officially begun for both the party's supporters and opponents. For the AKP the victory would mean speeding up and intensifying the party's project of building the 'new Turkey': a conservative and wealthy nation in which Islamic society conformed to neo-liberal policies. For the opponents, as well as those who had strayed from the party, this vision for the 'new Turkey' had been heading in the wrong direction—one that was distinctly more authoritarian, majoritarian, exclusionist, and brutal in terms of capital accumulation. The government policies and discourses had led to increasing discontent and unrest among the secular middle class, liberals, left-wing intellectuals, Alevis, feminists, LGBTs, anti-capitalists, as well as religious groups. Additionally, the anti-environmental and anti-democratic urban policies of the government had been critiqued by a number of people. The Gezi Park Protests of May 2013 were instigated by these conflicts.

Demonstrations began on the 28th to protect Gezi Park but escalated into full-blown manifestations across Turkey that lasted for months.[108] Protesters demanding basic rights and freedom were branded 'a bunch of looters' by Prime Minister Erdoğan.[109] The government imposed gag orders on coverage of the Gezi Park protests and when television stations aired independent coverage of the protests in June, they were fined for inciting violence. The fact that nearly all mainstream media organizations were owned by giant companies with ties to the ruling political party, or with business interests in other industries, led to effective self-censorship. Case in point: CNNTURK aired a documentary on penguins instead of offering live coverage of the protests and the police use of tear gas. News Channels like NTV and CNNTURK were criticized for not covering the demonstrations and themselves became the subject of protests. Using humor, protestors turned the CNNTURK images into resisting penguins, which became a symbol of media's concealment of reality.

Dozens of journalists were fired or forced to resign in the aftermath of the Gezi protests, apparently in retaliation for their sympathetic coverage of the demonstrations. Prime Minister Erdoğan called social-media a 'nuisance' and

---

108 Alternative Informatics Association (*Alternatif Bilişim Derneği*) of Turkey reports the process after Gezi Park Protests and the situation of traditional media at https://www.alternatifbilisim.org/wiki/An_analysis_of_Gezi_Parki

109 As the Ministry of Interior's report shows, 3.6 million people attended the demonstrations, 5513 people were detained, and 189 were arrested. According to an assessment made by the Turkish Medical Association (TMA) on July 15, 2013, 8163 people were injured and 5 protestors lost their lives in demonstrations across Turkey. The online survey conducted by TMA reveals that 11,155 people were exposed to chemical weapons and riot control agents. See the document released by the Documentation Centre of the Human Rights Foundation of Turkey (HRFT) at http://www.fidh.org/en/europe/turkey/hrft-fact-sheet-on-gezi-park-protests-as-of-july-16th-13688

platforms such as Twitter, which was instrumental in the protests, as a 'menace to society.' Moreover, some Twitter users were detained for their online activities.[110]

Aside from all the pressures to restrict, censor, and block, there is no doubt that we owe freer and quicker flows of information to the Internet. Certainly, it is not the Internet itself but the uses of the Internet that reveal the democratic potential of this medium. A recent example of the use of social media for political activism was the 'Diren Gazetecilik' (Resist Journalism) campaign, which was organized for the July 24 Journalists and Press Day (celebrated since 2013 as the 'Struggle for Press Freedom Day'.)[111] The campaign was initiated by The Platform for Journalists' Freedom (GÖP), composed of 94 press occupational organizations.

One of the main questions that I will ask in this chapter is: 'Do the current conditions of the digital environment promote better journalism in Turkey?' I begin with an overview of world press freedom, focusing on journalism in Turkey during and after the Gezi Park events. I then reflect on the future of journalism in Turkey, considering both the technical and political aspects.

Crisis in Journalism and Hard Times for Journalists in Turkey

Journalists have always been a litmus test for freedom in their societies. When journalists are under pressure, this is usually a sign that thought itself is being restricted in society, along with the rights of women, LGBTs, and minorities. Journalists experience this pressure in many ways: as imperatives to self-censor, as a state of emergency, through intimidation and psychological or physical violence and as threats of political or economic sanctions. It's not just the threat of imprisonment that journalists contend with; they often become the targets of governments or hate campaigns when they report on subjects that interest groups or the state consider sensitive. They work under precarious conditions and face the possibility of losing their jobs whenever they challenge the dominant political and financial interests.

After September 11th, 2001, Western Europe and the US entered a period of intensive security measures directed against terrorism. On World Press Freedom Day in 2011, IFJ (*International Federation of Journalists*) President Jim Boumelha pointed out that the period following 9/11 was one of degraded press freedoms, as governments adopted a hard line in the fight against terror. He said, 'journalists have been among the prominent victims of a widespread assault on the democratic

---

110 'Turkey', http://freedomhouse.org/report/freedom-world/2014/turkey-0#.UvOwSKW2A8N
111 'Journalists of Turkey stage resistance campaign', http://bianet.org/english/freedom-of-expression/157394-direnmedya-journalists-of-turkey-stage-resistance-campaign

rights of all citizens.'[112] A free press is expected to expose—to keep in check—the tendency of government officials to abuse their power (Werhan, 2008); an attack on journalism is thus an explicit abuse of governmental power. Through the excuse of national security or prosecuting crimes, governments legitimize these restrictions on the free press. Typically, state interests—couched in term of security—override the principles of press autonomy.

IFJ highlights that over the past 12 years, more than 1100 journalists and media staff have been killed in the line of duty. Journalists over the world have died in war zones and others were targeted by brutal assassins. Yet, national and international solidarity can protect and strengthen journalists. For example, the IFJ Safety Fund was launched in 2003 to expose the attacks and threats against press freedom and the rights of journalists.[113] IFJ's *Journalists and Media Staff Killed in 2012* global report shows that 121 journalists were killed and 33 injured in one year. The Middle East is the region with the most deaths; 43 journalists were killed in 2012, 33 losing their lives in Syria.[114] Since Turkey's first journalist murder—that of Hasan Fehmi Bey, in 1909—61 others have been killed.[115] Thirty-seven of the murders occurred in the 1990s, the darkest years of Turkey in terms of human rights violations. There are many unsolved murders from that decade, especially of Kurdish politicians, activists, and journalists.

Since the last journalist murders—that of Hrant Dink in 2007 and Cihan Hayırsevener in 2009—Turkey has become a relatively safe country for journalists in terms of the danger of losing one's life. At the same time, however, Turkey has become the 'world's biggest prison for journalists,' according to the 2013 report on imprisoned journalists by the *Republican People's Party Prison Examination and Watch Commission*. Seventy-one media professionals and four media workers were in prison at the time of the report's completion. In fact, this number shows that, in terms of imprisonment, the situation is graver for journalists today than it was during the 1980 coup period, when 31 journalists were arrested.[116] Apart from the number of jailed journalists, more than 100 journalists are currently on trial and facing charges.[117] Arbitrary and unlawful deprivations of liberty and arrests and detentions without reasonable cause are a huge problem in Turkey. Legal measures such as Article 9(3) of the International Covenant on Civil and Political Rights,

---

112 'Attacks hangs over journalism', http://www.radiovop.com/index.php/national-news/6226-shadow-of-9-11-attacks-hangs-over-journalism-ifj.html
113 'IFJ International safety fund', http://ifj-safety.org/en/contents/ifj-international-safety-fund
114 'In the grip of violence: Journalists and media staff killed in 2012', http://ifj-safety.org/assets/docs/202/117/0b958ca-3d47c75.pdf
115 For the full list of murdered journalists, 'Öldürülen gazeteciler', http://www.tgc.org.tr/oldurulen-gazeteciler.asp
116 'CHP'nin tutuklu gazeteciler raporu, Temmuz 2013', http://www.cgd.org.tr/index.php?-Did=275&Page=1
117 'Gazetecileri susturamazsınız', http://www.tgs.org.tr/index.php?option=com_frontpage&Itemid=1

Article 7(5) of the American Convention on Human Rights and Article 5(3) of the European Convention on Human Rights state that every detainee is entitled to a trial within 'a reasonable time' or should be released pending trial. This is an appropriate measure to ensure that one is presumed innocent until proven guilty and that deprivation of liberty only occurs in exceptional circumstances.[118]

Authorities claim that journalists are not arrested for journalistic activities but for their activities against the state. They are charged with being members of terrorist organizations, aiding and abetting terrorist organizations, or serving the purpose of the organization by supporting its propaganda. Some journalists are charged with denigrating Turkishness or influencing court proceedings. But it is well known that when freedom is discarded for the sake of national security policies it always brings more authoritarianism and fewer civil rights. The fact that Turkey has fallen in the international ranking for press freedom and human rights means that vague and broadly defined anti-terror laws are easily turned into violations of freedom of thought and belief.[119] According to the CPJ (Committee to Protect Journalists), Turkey jailed more journalists in 2013 than any other country, including China and Iran.[120]

The 2013 *Reporters Without Borders World Press Freedom Index* shows that the same three countries—Finland, followed by the Netherlands and Norway—have consecutively held the highest rankings for respect of press freedoms. Out of 179 countries, the lowest ranked countries are Turkmenistan, North Korea, and Eritrea, immediately preceded by Syria (176th), where a deadly information war is being waged and Somalia (175th). Iran (174th), China (173rd), Vietnam (172nd), Cuba (171st), Sudan (170th), and Yemen (169th) complete the list of the ten countries that respect media freedom least. Turkey (154th) has fallen in the index, dropping from 148th to 154th.[121]

118 'Human rights and arrest, pre-trial detention and administrative detention', http://www.ohchr.org/ Documents/Publications/training9chapter5en.pdf
119 For a short article about counter- terrorism and its risks for jeopardizing freedom see 'Counter-Terrorism: Guaranteeing security or jeopardising freedom', http://www.eurotopics.net/en/home/ presseschau/archiv/magazin/politik-verteilerseite/anti-terror_2007_07/terrorbekaemp-fung_schneider_mueller/
120 'Turkey's hidden truths', http://www.bbc.co.uk/programmes/p01qnc1y?ocid=socialflow_facebook
121 The index has been published regularly since 2002. See 'World press freedom index 2015', http:// en.rsf.org/

Table 11.1. Turkey in RSF World Press Freedom Index

Year	Number of Countries	Rank
2002	139	99
2003	166	115
2004	167	113
2005	167	98
2006	168	98
2007	169	101
2008	173	102
2009	175	122
2010	179	138
2011-2012	179	148
2013	179	154

Source: 2013 Reporters Without Borders World Press Freedom Index

Published annually since 1972, *The World Freedom Report* makes comparative assessments of political rights and civil liberties in 195 countries. The electoral process, political pluralism and participation, the functioning of government, freedom of expression and belief, associational and organizational rights, the rule of law, personal autonomy and individual rights are the indexes used to rate the freedom of each country. Turkey's 2014 freedom score is 3.5 (1=most free; 7=least free), which makes it a relatively free country. Turkey has similar scores for Internet freedom. Freedom House's *Freedom on the Net 2013* report shows that Turkey is a relatively free country with a score of 49 (0=most free; 100=least free). Turkey's ranking has worsened since 2012, from 46 to 49. The scores that measure the level of Internet and digital media freedom in 60 countries are prepared according to three criterions: Obstacles to access, limits on content and violations of user rights. The report shows that Turkey's score is worse than others' when it comes to violations of user rights.[122]

Turkey's population is 85 million and the number of Internet users is 35 million, which means that almost 40 percent of people use Internet. The Turkish government has been working hard to regulate Internet media, which means controlling and restricting a relatively free medium with a large user base. Especially during and after the Gezi Park events, Internet regulation turned into one of the most serious agendas of the government. Journalism, and media more generally, has been dramatically influenced by the Gezi Park events.

---

122 'Freedom on the net 2015', http://www.freedomhouse.org

Journalism After Gezi

On July 26, 2013, the Turkish Journalists' Union announced that 59 journalists had been fired or forced out. The opposition Republican People's Party (CHP) compiled a list of 77 journalists who were fired or forced out due to their coverage of the protests.[123] Some media employees cite much higher numbers. *NTV Tarih*, a history magazine owned by *NTV*, was shut down entirely and its staff let go after the magazine's editors prepared a special 'Gezi edition.' The Gezi firings continued throughout the fall. In November, the public broadcaster TRT fired two employees who used social media to voice their support for the protests (Corke et al., 2014, p. 8). From the beginning of the protests in May, until the end of September 2013, 153 journalists were injured, 39 were detained, 3 were arrested, and 2 are still in jail.[124]

The coverage of protests also caused smear campaigns against the journalists of international news corporations. For example, CNN and BBC were attacked by the Turkish state (and its supporters) in social media and accused of being enemies of Turkey. Following her reporting of Gezi protests, the BBC's correspondent Selin Girit was the target of a Twitter hate campaign initiated by a senior Turkish politician. Being accused of 'treachery to her nation,' she received threats of rape and murder.[125]

The conventional media of Turkey failed to inform the public during the protests because of established cooperation with or strong pressure from the Turkish government. While Turkey's news channels—CNNTÜRK, NTV, and Habertürk— censored their coverage of Gezi Protests, the people relied on international media, independent press, and Internet for the latest news about the protests. People's frustration with Turkish media was channeled into the protests and demonstrations themselves.

Another effect of the Gezi Events was a rise in people's interest in newspapers. As the tables below indicate, the total number of newspapers circulating right after the events increased and continued to do so during the second week of the protests:

---

123 The December 17 corruption scandal has produced another string of firings of prominent columnists.
124 'Habercinin Gezi'si: Saldırı, gözaltı, istifa, işsizlik', http://bianet.org/bianet/ifade-ozgurlu-gu/150722-habercinin-gezi-si-saldiri-gozalti-istifa-issizlik
125 'Turkey's hidden truths', http://www.bbc.co.uk/programmes/p01qnc1y?ocid=socialflow_facebook

Table 11.2. Circulation of Newspapers in the First Week of Gezi Protests

During Gezi Events: 27.05.2013 - 02.06.2013		
Total: 5 056 081	Previous Week: 5 015 273	Difference: 40 808

Source: www.medyatava.com

Table 11.3. Circulation of Newspapers in the Second Week of Gezi Protests

During Gezi Events: 03.06. 2013-09.06.2013		
Total: 5 122 974	Previous Week: 5 056 081	Difference: 66 893

Source: www.medyatava.com

Table 11.4. Circulation of Newspapers a Week Before Gezi Protests

Before the Gezi Events: 20.05.2013 - 26.05.2013		
Total: 5 015 273	Previous Week: 5 019 546	Difference: -4 273

Source: www.medyatava.com

Significantly, those newspapers whose circulation increased the most were left-leaning or opposed to the government. The leftist newspapers *Sol* and *BirGün* increased their circulation by 48 percent and 34.5 percent respectively and the oppositional/Kemalist newspaper *Sözcü* by 28.5 percent; whereas the Islamist and pro-government newspapers *Akit* and *YeniŞafak* increased by 16.1 percent and 12.4 percent respectively. The visitors of independent news websites also increased substantially; the left-wing news and commentary website sendika.org had 327,670 visitors a month before the Gezi events and 1,188,964 directly after the protests had begun (Bulut, 2013, p. 87).

What is not clear is the extent to which this increasing circulation and traffic of alternative or oppositional journals is permanent or temporary. The extent to which these newspapers maintained their high levels of readership long after the Gezi events remains an open question.

Table 11.5. A Comparison of the Circulations of the Leftist/Oppositional Newspapers

Newspaper	Before Gezi Events (31.3-28.4 2013)	During Gezi Events (3-30.6. 2013)	One month After Gezi Events (1-14 July 2013)	One year after Gezi Events (1st Anniversary) (26 May-1 June 2014)	One Year after Gezi Events (7-13 July 2014)
Birgün	7.953	10.678	10.488	25.461	26.159
Sol	12.760	18.940	18.427	14.639	No print version anymore. Online news portal Digital-only format
Radikal	23.555	25.865	25.211	22.651	No print version anymore. Digital-only format
Cumhuriyet	51.331	57.108	56.129	52.333	51.759
Evrensel	5.838	6.555	5.638	7.569	12.174
Sözcü	288.807	371.050	366.763	337.390	348.246

Source: The first three columns on left showing the circulation numbers are taken from Bulut's (2013, p. 87) work. And the last two columns on the right are prepared by using the data of medyatava.com

Of six newspapers, *Birgün*, *Sözcü* and *Evrensel* have kept their relatively high circulation numbers. Their slightly higher circulation numbers in July of 2014 were partially the result of print closures in two other left newspapers, *Radikal* and *Sol*.[126] These examples of the digitalization of print newspapers in Turkey regenerated discussions on the future of journalism because so many well-respected journalists lost their jobs in the process.

---

126 *Radikal* was first published in 1996, with the intention of making a rights-based journalism focused on issues related to the environment, minorities and LGBTs. On June 21, 2014, *Radikal* was printed and distributed for the last time and headed into digital-only format. Similarly *Sol* newspaper printed the last paper version on June 4, 2014.

New Forms of Journalism in Turkey?: Journalists without Journals, Journals Without Journalists, and More

In this section, I will ask a broader question: What is digital journalism? What are the advantages and disadvantages of online journalism for all sides: namely, employers, employees, and readers. Certainly, the expanded use of the Internet has changed the way that journalism is produced, distributed and used. This situation raises the question of whether a path has thus been opened for better and more independent journalism. Some have suggested that the changing digital media landscape has led to a creative explosion in diverse forms of journalism, while others claim that the field of journalism is now in crisis.

When Terry Flew published his book *New Media: An Introduction* in 2002, digital media and journalism referred to the presence of computers in the newsroom, the use of Internet to research news stories, online web sites of long established news organizations, and possibly the use of digital cameras to record audio visual footage. In the 10 years that have passed since the publication of this book, an entirely new vocabulary has entered news journalism: blogging, Twitter, Wikipedia, Wikileaks, citizen journalism, iPads, smart phones, YouTube, and social media. The rise of user-created content and participatory media has led to the blurring of lines between media 'producers' (Axel Bruns, 2008; Flew, 2012, pp. 3,4) and consumers. John Pavlik (2013, p. 183) has identified four principles that underpin recent innovations in news media: intelligence or research, commitment to freedom of speech, dedication to the pursuit of truth, and accuracy and ethics.

Pavlik emphasizes that the methods and truth claims of the traditional model of objective journalism have been challenged with new and alternative ways of accessing the reality and translating it into public knowledge and understanding. Arianna Huffington (2013) sees the future of journalism as definitely a hybrid one, combining the best practices of traditional journalism—fairness, accuracy, storytelling, deep investigations—with the best tools available to the digital world—speed, transparency and, above all, engagement.

Others have pointed to changes in logic, structure, and indeed, the very definition of journalism (Hermida, 2010). Twitter now facilitates the immediate dissemination of digital fragments of news and information from official and unofficial sources over a variety of systems and devices. As Hermida notes, Twitter works as a kind of 'awareness system'; it alerts the reader to a news fragment, which he or she then actively pursues in more detail through other print, broadcast, or online channels. Twitter journalism also provides an awareness of what others in your network are reading and what they consider important.

The major transformations in journalism relate to both the digital environment in which journalists now work and the users who more actively participate in the production of news content. Van der Haak et al. (2012) writes that:

New facts are being unearthed daily; more audience feedback is being integrated; more voices are being heard; more diverse perspectives on the same news stories are being presented; more stories are available, archived and searchable for longer periods of time; more men and women of power are being watched more closely; and more people are engaged more actively with the changes in the world—by taking photos or making videos of key moments, by commenting on blogs, or by sharing the stories that matter to them. (p. 2923)

In this way, the transformations in journalism can be evaluated according to two main aspects: The first is 'citizen journalism,' which refers to the citizen's active participation in journalism activities, such as news gathering and sharing, as well as the active use of digital tools by media professionals or activists for alternative, independent media experiences. The second aspect is the mainstream media's use of Internet journalism, which involves the adoption of social media and other online tools.

'Citizen journalism' typically refers to the use of computer, Internet, and smart phones by average people. The data they collect, the stories they share, and the questions they ask cumulatively shape the content of online journalism. Optimistically, this trend is interpreted as an expansion of free and democratic communication. As Hintz (2013) notes, people have been transformed from 'audience' into a generation of 'netizens,' putting into practice the now-classic media adage: 'Don't hate the media, be the media!' (p. 146). Apart from being an active producer of news content, by demanding quick and reliable information, the citizen has also created a more dynamic and participatory flow of information. While Homero G. De Zuniga (2009) thinks that certain web uses contribute to political participation, civic engagement, and increased news consumption—especially for young people—he notes that others fear that news in the online environment may have resulted in societal fragmentation and displacement of community concerns.

Online versions of independent journals have become more prevalent comparing with print versions. A very well-known example is *Huffington Post*—a commercial online collaborative blog that is more visible in the United States than any other news outlet except for the *BBC*, *CNN* and the *New York Times* (Benkler, 2011, p. 53). In Turkey, journalists who were fired from the mainstream newspapers for political reasons or who preferred to be free from the limitations of conventional media, have created their own journalism environment, whether this be personal blogs, Twitter pages, or online-alternative journals (like *T24*). Political activists have turned to online facilities, creating alternative news and intellectual platforms. Especially after the Gezi events, platforms such as *ÖtekilerinPostası* and *Sendika org* have seen an increase in followers, readers and supporters. *Çapul TV* also started to make Internet broadcasting during the Gezi events, filling the void of mainstream coverage. During the Gezi events, one of the popular slogans of the demonstrators was 'the revolution will not be televised.'[127]

Online news facilities, like Twitter, have been adopted by big media institutions. This shows the compatibility of professional journalism with online-civic journalism. Traditional news sources migrated online via the emergence of an interconnected opinion space of personal journals, or weblogs (blogs), which started in the mid-1990s but really gained attraction after the turn of the century (De Zuniga, 2009). Newspapers and TV news stations are jumping on the bandwagon of participatory journalism, inviting the public to send in videos and stories (Bird, 2009). Most newspapers also have official Twitter accounts. Apart form these official accounts, most of the journalists in the mainstream media have their own Twitter accounts with a large number of followers.

Turkey's mainstream media uses social media effectively to compete for fast and accessible flows of information. Some mainstream newspapers admit that social media is the main instrument of the new journalism, so they work seriously to be a leading actor on this stage. For instance *Hürriyet,* which has been a strong agenda-setting power in the Turkish media for decades, is a leader in this regard, with three times as many Twitter followers as print readers.

Media institutions—both those aiming towards mainstream and independent journalism—use the support of readers and online communities for both financial and creative purposes. While corporate-sponsored media uses the contributions from the readers in content producing, the independent news platforms also accept financial support (donations). This practice of obtaining financial or productive support from people online (called 'crowdsourcing' and 'crowd funding') has been used widely to fund various emerging projects.

Many news organizations like *BBC* and *The Guardian* led the way in crowdsourcing and integrating user-generated content. *Al Jazeera* too invited viewers to upload their own photos and videos of the Israeli attacks on Gaza and offered the footage free of charge and with a Creative Commons license to provide a crowd-

---

127 A poem and song by Gil Scott-Heron.

sourced Arab alternative to the well funded, top-down media strategy of Israel (Van der Haak et al., 2012).

Table 11.6. Mainstream/pro-government/right-wing Newspapers (in the Order of Circulation Rates)

	Newspaper circulation (23-29. 09. 2013)	Facebook followers (03.10.2013)	Twitter followers (03.10.2013)
Zaman	943.490	310.375	340.757
Posta	441.098	143,592	38.628
Hürriyet	386.025	435.806	**985.067**
Sözcü	347.465	456.033	178.297
Sabah	309.718	295.387	223.364
Habertürk	225.128	499.818	947.394
Türkiye	184.220	51.323	18.220
Milliyet	167.953	453.942	589.582
Bugün	124.106	133.732	52.698
Star	121.594	83.536	96.710
Vatan	115.224	246.482	62.292
YeniŞafak	112.861	75.891	79.461
Akşam	104.059	53.059	35.607

The independent Internet journals and news platforms have been using crowdfunding to maintain a free and open source of news with reliable, up-to-date news content. America's *Democracy Now* is a example to that. On their web site they write that 'Democracy Now! is funded entirely through contributions from listeners, viewers, and foundations. We do not accept advertisers, corporate underwriting, or government funding. This allows us to maintain our independence.'[128] An example from Turkey is *T24*, who collected 100,000 Turkish Liras in a short time after they announced that they were doing crowd funding and requested donations from their readings to improve their project. Since September 2009, when they started independent journalism online, *T24* has reached almost 85 thousand followers, becoming one of the most effective independent news platforms in Turkey.

Some online news platforms have started using crowdsourcing in a totally different manner, namely, outsourcing news production to a third party, often to an offshore labor force. For instance, the online newspaper *Pasadena Now* was told by *NY Times* columnist Maureen Dowd to fire its entire *Pasadena* staff and outsource news coverage to writers in India who write news and features, using email, press releases, the web and live video streaming from a cell phone at City Hall. Dowd reports that Dean Singleton, chairman of the *Associated Press* and head of the *MediaNews* group, which publishes several major newspapers, announced his company is considering outsourcing almost all its operations (Bird, 2009).

Apart from crowdsourcing, online journalism provides choices like data visualization and immersive journalism. With data visualization, graphic design, data mapping, and interactive graphics become essential components of conveying information and storytelling,[129] while immersive journalism emphasizes the first-person experience in a news story. Innovation in camera technology also enables new forms of point-of-view journalism in reporting and constructing the story from a specific person's position inside a real-life situation (Van der Haak et al., 2012, pp. 2930-2932). Visual journalism is a method that integrates text, video and audio sources into storytelling. By integrating video sources in online news articles, journalism increasingly becomes both visual and textual.

Data journalism uses different data visualization tools to give readers compelling stories with large amounts of information in a digestible form. Data journalism helps a journalist tell a complex story through engaging infographics.[130] Journalists are needed more than ever to curate, verify, analyze, and synthesize a wide range of data. Taken together, these emerging forms of journalism can be understood as media's attempt to adapt and respond to changes in the information environment by using multi-dimensional story-telling methods and providing readers with more interactive ways of exploring the sources underlying the news,

---

128 'About democracy now', http://www.democracynow.org/about

129 For example, journalists *of The Telegraph* in London used moderately sophisticated software to find connections among hundreds of thousands of documents when the newspaper obtained copies of expense reports by some members of Parliament and showed how officials were abusing their allowances to buy second homes, pay personal expenses, and duck taxes (van der Haak et al., 2012).

130 See more 'What is data journalism', http://datajournalismhandbook.org/1.0/en/introduction_0.html#sthash.WLo1Itzj.dpuf

thereby encouraging them to participate in the process of creating and evaluating stories (Gray et al., 2012).

Crisis in Conventional Journalism

Besides the technical innovations and reforms in journalism, there is a remarkable crisis in the traditional models of journalism, particularly in corporate media institutions. In addition to the pressures of ownership, monopolization, political and, economic power and the precarious working conditions of average media professionals—which has been the major handicap for a free media—traditional media also faces financial dilemmas in adapting traditional media methods to online journalism, namely, the intense competition among Internet media and the decline of interest in conventional newspapers and print materials in general.

Print and broadcast journalism has to compete with online journalism practices that present free, quick, and interactive flow of news. Most media owners have squeezed news organizations to do more with less. As a result, working conditions for many journalists have deteriorated and their workloads have increased. Multimedia reporting and publishing have become the norm without comparable investments in training or new staff (van der Haak et al., 2012, p. 2944). Increasingly, Internet journalists are forced to make their livings with 'day-job' careers. What this means for journalists starting out is that the expectations for journalistic careers are in the process of shifting significantly (Gitlin, 2009). The rise of the citizen-journalist is accompanied by a decline in jobs for trained journalists, with massive layoffs striking newspapers and TV news organizations (Bird, 2009).

Yet, the crisis in traditional journalism is not only caused by the tough competition with online journalism. Todd Gitlin (2009) argues that U.S. newspaper circulation has been declining, per capita, at a constant rate *since 1960*. Young people are not reading papers. While they say they 'look' at the papers online, it is not clear how much looking they actually do (Gitlin, 2009). The amount of time spent with newspapers is also declining. The average American newspaper reader is 55 years old. There is a decline in advertising revenues combined with a decline in the circulation of newspapers, which has badly damaged the profitability of newspapers. Since 2001, overall U.S. newspaper circulation has dropped by 13.5 percent for the dailies and 17.3 percent for the Sunday editions. The Pew Center's Project for Excellence in Journalism, 'State of the News Media 2012' report shows that the recent decline of newspapers is not as overstated as Gitlin claims. In the U.S., newspaper advertising revenues have dropped 48 percent since 2006 (Pavlik, 2013). But it does not mean that people are not interested in obtaining news. On the contrary, people who have tablet devices and smart phones read news more actively. The point is that the younger generations do not prefer print newspapers.

Guardian Online (U.K.) is now estimated to have 49 million online readers worldwide, as compared to fewer than 200,000 readers of its print product in the U.K. (Flew, 2012, p. 19).

Whereas newspaper circulation is declining in the advanced capitalist societies, it is expanding in India and most of the other developing countries because the countries in the first group are in the final stages of moving to new digital means of delivering content (McNair, 2009).

In Turkey, between 2005 and 2011, newspaper circulation encountered a substantial increase. In 2005, circulation of newspapers and journals was 1,616,814 40. In 2011 it raised to 2,265,538,153.[131] By 2014, the average newspaper circulation is around 4 million and on particular days of the year (New Year's or days of political crisis), it reaches almost 5 million.[132] Even though the newspaper circulation is not declining, Internet use in Turkey has been expanding. It means that the use of the Internet for news and information has made online-journalism more attractive for Turkish people, just like the situation in other advanced capitalist societies. According to recent research by *Turkish* Statistical Institute, the Internet use of individuals aged 16 to 74 was 47.4 percent in 2012 and 45 percent in 2011. The research shows that people spend 72.5 percent of their time on the Internet reading news, newspapers, or journals.[133]

The widespread use of Internet facilities to obtain news led media owners to search for less expensive solutions for journalism in Turkey as well. At the moment, the digitalization process of newspapers seems to affect left wing, relatively low-budget newspapers. As mentioned before, two of the leftist newspapers, *Radikal* and *Sol* decided to continue in digital-only form. The case of *Radikal* is a bit different from *Sol* because *Radikal* is one of the newspapers published by a media conglomerate, Doğan Media Group. The main reason for the paper's abandonment of the printed version was its low circulation rate.

Also, the newspaper declared that its aim was to embrace the digital era and be the initiator of digital journalism in Turkey. In that process, experienced correspondents and columnists paid the cost and lost their jobs. Even though some well-experienced and respected journalists continued working there, *Radikal* faces a real risk of turning into a model of 'copy-paste journalism'.

Pınar Öğünç, one of the many talented journalists at Radikal, questioned the glitzy promotion of digital media in her farewell column:[134]

---

131 These numbers are from *Turkish* Statistical Institute, http://www.turkstat.gov.tr/PreTablo.do?alt_id=1086

132 For the actual circulation numbers, see '02 Kasım 2015 08 Kasım 2015 haftası tiraj tablosu', http://www.medyatava.com/tiraj/

133 'Hanehalkı bilişim teknolojileri kullanım araştırması, 2012', http://www.tuik.gov.tr/PreHaber-Bultenleri.do?id=10880

134 'Radikal newspaper curtsies goodby and takes leave from Turkey's sick sector', http://www.hur-

Digital media in Turkey has flourished as a channel where disregarding ethical concerns to obtain more hits is considered acceptable, news stories that would not be chosen to be printed are 'promoted,' and editorial supervision has become more lax due to speed and the lack of personnel. Meanwhile, the employer shifts the blame onto the worker for not making enough profit in this new media universe, which has added new methods of exploitation to the ones that were already known in the sector ... When you dare to criticize all these things, to stand on the side of rights and labor, they are able to treat you as an 'old-fashioned' journalist who is not capable of seeing where the media is headed in the world. However, the direction where journalism in the world is headed is a place where original content, language and refinement—in other words, 'production'—become all the more valuable, as they are enriched with the possibilities offered by digital technology.

Towards More Freedom or More Pressure?

Even though online journalism and Internet media present real possibilities for liberation from strict corporate and governmental control, the other side of the mirror should also be considered.

Emerging communication platforms, such as Facebook, Twitter and YouTube, have provided a human narrative on the activities and effects of oppressive regimes, especially in Middle East and North Africa region, and they have served as important tools in the fight for freedom and democracy. Indeed, social media helped dissidents to organize protests and voice anger, changed public perceptions of Turkish authorities and established hierarchies, and helped make the citizen an active participant in the construction of knowledge (Saleh, 2013, p. 236). The Tunisian revolt was in part aided by amateur videos of demonstrations, uploaded to a *Facebook* page of an activist, Lotfi Hajji, and then retransmitted around the Arab world by *Al Jazeera*. Video taken by protesters was mixed with that taken by professional journalists to depict the revolt in Egypt. During the Iranian reform movement protests in 2009, videos and images created by users on the ground became the sole video feed for international news outlets (Benkler, 2011, pp. 52-66). During the Iranian election protests of June 2009, the volume of tweets mentioning Iran peaked at 221,774 in one hour, from a flow of between 10,000 and 50,000 an hour (Hermida, 2010). Similarly in Turkey during the Gezi Park Protests, Twitter and Facebook were the main channels for keeping up with the

riyetdailynews.com/blog-radikal-newspaper-curtsies-goodbye-and-takes-leave-from-turkeys-sick-sector-.aspx?PageID=238&NID=68238&NewsCatID=341

latest news, organizing new protests, and providing safe ways of communicating between protestors and reacting against the government's policies.

Just as social media have been used by activists to advance political change, they have also been used by governments to control and deter such action. Specifically, social media was used to identify protesters in Tunisia, Syria, Iran (Hintz, 2013), and more recently in Turkey.

Governments are worried about the widespread use of social media by the public. They think the Internet undermines sovereignty, much in the way that states previously considered telegraph's capacity to cross borders as a direct threat to their sovereignty (Gripsrud et al., 2010, p. 248). Turkish Prime Minister Recep Tayyip Erdoğan branded Twitter 'a scourge' and accused some social media users of provoking people against the government during the Gezi Events. Even though the government authorities find Twitter a real troublemaker, they do their best to manipulate the Twitter trend topics and use trending lists for propaganda.

The use of the Internet during the huge protests against government led the authorities to restrict Internet use. On February 5, 2014, a new Internet bill, tightening government control over the Internet, was approved in Parliament. The new law will allow Turkey's telecommunications authority to block websites without first seeking a court ruling. It will also force Internet providers to store data on web users' activities for two years and make it available to the authorities.[135] Turkey's previously existing Internet law (Law 5651) has already been used to block thousands of websites by court order. According to Google, Turkish authorities issue three times more requests to remove content than any other country.

The Committee to Protect Journalists (CPJ) called on Turkish President Abdullah Gül to veto the Internet bill passed by the Parliament.[136] The European Commission also lashed out at the bill, saying it raised 'serious concerns' in light of Turkey's candidacy for European Union membership. 'The Turkish public deserves more information and more transparency, not more restrictions,' European Commission spokesman Peter Stano said. He told reporters that the law 'needs to be revised in line with European standards.' The government has rejected accusations that the bill amounts to censorship, insisting it would protect privacy. Internet freedom activists, however, believe that their government designed the bill to rapidly silence its critics.[137]

---

135 ' Turkey passes law tightening control of internet', http://www.bbc.co.uk/news/world-europe-26062038
136 'Turkish president should veto internet bill', https://www.cpj.org/2014/02/turkish-president-should-veto-internet-bill.php
137 'Turkish parliament adopt internet censorship bill', http://america.aljazeera.com/articles/2014/2/6/turkish-parliamentadoptsinternetcensorshipbill.html

The use of the Internet as a form of public sphere directly depends on the political culture and the effectiveness of democratic institutions in a nation. For the state, social media is used for more control, propaganda, information gathering, and pressuring users. On the citizen's side, social media is used to keep the state accountable and to monitor and critique its activities, while making demands, sharing information, organizing, and resisting.

As the case of Egypt in 2011 showed, when social media applications or even the Internet itself becomes a threat to an existing political order, they can be shut down. We are witnessing increasing online surveillance and filtering and new forms of censorship (Hintz, 2013, p. 147). The filtering of Web content has become a particularly common practice across the globe. According to the OpenNet Initiative (2012), 47 percent of the world's Internet users experience online censorship, with 31 percent of all Internet users living in countries that engage in 'substantial' or 'pervasive' censorship

While the Chinese 'Great Firewall' and filtering practices in other authoritarian countries have been well documented, filtering in Western democracies has not received the same attention, despite the fact it is prevalent. Often initiated with the rationale of restricting illegal or otherwise unacceptable content (such as child pornography), surveillance and censorship are increasingly expanding to other fields (as evidenced in the case of Wikileaks and Julian Assange). The US debate over an Internet kill-switch and UK government proposals of temporary blockages of social networking platforms in times of political turmoil have further demonstrated the willingness of government to interfere with online communication and have highlighted the vulnerability of the supposedly borderless cyberspace. With the ubiquity of electronic communication, the capacity of the state to gather and process information about its citizens is growing. Globally, Internet activists who provide communications infrastructure for social movements or publish oppositional content have been subject to police operations such as house raids (Hintz, 2013, pp. 149, 153, 156).

In spite of all these pressures by governments, it is not possible for governments and corporations to enforce highly effective censorship in the digitally networked age. Indeed, censorship is difficult because information circulates in the global Internet networks, open to public view. When information is censored in some countries, the open, networked structure of the Internet (UProxy, VPN etc.) allows a continual distribution of information that can be accessed through multiple platforms. This is also true of countries like China and Iran. Moreover, countless citizen journalists contribute with their reports, images, information, and opinions, making it possible for the practice of journalism to broaden the scope and diversity of its sources (van der Haak, 2012, p. 2934). But there is no doubt that governments will continue to search for the ways to restrict freedoms to keep control and power.

Conclusion: 'So what?'

Inspired by Karl Marx's words on press and censorship (1842), it can be very simply said that the struggle for freedom of the press is a battle between people who love freedoms and those who detest it. Those journalists who love freedom have found themselves in jails, in courts, and in the company of protestors on the streets; they've also found themselves at risk of losing their jobs. Many continue to hang onto their jobs by a thread under pressures from editors, bosses, or political powers.

There is a clear need for international solidarity with journalists in the struggle for greater press freedoms. There is widespread acceptance of political restraints on the part of journalists, politicians, and ordinary citizens. They might say, 'Yes, there is censorship, but so what?' In Turkey, this complacency is well entrenched. The pressures from the state (government and military) have always been a major problem for Turkish journalists.[138] Even though the recent government of Turkey is praised for implementing an end to military dominance and its control over the media, state control did not cease.[139] The current evidence of this is the voice recording of conversations between the Prime Minister and the deputy chairman of one of the mainstream media groups. According to the voice recordings, the Prime Minister gives instructions to change the news content. After those voice recordings were uploaded on YouTube and provoked a debate on press freedom in Turkey, none of the recorded men denied the situation. The editor-in chief remarked that, 'There have always been interventions. I have been doing this job for 32 years. Governments have always attempted to intervene in the media. The interventions are proportional to the strength of the governments. The stronger the governments, the more intense the interventions.'[140] At the beginning, the response of government to the allegations about media manipulation was silence and denial. But after the voice recordings were made public, the prime minister's position changed 'so what?'[141]

---

138 For a recent research on censorship in Turkish press, see Arsan (2013).
139 For the last 10 years of freedom of expression in Turkey, see Çaylı and Depeli (2012).
140 'Editor's confession concrete evidence of gov't pressure on media: observers', http://www.today-szaman.com/news-339145-editors-confession-concrete-evidence-of-govt-pressure-on-media-say-observers.html
141 'Turkey media manipulation: from denial to so what?', http://www.al-monitor.com/pulse/originals/2014/02/turkey-media-manipulation.html#

So what? This question must be redirected to the main subject of this chapter: The information technologies have advanced. So what? Digitalization has improved journalism facilities dramatically. So what? The Internet has opened up new spaces for participation and activism. So what? What if we have media but do not hear, do not see and do not speak:

They have hearts with which they understand not, they have eyes with which they see not and they have ears with which they hear not (the truth)

Surah Al-Araf (Verse 179)142

References

Arsan, E. (2013). Killing me softly with his words: Censorship and self-censorship from the perspective of Turkish journalists. *Translate For Justice.com.* Retrieved from http://translateforjustice.com/tag/esra-arsan/

Benkler, Y. (2006). *The wealth of networks: How social production transforms markets and freedom.* Yale University Press.

Bird, S. (2009). The future of journalism in the digital environment. *Journalism, 10,* 293-295.

Bulut, G. (2013). Direniş ve Medya: Gözümüzün İçine Baka Baka. *Praksis,* Ağustos. 79-93.

Çaylı, E., & Depeli G. (2012). İfade Özgürlüğünün 10 Yılı. IPS İletişim Vakfı Yayınları.

Corke, S. (2014). Democracy in crisis: Corruption, media and power in Turkey—A Freedom House Special Report. *Freedom House.* Retrieved from www.freedomhouse.org.

De Zuniga, H. (2009). Weblogs, traditional sources online and political participation: An assessment of how the Internet is changing the political environment. *New Media & Society, 11,* 553-574.

Flew, T. (2012, October 12). *The digital transformation of 21st century news journalism.* Presentation to the School of Communication, Conference on Digital Media and Journalism, Ming Chuan University, Taipei, Taiwan. Retrieved from http://www.academia.edu/2045520/THE_DIGITAL_TRANSFORMATION_OF_21ST_CENTURY_NEWS_JOURNALISM.

Gitlin, T. (2009, May 19-20). *A surfeit of crises: Circulation, revenue, attention, authority and deference.* Keynote Presentation to Journalism in Crisis conference, University of Westminster, London. Retrieved from http://www.westminsternewsonline.com/wordpress/?p=1951

Gray, J., Bounegru, L., & Chamers, L. (2012). *Digital journalism handbook.* Retrieved from http://datajournalismhandbook.org/1.0/en/front_matter_2.html

---

142 This Surah is the one that Turkish Prime Minister mentions most in his various speeches.

Gripsrud, J., Moe, H., Molander, A., & Murdock, G. (2010). (Eds.). *The Idea of the public sphere*. Plymouth: Lexington Books.

Hermida, A. (2010). Twittering the news: The emergence of ambient journalism. *Journalism Practice, 4*(3), 297-308.

Hintz, A. (2013). Dimensions of modern freedom of expression: WikiLeaks, policy hacking and digital freedoms. In B. Brevini, A. Hintz & P. McCurdy (Eds.), *Beyond WikiLeaks: Implications for the future of communications, journalism and society* (pp. 146-166). London: Palgrave Macmillan.

Marx, K. (1842, May 5). Prussian Censorship. Rheinische Zeitung. No. 125, Supplement. Retrieved from http://www.marxists.org/archive/marx/works/1842/free-press/ch01.htm

McNair, B. (2009). Journalism in the 21st century: Evolution, not extinction. *Journalism, 10*(3), 347-349.

Pavlik, J. V. (2013). Innovation and the future of journalism. *Digital Journalism, 1*(2), 181-193.

Saleh, I. (2013). Wikileaks and the Arab Spring: The twists and turns of media, culture and power. In B. Brevini, A. Hintz & P. McCurdy (Eds.), *Beyond WikiLeaks: Implications for the future of communications, journalism and society* (pp. 236-245). London: Palgrave Macmillan.

Tuğal, C. (2014). Resistance everywhere. *New perspectives on Turkey.* Retrieved from http://www.newperspectivesonturkey.net/Content/Npt/Issue_32/Lecture_34/157-172_49_NPT_Fall.pdf

Van der Haak, Parks, M., & Castells, M. (2012). The future of journalism: Networked journalism. *International Journal of Communication, 6*, 2923–2938.

Werhan, K. (2008). Rethinking freedom of the press after 9/11. *Tulane Law Review, 82*, 1561-1606.

13.
AFTERWORD

The Willpower of the Working Class and the Burning Questions of a Unified Movement in Turkey

Gamze Yücesan-Özdemir

When we lend an ear to the voices from the streets of Turkey, we realize that left/socialist values and social forms are gaining recognition and acquiring meaning. And yet, it seems that despite its increasing significance, the left has not forced the hand of political power towards comprehensive changes. In other words, while socialist values certainly had an important role in the resistances and revolts discussed in this volume, they did not develop into a political power. This is due to the absence of the *willpower* of the working class against the dominant economic and political structures of power in Turkey. Therefore, it is important to discuss how a unified movement toward constructing the willpower of the working class could be achieved.

Part of the class struggle involves a battle over ideas. As Lebowitz (2006, pp. 25-26) says, 'The battle of ideas begins here by communicating knowledge of the nature of capitalism—by demonstrating that poverty in not the fault of the poor, that exclusion is not the fault of the excluded, that the wealth is result of the chain of human activity.' Lebowitz continues, 'Therefore, the knowledge that we need to build up and maintain human society as an alternative society is necessarily 'democratic, participatory and protagonist.'' In the course of discussion, we can ask questions and seek answers about three issues: Who are the subjects and interlocutors of the unified movement? What political form should this movement take? What language and discourse would be most effective for such a movement?

To the question of who is the subject and interlocutor of the movement, the answer is, of course, the working class. We have encountered the working class in all of the resistances and struggles discussed in this book. Yaşlı argued in Chapter 3 that the TEKEL resistance was 'the moment when the working class became visible after a decades-long silence.' It was a turning point in the contemporary history of class struggle, in which the workers uncloaked the oppressive and conservative cover of the regime and took to the streets. As Yaşlı said, TEKEL workers gathered under a common identity, beyond ethnic affinities; Kurdish and Turkish workers overcame the determining influence of nationalism and focused on their common struggle as workers.

Student opposition is another site of the working class revolt. The three nemeses of student opposition, says Kaya in Chapter 4, are commodification, commercialization, and conservatization. The objective position of students in this struggle is that of the potential working class. Their schools are preparing them to take their place in the white-collar labor market with their qualifications in hand. And yet, capitalism has guaranteed unemployment or underemployment for many of them. These graduates will join the ranks of the reserve labor and the working class (Boratav, 2013).

Turkey's unappointed teachers, as Durmaz shows in Chapter 8, are making working class objections to their precarious employment. Indeed, we are experiencing the re-proletarianization of youngsters who are endeavoring to be teachers in the public sector. As Yıldırım and İlhan demonstrate in Chapter 6, working class objections are also clearly evident in the struggle of the people against the destructive urban projects that are threatening their homes and livelihood. Far from being oriented to 'regeneration,' these projects dispossess the poor in the service of profit making.

The working class objections are also central to the agenda of women's movements in Turkey. The position of women in the labor market, Balta emphasizes in Chapter 7, is one of the main topics of discussion in the movement; flexibilization and precarization of labor and women's exclusion from the public sphere are strongly critiqued. In the face of neoliberal attacks, there is no better way of disciplining working class men (most of whom are engaged in manual labor) than to render them entirely responsible for their dependent wives and children at home. On the other hand, women's narrowly defined identity as housewives reduces their participation in the ranks of jobseekers. Women are encouraged to find home-centered, flexible work; hence employment costs are kept low and the state offloads its responsibilities of social reproduction onto mothers.

The debate about the role of the middle class in resistance has been sparked in the context of the Gezi uprising. In Chapter 2, Saraçoğlu and Yeşilbağ argue that it is problematic to read the Gezi uprising as the resistance of a 'new cultural bourgeois,' consisting of intellectuals, professionals, and urban middle class and oriented to defending or increasing their cultural capital against the dominant economic and political powers. This problematical middle class analysis misconceives the Gezi uprising by confining it a) *temporally* to a certain moment without regarding it as a process and b) *spatially* to a park without regarding its spread across the country. Besides, those who charge that the 'Gezi uprising belonged to the middle class' are relying on a faulty methodological individualism.

Marx's understanding of 'class' in general, and 'working class' and 'proletariat' in particular, derived from the historical processes and dynamics of capitalism that Marx was observing and analyzing in his time. Marx locates the essence of class not simply in 'structural positions' but in relationships—the relationships of exploitation, conflict, and struggle that provide the impulse to processes of class formation. While presenting the working class as a revolutionary subject in process, he conceived it as a camp that only gains transformative potential and visibility within class struggles rather than as a sum of individuals or segments.

The new industries, jobs, and employment fields that have emerged during the historical development of capitalism have necessitated a reconsideration of the class map. The Marxist class analysis has been disclaimed as incapable of explaining the increasing complexity of production processes. This shallow approach, which argues that Marx split capitalism into two main classes (bourgeoisie and proletariat) and defined 'blue-collared, muscled male workers' who labor in the industrial sector as proletariat, repeated the same simple critique again and again as the service sector expanded: 'Unfortunately, life is not as easy as Marx states.' While the thesis that the working class has vanished has been in circulation for some time, no one asks whither the bourgeoisie (Bensaid, 2009, p. 49). Yet, if there is the bourgeois, there is also a working class.

Do the different strata of the working class show enormous differences in terms of their labor processes, everyday life experiences, identities, and cultures, as social scientists often repeat? Bourgeois social scientists often search for differences when they view the working class; seeking and finding common grounds is almost unscientific for them. Yet, precarity and the indefinite future is a reality that crosscuts the different strata of the working class. Özuğurlu's (2010) analysis is important here:

In fact, forms of employment are highly diversified in the name of t h e flexibilization of labor market. This deepened the differences within the working class and caused reinforcement of differentiation. This is the fact. And there is another fact as well: A fundamental tendency that thoroughly transcends the partitioned labor market and diversified employment forms and therefore re-homogenizes differences within the working class on the line of common fate. This tendency is the precarization of work. Thus, the reminder should be placed here: The new working class is those whose fate is united while their lives are fragmented' (pp. 46-47).

The second question that preoccupies us here is: What political form should this movement take? This involves constitutive questions of organization, willpower, protagonism, and spontaneity. These are the most difficult and complicated questions for left/socialist analysis, as their answers lie within coordinated processes: Political forms and practices of the movement are actually produced together with the working class.

Recent discussions about the spontaneous revolts among youth have challenged perceptions of youth as apolitical, individualistic, and hedonistic. Turkish youth, as Kaya tells in Chapter 4, staged protests and resistances with remarkable spontaneity. Students at ODTÜ stood up against the regime, politicians were welcomed with an egg festival, and canteens were occupied.

Spontaneity has also found expression under the name of different associations, organizations, and formations, as well as committees, circles, and initiatives. It revealed itself during Gezi uprisings, within local revolutionary-popular experiences, in objections to urban regeneration and in anti-HES resistances. To be sure, defending and making use of this spontaneity is crucial. Park forums, neighborhood assemblies, and organized common grounds are offering experiences worth further analysis. And yet, there is a real threat that 'classless' spontaneity is prioritized in future struggles. Left-liberals particularly are celebrating what appears to be publics devoid of class identities and attempts to replace all the emblems and flags of archaic organizational forms with the motto of 'a more livable capitalism or capitalism with human face.' Class politics would thus defend and appropriate spontaneity but in a way that affirms the centrality of class relations in organized protest. While considering political forms and activities, one should not give credit to the organization model that has severed its ties with the working class, stating 'My cadres are ready, my program is ready, only the working class is absent.'

Rosa Luxemburg's analysis is still relevant for our understanding of the political form and activities of the movement. Luxemburg ([1906] 1996), who advocated for mass activities, democracy, and spontaneity, always warned against the tendency towards decentralization. She saw spontaneity as the means by which the masses could move the party and the struggle forward, by eliminating the potential for inactive leadership within the party; she did not, however, regard it as a centerless, complex or nondescriptive orientation. Luxemburg (1906) wrote that 'the window of the party should always stay open. Voices of the street should reach to the party.'

The third question with which we are concerned is: What language and discourse would be most effective for such a movement? Central to our answer is the need for a reversal of ideological dispossession in the movement's discourse. As Saraçoğlu and Yeşilbağ argue, the movement must expose capital as it is accumulated through dispossession and political and ideological seizure. What lies beneath the 10-year-long rise of the AKP power is precisely the success of its ideological and political mechanisms in accompanying and supporting accumulation through dispossession. In other words, the AKP seized the very ideological and political means that could otherwise have equipped the discourse of the labor struggle. It appropriated workers' reactions and incorporated them into its own strategy and ideological field. Thus, the resistance that was ignited in Gezi Park and spread across Turkey should be read as throwing a wrench in the AKP's strategy of ideological dispossession. The terms, 'freedom,' 'justice,' and 'equality' were reclaimed from the AKP, which had earlier appropriated and redeployed them in the rhetoric of the 'national will.' These terms have now become the political vocabulary for those longing for another Turkey.

The language and discourse of the movement would be formed with the active participation of the working class and would articulate both their experiences and their desire for change. The values generated in the process would produce political attitudes capable of making another society possible. Freire's (2000) analysis of alternative, critical, and liberating processes could be a guiding light within this process. Freire proposes 'cultural action' against 'cultural invasion.' According to Freire (2000, p. 181), cultural action, as historical action, is an instrument for superseding the dominant alienated and alienating culture. In cultural action, there are no spectators, the object of the actors' actions is the reality to be transformed for the liberation of men and women. There are actors who critically analyze reality (never separating this analysis from action) and intervene as subjects in the historical process. This is challenging work, as existing conditions constrain such exercises of interpretation, definition, and expression. Nevertheless, all efforts should be made in this direction.

Working class cultural activism requires communication—something that all of our contributors discuss to some extent. As Hamsici says in Chapter 5, resistance against HES projects enabled unprecedented communication between villages that were previously isolated from one another. The collectivization of resistance against HES projects brought together different villages and societies. Thus, voices and hands—playing accordion, kemençe, bagpipe, and drum—joined together for the first time in the struggle for basic rights.

Another important matter for communication is collective time and space. Communication between socialist organizations and the working class became possible during the TEKEL resistance, in which participants were concentrated geographically and temporally. In Chapter 3, Yaşlı showed us that socialist organizations re-established their ties with the working class. Although those socialist organizations that remained under the influence of old habits tried 'to transfer consciousness,' the majority endeavored 'to learn together.' Young members of the leftist organizations directly witnessed a manifestation of class struggle and actually became part of it. On the other hand, the workers made contact with young and educated men and women in a common public space despite their different cultural codes.

Improving communication and organizing means is vital for defending the collective rights of workers. RedHack, as Etike highlights in Chapter 11, became one of the natural leaders in the resistance. Besides providing communication and coordination, the cyber-attacks that they staged in protest of police violence and political developments enabled RedHack to gain support. RedHack's activities, which were not limited to the Gezi Uprising, took place on two fronts: First, in moments of crisis and protest, they provide methods of coordination between protesters; Second, they staged cyber attack protests against unjust political and social practices. In Chapter 12, Çaylı discusses new forms of journalism that could expand the boundaries of communication and freedom of expression in Turkey.

Working class cultural activism also requires the development of its own symbolic codes. While discussing the discourse and symbols of the movement, significant experiences emerge from the anti-HES struggles. In chapter 5, Hamsici explains how items intrinsic to everyday life and culture—the yellow scarf, accordion, bagpipe, and kemençe—have turned into symbols of the anti-HES resistances in different regions and neighborhoods of the Black Sea region. Moreover, as Etike underlines in Chapter 11, RedHack combined traditional symbols, like the hammer and sickle, with contemporary technological means in the resistance.

The language and discourse of the movement can be discussed according to different levels of abstraction. We might think of these as corresponding to the three contexts that Durmaz identifies as loci of resistance in Chapter 8: the labor process, syndical organization, and political regime. While the dynamics of the labor process and syndical organization are bound by a discourse oriented towards improving precarious working conditions, the political discourse and activity must be oriented to overthrowing the existing regime and replacing it with something else. As Durmaz argues, 'If the focus of analysis is the practices of the political regime in social life, then the locus of resistance is neither the individual nor labor unions; on the contrary, it is the social opposition.'

The language and discourse of the movement should, of course, be oppositional; it must say 'no!' One kind of protest is directed against the agents currently responsible for the execution of the neoliberal agenda. As Kaya reveals in Chapter 4, these protests—involving everything from tossing eggs to battling the police on campus—are too easily interpreted as frivolous and fragmented instances of revolt with limited social or political gains.

The language and discourse of the movement could also raise its demands within the limits of bourgeois democracy as well. In Chapter 9, Özdemir stresses that current labor legislation in Turkey is more backwards than that of states linked to the international capitalist system and suggests that a struggle should be conducted against capitalism. As he argues, 'the current system can surely be partially ameliorated, through struggles. The act of pushing the limits is the precondition of a struggle against capitalism.'

The language and discourse of the movement should express the hopes for a different tomorrow, together with an anger that objects and refuses. After all, beyond the 'dark' analyses of capitalism, the applicability, probability, and actuality of socialism must be heard and discussed. Producing left/socialist demands within the language and discourse of the movement is crucial. Working class cultural activism aims at surmounting the antagonistic contradictions of the social structure, thereby achieving the liberation of human beings. The movement thus has the challenging task of expressing the demands and expectations of that part of the working class that experiences the most severe forms of inequalities and injustices, while generating new paradigms of labor based on the values of equality, democracy, participation, and solidarity. Albeit difficult, producing socialist social policy demands within a capitalist society is possible. However, to achieve this, collective rights must be advocated on the grounds of society's collective property—the owners of which are those who form social labor power. We can neither imagine socialness without laborers nor a socialist republic without laborers' right to unlimited organization.

The language and discourse of the movement should push forward the potentialities of a proletarian public sphere. As Kaya says in Chapter 4, the canteen occupations and the Starbucks protests constitute another aspect of the students' struggle against neoliberalism. Such forms of protests demonstrate that this struggle is not merely reactive and does not simply remain at the level of problematizing the political rule of the AKP, while failing to notice the social and economic relations and mechanisms behind it. The students are trying to reclaim their on-campus social spaces from the neoliberal transformation of the university. This amounts to the creation of a counter-public sphere on campus.

Another example of a proletarian public sphere is the revolutionary-popular local governments that Gültekin discusses in Chapter 10. Underlying this alternative form of local administration is a commitment to popular and direct democracy. The direct participation of people's assemblies (with sub-commissions of women, youth, workers, villagers etc.) in the administration is very valuable. Moreover, these forms of administration depend upon the practice of managing resources by the people and their collective participation within legal procedures. These local forms of government do not merely advocate for the management of resources on behalf of the people; rather they are remarkable for their explicit inclusion of the community in decision-making processes.

The language of the movement should be courageous, self-confident, outraged, and humorous. This is precisely the language with which RedHack influenced the Turkish public during the Gezi Uprising. As Etike demonstrates in Chapter 12, RedHack was outraged but humorous at the same time. Humor directed at power provided a psychological relief from oppression and exploitation. It also revealed that the political regime is the weaker opponent against the intelligence of the people. It is obvious that RedHack successfully associated the conventional left discourse with the humorous language and culture of the Internet, which tends to say everything in 140 characters or fewer.

Social movements in Turkey today articulate a different social order where media organizations are independent of capital, where the unemployed, students, and pensioners participate actively in institutions that represent them, where freedoms of expression are exercised without restraint, where hospitals and universities are accessible and responsive to workers' needs and where precarity and insecurity is reduced. Our efforts in academia and politics should be oriented to paving the path to such a future. To this end, it is important to complement the struggles in the streets with more clear suggestions and analyses about how education, healthcare, and the economy would be transformed in socialist Turkey. This will enable us to better communicate how socialism remains an achievable and realistic alternative. We close with the imperative to 'Take the Power in Your Own Hands,' as Lenin said in 1917, and to 'undertake the work on your own, start[ing] from the very bottom and ... not wait[ing] for anybody' to do it for you.

References

Bensaid, D. (2009). *Marx, mode d'Emploi.* La Decouverte Poche.

Boratav, K. (2013, June 22). Olgunlaşmış bir Sınıfsal Başkaldır. *Sendika.* Retrieved from http://www.sendika.org/

Freire, P. (2000). *The pedagogy of oppressed.* Bloomsbury Academic.

Lebowitz, M. (2006). *Build it now: Socialism for the 21st century.* Monthly Review Press.

Lenin, V. I. ([1917] 2008). *Lenin: Revolution, democracy, socialism: Selected writings* (P. Le Blanc, Ed.). London: Pluto Press.

Luxemburg, R. ([1906] 1996). *The mass strike, the political party and the trade unions.* Bookmarks.

Özuğurlu, M. (2010). Tekel Direnişi: Sınıfsal Mücadeleler Üzerine Anımsamalar. In G. Bulut (Ed.), *Tekel Direnişinin Işığında Gelenekselden Yeniye İşçi Sınıfı Hareketi* (pp. 40-53). Ankara: Nota Bene.

ABOUT THE AUTHORS

Ahmet Kerim Gültekin is an ethnologist who is currently working as an assistant professor at the Tunceli University sociology department. He received his doctorate in Ethnology from the University of Ankara (2013), where he also did his MA (2007) and BA (2004) in Social Anthropology and Ethnology. His areas of interest are mainly anthropology of religion, the cults of sacred spaces (ziyaret), folk legends and beliefs, cultural anthropology, identity politics, types of social organizations and memory studies. His publications are mainly on the anthropology of religion, specifically Alevism. Some of his articles are published in the monthly journal Bilim ve Ütopya. He is the author of the books *Tunceli'de Sünni Olmak*, 2010 [*Being Sunni at Tunceli*] and *Tunceli'de Kutsal Mekan Kültü*, 2004 [*Sacred Place Cults in Tunceli*].

Ali Murat Özdemir received his Bachelor's degree in Law from the Faculty of Law, Ankara University, Ankara, Turkey, received his M.A. degree in international commercial law from the Centre for Legal Studies, Sussex University, UK and his doctorate degree from the Department of Political Science and Public Administration, Middle East Technical University, Ankara, Turkey. He has published widely on the sociology of law and political economy in general and on the political economy of the Turkish legal system in particular both in English and Turkish. He has a forthcoming book on the political economy of labor law (*Political Economy of Labor Law: the Case of Turkey*, Roman Books) and some of his articles are published in *South East Europe Review* and *Economic and Industrial Democracy*.

Cenk Saraçoğlu is a full-time faculty member in the Department of Journalism, Faculty of Communication, Ankara University. He received his undergraduate diploma from Bilkent University, International Relations Department in 2002 and earned his Ph.D. degree in Sociology from the University of Western Ontario, Canada, in 2008. He worked at Middle East Technical University, Northern Cyprus Campus as an assistant professor between 2009 and 2012. He is interested in migration, natonalism, urban transformation, and ethnic relations with a particular focus on Turkey. He is the author of the book *Kurds of Modern Turkey: Migration, Neoliberalism and Exclusion in Turkish Society* (I.B Tauris, London: 2011), Şehir, Orta Sınıf ve Kürtler [The City, Middle Class and the Kurds] (İletişim: İstanbul: 2011) as well as some articles published in *Ethnic and Racial Studies*, *Patterns of Prejudice*, *Toplum ve Bilim* (Turkish Quarterly) and *Praksis*.

Ecehan Balta is an independent researcher based in Ankara (BA Sociology, Middle East Technical University, Ankara, Turkey, 1996; MA in Political Science, Ankara University, Ankara, Turkey, 1999). She is a Ph.D. candidate in political science, Ankara University, Ankara. Her areas of interest are political science, political sociology, feminism, race, and ethnicity. She is author of articles on Turkish politics.

Emek Çaylı is assistant professor of communication sciences, Hacettepe University, Ankara (Ph.D. in Radio, Television and Cinema, Ankara University, Ankara, Turkey, 2009; MA in Radio, Television and Cinema, Ankara University, Ankara, Turkey, 2003; BS in English Linguistics, Hacettepe University, Ankara, Turkey, 2000). Her areas of interest are biopolitics, gender and media, freedom of the media in Turkey, and critical analysis of popular culture. She is the co-author of the book, İfade Özgürlüğünün On Yılı: 2000-2011 [*Ten Years In Freedom of Expression: 2000-2011*] (İstanbul: IPS İletişim Vakfı Yayınları, 2012). She has published articles on public sphere and media, everyday life and literature, media ethnography, and domestic violence in various journals.

Ezgi Kaya is a research assistant, Ankara University, Faculty of Communication (MS in Political Science, Boğaziçi University, Istanbul, Turkey; BS in Political Science, Boğaziçi University, Istanbul, Turkey; BS in Philosophie, Boğaziçi University). She is a Ph.D. candidate in political science at Middle East Technical University, Ankara, Turkey. Her areas of interest are labor processes of journalists, labor relations in media industry, and youth.

Fatih Yaşlı is assistant professor of political history, Abant İzzet Baysal University, Bolu (Ph.D. in Political Science, Ankara University, Ankara, 2008; MA in Political Science, Abant İzzet Baysal University, Bolu; BS in Finance, Gazi University, Ankara, 2001). His areas of interest are political thought, political thought in Turkey, the political history of Turkey, and rightist ideologies in

Turkey. He is the author of the books *Nietzsche ve Marx: Hayatın Olumlanması Olarak Felsefe*, 2008 [*Nietzsche and Marx: Philosophy as the Affirmation of Life*], *Kinimiz Dinimizdir: Türkçü Faşizm Üzerine Bir İnceleme*, 2009 [*Our Hatred is Our Religion: An Analysis of Turkist Fascism*] and *AKP ve Yeni Rejim*, 2012 [*The AKP and the New Regime*]. He also co-edited with Çağdaş Sümer, *Hegemonya'dan Diktatoryaya Liberal Muhafazakâr İttifak*, 2010 [*Liberal Conservative Alliance from Hegemony to Dictatorship*].

Fatma Yıldırım is an assistant professor, Ankara University, Faculty of Medicine (MA in Labor Relations, Ankara University, Ankara, Turkey, 1988; MA in Psychology in Hacettepe University, Ankara, Turkey, 1996; Ph.D. in Psychology in Ankara University, Ankara, Turkey, 2002). Her areas of interest are social policy, social psychology, organisational psychology, and disadvantaged groups. She is the author of various articles in *International Journal of Public Health* and *Social Psychiatry and Psychiatric Epidemiology*

Gamze Yücesan-Özdemir is professor of social policy, Ankara University, Ankara (Ph.D. in Development Studies, University of Sussex, Brighton, UK, 1998; MA in European Studies, University of Reading, Reading, UK, 1993; BS in Management, Middle East Technical University, Ankara, Turkey, 1992). Her areas of interest are labor process, social policy, labor markets, labor politics, and trade unions. She is the author of various articles in *Economic and Industrial Democracy, Capital and Class, Turkish Studies, South East Europe Review and International Union Rights*.

İnci Özgür İlhan is a assistant professor, Ankara University, Faculty of Medicine (MS in Medicine, Ankara University, Ankara, Turkey, 1993; Ph.D. in Medicine, Ankara University, Ankara, Turkey, 1998). Her areas of interest are alcohol dependency, obsessive-compulsive disorders, and public health. She is the author of various articles in and *European Addiction Research*.

Mahmut Hamsici currently works for BBC Turkish (MA in International Relations, Galatasaray University, İstanbul, Turkey; BA in Economics, İstanbul University, İstanbul, Turkey). He has worked as a journalist for various national and international newspapers, including *Radikal* (Turkish daily) and *Tageszeitung* (German daily). He is the co-author of *Yerüstünden Notlar* [*Notes from the Earth*] (Nota Bene: Ankara, 2011) (with Alaattin Timur) and the author of *Dereler ve İsyanlar* [*Brooks and Uprisings*] (Nota Bene: Ankara, 2011).

Melih Yeşilbağ is a research assistant in the Department of Sociology, Ankara University (MA in the Atatürk Institute for Modern Turkish History, Boğaziçi University; BA in Electrical and Electronic Engineering, Boğaziçi University). His doctoral education is still in progress. His areas of interest are development studies, international political economy, state and capital relations, and economic sociology.

Orkun Saip Durmaz is a research assistant in the Department of Labor Economics and Industrial Relations, Kocaeli University (Ph.D. and MA in Labor Economics and Industrial Relations, Ankara University, Ankara, respectively in 2014 and 2007; BS in Political Science and Public Administration, Middle East Technical University, Ankara, 2003). His areas of interest are the labor process, processes of proletarianization, class formation in Turkey, educational policies, political history, and the epistemology of the research methods. He is the author of articles concentrating on the issues of teaching abut the labor process and educational policies.

Şafak Etike is as a research assistant, Ankara University, Faculty of Communication, Department of Journalism (MA in Journalism, Gazi University, Ankara, Turkey, 2011; BS in Journalism, Ankara University, Ankara, Turkey, 2004). Her doctoral education is still in progress. Her areas of interest are social media, technology, and imperialism. She has various papers presented at conferences.

www.ingramcontent.com/pod-product-compliance
Lightning Source LLC
Chambersburg PA
CBHW030733280326
41926CB00086B/1273